a reader's guide to
Dylan
Thomas

WILLIAM YORK TINDALL

OCTAGON BOOKS

A Division of Farrar, Straus and Giroux

NEW YORK 1973

Reprinted 1973

OCTAGON BOOKS
A Division of Farrar, Straus & Giroux, Inc.
19 Union Square West
New York, N.Y. 10003

Library of Congress Catalog Card Number: 73-4641

ISBN 0-374-97948-0

to Cecilia herself

Acknowledgments

For permission to quote passages from *The Collected Poems of Dylan Thomas* (copyright 1952 by J. M. Dent & Sons, Ltd., copyright © 1957 by New Directions) I am indebted to J. M. Dent & Sons and New Directions, the English and American publishers. For permission to quote from *Adventures in the Skin Trade and Other Stories* (copyright 1955 by New Directions) I am indebted to New Directions. The Estate of Dylan Thomas and David Higham Associates, Ltd. have kindly permitted quotation from the manuscripts and letters of Dylan Thomas. I am no less grateful to The Lockwood Memorial Library of The University of Buffalo, which generously allowed me to use the manuscripts in its keeping, and to The Columbia University Council for Research in the Humanities for a grant that enabled me to complete this book.

W. Y. T.

Columbia University,
October 7, 1961

Bibliographical abbreviations

Adam   *Adam International Review*, Dylan Thomas Memorial Number, Vol. XXI, No. 238 (1953).

Casebook   Brinnin, John Malcolm, editor, *A Casebook on Dylan Thomas*, New York, Thomas Y. Crowell, 1960.

Fraser   G. S. Fraser, *Dylan Thomas*, London, The British Council, 1957.

Olson   Olson, Elder, *The Poetry of Dylan Thomas*, Chicago, University of Chicago Press, 1954.

Stanford   Stanford, Derek, *Dylan Thomas*, London, Neville Spearman, 1954.

Tedlock   Tedlock, E. W., editor, *Dylan Thomas: the Legend and the Poet*, London, Heinemann, 1960.

Treece   Treece, Henry, *Dylan Thomas*, London, Lindsay Drummond, 1949.

Watkins   Watkins, Vernon, editor, *Dylan Thomas: Letters to Vernon Watkins*, London, J. M. Dent and Faber and Faber, 1957.

Contents

The Map of Love, 1939

Deaths and Entrances, 1946

In Country Sleep, 1952

A READER'S GUIDE TO *Dylan Thomas*

Introduction

Thomas wrote sixteen great poems—give or take a couple. Few poets have written so many. If I were making an anthology of the hundred best lyrics in English, I should include two or three by Thomas along with half a dozen or more by Yeats. To those who want to know which sixteen of Thomas' poems I have in mind I offer a list of seventeen: "I see the boys of summer," "The force that through the green fuse," "Especially when the October wind," "To-day, this insect," "Hold hard, these ancient minutes," "Altarwise by owl-light," "We lying by seasand," "After the funeral," "A Refusal to Mourn," "Poem in October," "Ceremony After a Fire Raid," "Ballad of the Long-legged Bait," "Fern Hill," "In Country Sleep," "Over Sir John's hill," "Lament," "In the White Giant's Thigh."

Value judgments of this sort, notoriously subjective and uncertain, are not unlike the reports of a winetaster, which depend upon experience in tasting. Saying that Thomas wrote sixteen great poems means that, having read his poems again and again and having read many others through the years, I find these sixteen agreeable. Impressions are harmless and, if they provoke agreement or disagreement, useful. Nothing more useful than what makes readers consult themselves and the text before them.

Taste and judgment, comfortable in the presence of Shakespeare, are challenged by novelty. In 1933, when Thomas burst upon London with his marvels, readers were dazzled. Here, the better sort felt, were things beyond them yet their own, things from the madhouse or the analyst's couch, craftily rearranged. Here, dense to the point of clotting, was something rich and strange. As if Victoria had never laid her hand on Britain, here was something of more than Elizabethan abundance—deeper than the roots of aspidistras. Nothing in these extravagant riddles like the sociable verses of Auden or the austerities of Eliot, who had just proclaimed himself royalist, classicist, and Anglo-Catholic. When, in 1950, Thomas burst upon New York, he proclaimed his individuality: "First, I am a Welshman. Second, I am a drunkard. Third, I am a heterosexual."

To proclaim this suddenly at a party on West 11th Street was to disconcert decorum. Part of Thomas' impact was personal. He displayed his person everywhere: in bars, in parlors, on platforms, and on campuses, where he would have chased the girls had he been able to run. Almost everyone in London, New York, and Oklahoma saw, heard, or met him. Since I was around at the time, I knew him a little, too. Sometimes a little seemed enough; but sentiment always broke through. In my closet, held in trust for posterity, is an empty Dylan Thomas beer bottle (Budweiser) which I mean someday to present to a museum.

More of us loved than hated the irresponsible, charming, outrageous man; for he was our bourgeois idea of what a poet should be. Wallace Stevens looked and acted like an insurance man. Thomas looked and acted like a poet. There he was, prancing, eloquently declaiming, lying in his puke, puzzling us. Enchanting us, too. Little wonder that he became a popular poet, as popular as any in our time—be the rival Eliot or Frost.

Thomas was our Bunthorne. The analogy, however, is inexact; for although Thomas talked about the daisies in deep, transcendental phrases and although heavy dragoons hooted their displeasure as lovesick ladies followed the "greenery-yallery" young man about, he was not an "aesthetic sham." As he talked, what his followers liked most about him was his voice—not what he said (which, after all, they could not understand) but how he said it. No triumph here of sense but of tone. Whether on academic stages, on phonograph records, or broadcast through the air, this voice, we knew, was the true voice of feeling. Whether he read the poems of others or his own, this voice, delivering words from the printed page and bringing them to the ear, seemed poetry's proper vehicle or poetry itself. A poem, we found, is something to be read aloud by Thomas; and even as we accosted his poems silently, we could hear him read. Lacking experience or memory, we could put another record on the gramophone. The personality of the poet may still get between us and the poems, but not this voice.

Inevitably, a great poet with this voice and that presence displeased as well as pleased. England was crowded with heavy dragoons, for whom the trouble with Thomas was that he came from the lower middle class. His father was a schoolteacher. Thomas wore no old school tie, his upper lip was far from stiff, and everything about him seemed too much. In short, he was a slob. It may be that he was not born in Dublin, but Swansea is almost as outlandish. The shouts of the uniformed establishment —or its remnant, flying high above the aspidistra but sure Victoria is still around—made the higher praise of Dame Edith all but inaudible. Hers was not alone, of course. Many Englishmen were generous and perceptive from the start; but the opposition, always louder, has been growing, despite the death of *Scrutiny*, since Thomas' death. What the unfortunate outsider left us offers nothing to survivors of F. R. Leavis in the age of C. P. Snow. Without earnestness or any sense of its importance, Thomas would have seemed uncommitted in the committee room, where his poems would seem irreverent. He has an idiom of his own— and style. Incapable of understatement, dullness, or discourse in the manner of George Eliot, he has joined Joyce among established villains. Neither is like Anthony Powell, still less like John Betjeman.

The opposition, more amusing than the loyal support, demands more notice here. It is likely that T. S. Eliot's disapproval, in the third of his *Four Quartets*, of those who explore womb, tomb, and dream by "recurrent" images of "pre-conscious terrors" means disapproval of Thomas. But Sweeney's approval of birth, copulation, and death, Thomas' area, proves that Eliot's disapproval of these precedes his acquaintance with Thomas. Eliot's objections to what Thomas stood for are as impersonal as the objective correlative. Not so the more recent objections of Kingsley Amis, who, in "A Poet's Epitaph" (1957), says that "drunk with words," this poet "should have stuck to spewing beer, not ink." Thomas is even more plainly suggested by the satiric portrait of Probert, the ignominious Welsh poet, in *That Uncertain Feeling* (1955), Amis' second novel. From Probert's middle-class mouth, which has "all the mobility of a partly-collapsed inner-tube," come repulsive sounds, "woaded with pit-dirt and sheep-shit." Turning bits of the Bible back to front ("In the word was the beginning," for example) and slapping "Dai Christ" on the back, this outsider fills his poetic play with lines like these: "But, Bowen *bach*, they buried you at batlight . . . under the woman's hair of grass, you and your wound." Buried Bowen replies: "I was Bowen Thomas, tailor of Llados"—or Sodall backwards, a witty variant upon Thomas' Llareggub, which, in the interests of delicacy perhaps, the English publisher of *Under Milk Wood* has changed to Llaregyb.

New Lines (1956), an anthology of poems to which Amis contributed, summarizes the recent reaction. Although unnamed in the introductory manifesto, Thomas is plainly there, supporting "the debilitating theory that poetry *must* be metaphorical." In place of his "diffuse and sentimental verbiage or hollow technical pirouettes," his "arrangement of images of sex and violence tapped straight from the unconscious," and his "*naïvetés* and nostalgias of childhood," let us, the editor implores, have decent, rational verse, something like that of John Betjeman or like the prose of George Orwell. Plainly, Thomas is out of fashion. Amis' "Against Romanticism," a poem exemplifying the ideal of this fashionable group, calls for pedestrian decency, "pallid" and "plain." Let no spellbinding complexities or swooning images divert us from our road to a temperate zone. Amis likes it there.

Robert Graves, late of the Royal Welch Fusiliers, lent his voice to the decent chorus. What the manifestoes of Sir Charles (better known as Sir C. P.) say about Joyce could be applied to Thomas—though Lady Snow found him congenial. Many of his friends, Geoffrey Grigson among them, joined his enemies, who forgot thát, whatever their distaste, Thomas remains a great poet. Look down your nose at him and you look up.

American taste, commonly lagging ten or twenty years behind British, still finds Thomas all right. Students in school and college adore him, convinced that "if this young man expresses himself in terms too deep for *me,/* Why, what a very singularly deep young man this deep young man must be!" Deep critics, still under Empson's spell, rush to the *Explicator* with explications, and rush back to quarrel with rivals. Incorrigibly analytic, we welcome all complexities. Joyce and Thomas are still our darlings, whatever their status in Britain. Whatever the British reaction against symbol, image, and all romantic trickery, we are still romantics, and who more romantic than Thomas? That he was lower-middle-class or indecorous means little here, where Llareggub is still Llareggub. He died, we think, a poet's death as he had lived the life of a poet; and his death was suitably here. Maybe Thomas was not at home with "strangers" of our sort, but we are at home with him.

My survey of the British and American criticism of Thomas, both favorable and unfavorable, has uncovered several widely-held notions about him: that, a sport among the poets of the Auden generation, Thomas had no interest in politics and society; that he was a religious poet, a surrealist, a disciple of Freud, a composer of nonsense verse, and a student of Welsh "cynghannedd" —that he was deeply learned or incredibly ignorant. Though each of these notions has something to commend it, none fits Thomas exactly.

Concerning his political innocence: it is plain that obscure poems about womb, tomb, and childhood seem beside the concern and manner of the Party. Thomas sounds nothing like Stephen Spender or Hugh MacDiarmid. Yet, when asked whether he took his stand with "any political or politico-economic party or creed," Thomas replied (in "Replies to an Enquiry") that he took his stand "with any revolutionary body" that asserts man's right to share in the fruits of production. "Only through such an essentially revolutionary body can there be the possibility of a communal art." But it is up to a revolutionary poet to declare himself as unmistakably in poetry as in prose. Thomas' poetic method, surely not that of "communal art," hid the pinkness of his heart. "Our eunuch dreams" and "All all and all," despite unsocialistic obscurities, are as socialistic in theme as most poems of the period. My reading of "Our eunuch dreams" affords textual evidence and circumstance. For such discoveries you need nothing but a clue, close reading, and the liberal imagination.

Religion is more of a problem. Thomas called himself a "holy maker," whose poems are written "in praise of God." Indeed, God and Christ are rarely absent from his service; and the later poems, abounding in bells, books, and candles, are as ritualistic as anything by Hopkins or Eliot. Like Bunyan, Thomas was always asking what he could do to be saved. What, if not religious, would he want to ask for that for? Clearly there is something so holy about some of his poems that critics cannot be blamed for detecting it. But holiness of what kind? That of the church of St. Sulpice or that of the Muir Woods?

Father was a skeptic, but grandfather was a preacher. As a boy, Thomas attended Sunday school and chapel—Presbyterian, he told me—where he got "tipsy on salvation's bottle." His familiarity with the Bible, which remained a principal source of his imagery, and with *Pilgrim's Progress* dates from this time. "The black spit of the chapel fold" left it, never to return; but it had done its work on him, as on Lawrence. Both remained essentially Protestant without being Christian, and both remained Puritans. Anti-Catholicism is the chapel's heritage. Though Thomas loved the poetry of Hopkins, he loathed him as a Papist. One evening at dinner in my house, Thomas violently rebuked my wife for being a Catholic. Why, then, if he left the chapel and hated the church, did he fill "Altarwise" and "Vision and Prayer" with Christian imagery? Why and to whom was he always praying, and in what interests always exhorting?

Some of his prayers are to the devil, who, in "Incarnate devil" is God's creative colleague. In "Poem in October" God is mythical. "Death shall have no dominion," whatever its ritualistic manner, is far from orthodox. The Saviour who figures in "Altarwise" is dismissed in "There was a saviour." But, whether praised or dismissed, God and Christ are always around in Thomas' poetry—not in their proper capacities, however, but as metaphors for nature, poet, and their creative powers. "He did not believe in God, but God had made this summer full of blue winds."

Like any vegetable-loving romantic, singing "the green fuse" as transcendental Bunthorne once sang "an attachment *à la* Plato for a bashful young potato," Thomas found nature holy. "The country is holy," he says in the prayer for his daughter. A statement of this kind is extraordinary; for he preferred images. Those he had acquired from the chapel and from Hopkins or Joyce were handy and suitable for expressing natural holiness— and so were sermon, prayer, and ritual. God creates by the Word, and Jesus suffers for mankind. So too the poet. What better images for himself could he find? Both Lawrence and Joyce, who were always confusing themselves with God, Christ, or Lucifer, had anticipated Thomas. When, therefore, he talks about God or Christ, he has nature in mind or himself, as creator and sufferer. Creating by the word, he became the Word. The holiness of Thomas is a romantic holiness, at once diffused and concentrated, that finds its expression in the images and rituals of chapel and church. His churches have weathercocks, not crosses, on the steeples.

Some think Thomas a follower of Freud. The Biblical images of the early poems—water, towers, snakes, and ladders—must owe something to *The Interpretation of Dreams*. Indeed, behind these poems, in the capacity of patrons, Freud and monotheistic Moses appear to walk hand in hand. Many of Thomas' poems are dreams, and many seem constructed according to Freud's dreamwork: by condensation, displacement, and symbolizing. Delighting in the interpretation of his friends' dreams, according to elementary Freud, Thomas spent a happy half hour on one of my wife's dreams after he had forgiven or forgotten her religion—or else, keeping it wickedly in mind. Like Thomas himself, the hero of "The Mouse and the Woman," a manifestly Freudian story, "could translate every symbol of his dreams," and, when writing, "let the dream dictate its rhythm." When asked by the editor of *New Verse* (see "Replies to an Enquiry") if he had been influenced by Freud, Thomas said, "Yes." Like Freud, he continued, he brings the hidden to light; but, exceeding the master, he proposes to "drag further into the clean nakedness of light more even of the hidden causes than Freud could realize." Persuaded by such evidence, I used to think Thomas more of a

Freudian than he was. It is true that, like most of us, he had a smattering of Freud, picked up maybe from glancing through the book of dreams; and what he found he found use for in his poems and stories. But now I think Freud one of their lesser elements, useful for adding a dimension to the Bible, a greater element. That Jacob's ladder and Eve's snake were also Freud's seemed pleasing and instructive.

Surrealism, which diverted some poets from the Party in the middle 'thirties and brought others to it, is an application of Freud. That Thomas was a surrealist is another widely-received notion—and not without reason; for there is madness in his method. Open his stories at random and you find images like these: "four-breasted stems at the poles of the summer sea-ends, eyes in the sea-shells." Here surely is more than customary of the "irrational element" that Yeats thought a distinguishing mark of great poetry, and here are words for what Dali was doing in paint. The poems of Thomas also abound in strangely juxtaposed images of the same sort. Several of his poems and stories proved suitable for publication by *Contemporary Poetry and Prose*, the surrealist magazine. Roger Roughton, its editor, was a friend of Thomas, and David Gascoyne, the principal surrealist of England, was an acquaintance. At the Surrealist Exhibition of 1936, crowded with friends and acquaintances, Thomas carried a cup of boiled string around. "Weak or strong?" he asked, offering it to André Breton, Sir Herbert Read, and the buffoons of the unconscious. Reviewing *The Map of Love*, Thomas' third book, Sir Herbert, the patron of British surrealism, found it "necessary to introduce the spectre of surrealism here"; for "here, if anywhere we find that transcendence of reality through the paranoic faculty of the poetic imagination which is the avowed aim of the surrealist. . . . There is no evidence to suggest that Mr. Thomas has ever read Lautréamont, but the similarity is occasionally striking." It is, indeed, but with a difference. The ideal of surrealism was "psychic automatism" or writing without conscious control. Always deliberate, Thomas consciously controlled matters from the unconscious, or matters like them, for planned effects. Like Freud's dreamwork, surrealism offered another dimension—another method to complicate that of the Sunday school. Any good artist finds use for what he finds around him.

Surrealism, which he found there, is nonsense by definition. Even a marginal and artificial surrealist like Thomas, a fellow traveler at a distance and with maps of love, invites the displeasure of the rational and the polite. Distracted by surfaces, Robert Graves thought Thomas beyond rhyme or reason. Vernon Watkins, a sympathetic friend, threw up his hands at some of the poems, which, in his opinion, make no sense at all. Some readers are like Peter De Vries, who, when asked what he thought of the work of Thomas, replied: "It's nice work if you can get it. I don't get it." Other readers, taking the poems as Rorschach tests, find what they like in Thomas' meaningless blots and squiggles. Unable to follow the more formidable poems, one critic wrote a book to express his inability. But a semi surrealist surface, complicated by Freud and the Bible, does not guarantee nonsense. Close reading and comparison of texts prove Thomas as rational and orderly as any poet this side of Alexander Pope. Thomas is merely difficult. If his complex of methods sometimes resulted in clotting, we must remember that nobody is successful all of the time.

Thomas was a Welshman. Therefore, it is tempting to think him a student of Celtic lore and an adept at "cynghanedd" or the harmonious and complicated interweaving of sounds that the bards of Wales have always been adept at. Thomas the bard or wizard, casting dark-vowelled spells, was one of his masks. But ignorance of Welsh kept him from bardic poetry and its system. "Cynghanedd," he admitted in a letter, "is a foreign, and closed form to me." The occasional and unsystematic interweaving of sounds in his poems shows a likelier debt to Hopkins, who was a student of Welsh. Yet, second-hand though Thomas' trickery with vowels and consonants may be, it is more or less Welsh in character and feeling—almost as Welsh in respect of these as the poetry of Hopkins. Thomas once told me that he was content to hint the Welsh techniques he lacked. As for "the deep Celtic significance" detected by critics in image and theme, Thomas cheerfully disclaimed it. A poet of Swansea, after all, is Anglo-Welsh, and, unless a learned man, closer to the traditions of England than of Wales.

. Some critics think Thomas a second Eliot, deeply learned. John L. Sweeney in his introduction to *Selected Writings* finds Thomas all but Grierson's rival in knowledge of seventeenth-century metaphysical poetry. Though flattered, Thomas modestly admitted in a letter to Donald A. Roberts that Sweeney "pays tribute to an erudition I do not possess." Elder Olson finds Thomas a profound student of astrology, plotting amid astrolabes and symboled charts the zodiacal career of Hercules. Others, noting Thomas' references to pryamids and the "third eye," have found the poet an Egyptologist and an occultist. Nothing is unlikelier. All that Thomas knew of zodiac, pyramid, and the occult eye could have come—and probably did—from ten minutes at a friend's bookcase with some work by Mme. Blavatsky, A. E. Waite, or J. H. Breasted, opened at random. Never one to rummage public libraries and lacking a library of his own, Thomas, the graduate of Swansea Grammar School, was not the deeply learned man some think.

Others, going to the opposite extreme, think him deeply ignorant. His reading, they say, consisted of thrillers, detective stories, horror stories, and science fiction, the area he chose when book reviewing. It is certain that *Dracula*, with its red-eyed "undead" emerging by batlight from their sheets and tombs, was one of his favorite books. Its influence may be detected throughout his poems and stories. But that Thomas, ignorant as the dawn, warbled wood-notes wild is no less unlikely. Neither deeply learned nor deeply ignorant, he was, like most of us, somewhere betwixt and between. He differs from most of us in being able to use what he picked up here and there, unsystematically. It may be that he knew no book well, but he leafed through many. His poems, stories, letters, essays, and recitations make it easy to list the books he had a nodding acquaintance with and put to excellent use.

Yeats, said Thomas, was his favorite poet. Yet he did not own a copy of his favorite, and, when called upon by the B.B.C. to read some poems of Yeats, Thomas had to ask Vernon Watkins what to read. From him Thomas first heard about "Lapis Lazuli," which he recited at every college in America. We do not always know what we love. This seems the case with Joyce, another favorite. The effect of *Dubliners* and A *Portrait of the Artist* is evident in Thomas' stories, especially those of Swansea or "little Dublin." His obsession with portraits of the artist and with young dog-gods may owe something to Joyce, whose portrait he sketched

—or so I like to think—in "The Mouse and the Woman." The Thomistic hero of this story asks aid of a Joycean "wise old man," with whom he has read the "classic books": "On an Irish harp you would pluck tunes until the geese, like the seven geese of the Wandering Jew, rose squawking into the air. Father, speak to me, your only son." Our hero asks in vain; for the godlike old man has "a nest of mice in the tangle of the frozen beard." Thomas must have glanced *Ulysses* through without getting much help, except for that Wandering Jew; but *Finnegans Wake*, which he proclaimed the greatest book of our times and his favorite above all others, is another matter. Certainly Joyce's verbal play and his vision of cyclical process had an effect on Thomas; yet when I spent an hour or so with him over a copy of *Finnegan*, everything we came across seemed news to him. It is likely that Thomas had read a few pages of *Work in Progress* as it appeared in *transition*, a magazine he was familiar with. A few pages—and why turn more? —were all he needed to reveal the method and to establish love. Nobody has found better use for fewer pages of *Finnegan* than he.

The poems of Thomas suggest his acquaintance with Hopkins, not only with "The Windhover" and "The Wreck of the Deutschland," but with poems that few know, "Penmaen Pool" and "The Half-way House," for example. Hopkins, whose "womb-of-all, home-of-all, hearse-of-all" and "warm-laid grave of a womb-life grey" state Thomas' early theme, presides over his later rhythms as well as his approaches to cynghannedd and his customary confusion of sun and Son. Embarrassed by this heavy debt and uneasy with a Jesuit, Thomas spoke of him reluctantly, and, when he did, claimed independence. My poems, said Thomas, "came out of the blue of my head. . . . The only truth about my poems, is that I make them up."

Both firmly established in his head, Eliot and Auden helped make the poems up. Since, however, Thomas was busy declaring his independence of both, his references to them are not always cordial. "Pope Eliot" sometimes declined to publish Thomas' poems in the *Criterion*; and Faber and Faber, which published most good poets of the 'thirties, did not publish Thomas. In 1937 Thomas congratulated Auden on his "seventieth birthday." Wilfred Owen, more congenial than these, was a Welshman, skilled at dissonance. Thomas liked him as much as he liked Thomas

Hardy, Walter de la Mare, and Wm. Empson. Of American poets, Thomas singled Stevens out for dispraise and Hart Crane, some of whose lines (those of "Recitative," for example) seemed agreeable, for praise. Francis Thompson's "Hound of Heaven" and "Ode to the Setting Sun" were pleasing, especially the latter, which proclaims "Birth and Death inseparable on earth: / For they are twain yet one, and Death is Birth." What *Adventures in the Skin Trade*, the story of Samuel Bennet, does not owe to Dickens, it appears to owe to the images of enclosure in Samuel Beckett's *Murphy*, which, unaccountably abandoning thrillers, Thomas reviewed in the *New English Weekly* in 1938.

The debt to D. H. Lawrence is no less than that to Joyce, who rules Thomas' words as Lawrence his themes: rebirth, for example, and the world of bird, beast, and flower. Thomas, who read Lawrence's poems from beginning to end, must have come upon some of the novels on the shelves of friends or on their parlor tables.

Among estimable older writers, aside from Dickens, Whitman, Melville, Beddoes, and Tennyson, were Wordsworth and Blake, from whose *Book of Thel* Thomas quotes in "The Visitor." Worms, sick roses, and heaven and hell fascinated him.

T. S. Eliot had taught poets to esteem the seventeenth century. Thomas esteemed it. Surprising juxtapositions, elaborate metaphors, puns and paradoxes, discordant concords of above and below, of macrocosm and microcosm, of the secular and the divine—all the armory of wit—were what he needed to supplement Joyce, Hopkins, and Lawrence. Not a deep student of that century, however, Thomas seems commonly to have confined his reading to Grierson's anthology of metaphysical lyrics; for all but two or three of the poems he refers to are there, where, no doubt, he first came upon them. Of Donne, Thomas knew the more familiar poems, the most famous of the Devotions, and the equally famous, and even more suitably charnal, last sermon, "Death's Duell," with its wombs and tombs, winding sheets and worms, deaths and entrances: "Wee have a winding sheete in our Mothers wombe . . . for we come to seeke a grave." Donne left young Thomas little to say. Vaughan was a Welshman; and Grierson's Vaughan, who says "Others, whose birth is in the tomb, / And cannot quit the womb," proceeded to the glories of recaptured childhood, leaving riper—Thomas little to say. He read Marvell on worms and graves, Herbert on Easter wings, and Milton on Christ's Nativity, all in Grierson. Though sometimes as extravagant as Crashaw or as juicy as Cleveland, with his "jelly in a glove," Thomas passed both by.

Of the King James Bible, Thomas knew Genesis, the Gospels, some of the Epistles, and the Apocalypse. So much for Sunday school; but he had read some plays of Shakespeare in Swansea Grammar School. Such, then, is the extent of Thomas' effectual learning—so far as I see it now, though for all I know he may have dipped into a summary of Hegel, a pamphlet on agronomy, *The Undertaker's Manual*, or a treatise on Bartók, who, Thomas told me, was the composer for him.

So equipped, he began to write poems, at once physical and metaphysical, about womb and tomb, life and death, or the natural and supernatural process of creation and destruction. Creation, which includes world, child, and poem, may be cosmic, sexual, or aesthetic. The creator may be poet or God or both together with their common tool, the word—or any man, for whose tool Thomas found many words. In the process of creation and destruction he found what Baudelaire calls "the horror and ecstasy of life." When horror won life's duel, womb and tomb, indistinguishably one, seem a hole Thomas was trying to crawl back into. More cheerful than poems on this, his many poems on poems and his many portraits of the artist show the better side of creation and creator although these portraits are not without intimation of mortality and, whatever the implication of divinity, not without self-criticism. Even self-mockery may be solipsistic, but sometimes Thomas on Thomas is more devastating than his severest critic.

Take the picture of Samuel Bennet with a bottle on his finger in *Adventures in the Skin Trade*. A symbolic concentrate, this bottled boy suggests all we know about Thomas and all we need to know. According to Freud, a bottle is female; yet, a translucent shape and the product of a craftsman's breath, a bottle is an image of poetry. Stuck with both, the frustrated, helpless, and happy poet is also stuck with the bottle's contents; for once it was full of beer. Something to attract notice—a kind of passport to society, the bottle gets him into trouble in bars and bathrooms. Stuck in the bottle, a finger, more than phallic, is what a poet writes with. That this finger is his little finger adds to the fun. Nobody more pathetic, significant, and absurd than this oracle of the bottle.

No matter what the ostensible subject of his prose or verse, Thomas always wrote about himself. A poem by Thomas about Jesus, the zodiac, or a worm is about Thomas. What but Joyce did Joyce write about? And yet he wrote about the world, entirely.

Among Thomas' solipsistic poems some concern his dreams and some his fears, horrors, and anxieties. His myths and archetypal voyages reveal himself as hero or captain. Some poems, of the graveyard school, look through another's grave at his own or at himself as elegist. Some celebrate his wife, his troubles around the house, and his children; some his childhood, and some, the places he loved or loves: the park, the farm, and Laugharne with its cobbles and cockles. Some blast his enemies; and some, in the service of a Puritan conscience, denounce the wicked city, Bunyan's Vanity Fair. Some concern his fear of war and some the war itself. Some are the poems of a naughty boy; for naughtiness, another of his masks, was also the most natural thing in the world. In mood and tone the poems range from the meditative and resigned to the mantic and exuberant, from the merry to the severe and hortatory. The sadness of a man aware of time and death underlies them all. Of whatever kind and whatever the mood, these poems record his struggles from darkness to the light, or, since he never quite got there, toward it. Beer is dark and light, mild and bitter, and the light is bitter. "My poetry," he says in "Replies to an Enquiry," "is . . . the record of my individual struggle from darkness to some measure of light."

Though important, these themes are less important than his genius and his craft with words. Like Joyce, Yeats, and Hopkins, but like few Englishmen since Hopkins, Thomas was in love with words. "The word is too much with us," says the hero of "The Orchards," creating a "world of words." Marlais, this hero, is Dylan Marlais Thomas, whose most lovable book—neither *Finnegan* nor the poems of Hopkins—was the dictionary. Nobody since Joyce has put that handbook for wizards to better use. Among the spelling words of Thomas, which range in kind from slang to the jargon of disciplines, are obsessive favorites, which ran all but autonomously away with him: "weathers," for example, or "forked"; for every virtue carries its own excess. Excessive too, maybe, his verbal play, the derangements that renew the language of the tribe, reveal a craftsman's delight, and, by their gaiety, relieve black humor—and his was almost as black as Beckett's. Words were Thomas' matter, his tool, and his refuge; but so great his delight in them and in what Rimbaud called their "alchemy" that, as Thomas complains, they sometimes got between him and the object. Sometimes they became the object. It may be, as logical positivists affirm, that the trouble with words is their ambiguity; but for Thomas this was their glory. As he forked his meanings out, they forked, miraculously. Double talk became triple under his bottled finger, and often quadruple. Nobody's ambiguities are more accurate.

More than meanings working together or at war, words are also the sounds of meanings. "Poetry is sound," said Thomas, aware, however, that "to articulate sweet sounds together," as Yeats puts it, is to order agreeable meanings. Conspiracies of sound and sense, Thomas' poems are "many sounding minded." More than the shapes of sound, they are the sounds and meanings of shape. Nobody a more musical shaper since God and Satan "fiddled" in the garden time.

So fiddled, the fiddling shapes of words are pictures, too. Those who compare Thomas with Bartók must also compare him with Dali. "Image, all image," says Marlais, the wordy boy of "The Orchards." As the words of Marlais Thomas multiply, the images quarrel. So he says in a frequently-quoted letter to Henry Treece:

> A poem by myself needs a host of images, because its centre is a host of images. I make one image . . . let it breed another, let that image contradict the first, make of the third image bred out of the other two together, a fourth contradictory image, and let them all, within my imposed formal limits, conflict. Each image holds within it the seed of its own destruction, and my dialectical method, as I under-

stand it, is a constant building up and breaking down of the
images that come out of the central seed, which is itself
destructive and constructive at the same time.

We may be sure that the juxtaposition of incompatibles, whether
of sound or pictures, is Thomas' method; but that the process is
systematically "dialectical" I cannot be sure. It is clear, however,
that his poems, not only shapes of sound and meaning, are shapes
of quarrels among them. Sometimes the relationships among these
contenders are troubled by uncertainty of syntax, a further and no
less calculated ambiguity that allows the mind to go off in several
directions within what we trust are "imposed formal limits."

Ambiguities of syntax and words, concordant discords of word
and image are the cause of his effects and a cause of his obscurity. Privacy was another. Not even their Biblical or Freudian
possibilities make his images altogether public. His trees have more
branches than those of Genesis or the Gospels. His towers and
seas are taller or wider than Freud's. Such privacies could be protective: to conceal what he had to reveal. Maybe, agreeing with
the magazine *transition* and damning the plain reader, Thomas
thought poetry expression rather than communication. In any
case, he did his best—or so it looks—to make his readers his
"strangers."

Yet, somewhere below these manifest confusions lies that "central seed," the latent sense from which the surface sprouted
and flowered. Deeply planted, to be sure, the sense is always
there. Never only things in themselves or autonomous shapes, his
poems are also about things. In the beginning of each poem was
the word; but words embody image and idea, and to know one
you must find the other. Disappointed when readers made no
sense of his images, Thomas liked to translate them into ideas. He
rebuked Dame Edith for mistranslation. To him the poems were
simple transactions between plain sense and a dialectical process
of image, acting as sense's surrogate. His approach was easier than
ours. Knowing what he had in mind, he worked from idea to
limited images. We must work from unlimited images to hidden
idea and back to images, where we linger; for a system of images
is more than its translation, and what the poet makes may be
more than what he makes of it and more or less than what he

intends. Striding on two levels, his intricate images interact with one another and with their common origin. Striding on the double, the poem consists of these interactions. No matter what the critics say, density and obscurity are no sure signs of value; but maybe such interactions are.

Shapes of this kind—imagistic, suggestive, reflexive, and syntactically uncertain, with half the meaning somewhere else—invite a variety of interpretations, none of which can be final. I offer my readings without canonical assurance. Under each of them I append a list of readings by others—under each, that is, that has been read before. Though these examiners and I agree occasionally about what we find in the text before us, we disagree more often. But any examination that brings out parts of the text and the relationships among them is worth something. Hypothesis begets hypothesis, and each, if based on textual evidence, may lead to fresh discovery. Our approaches may help yours and our follies, improving your wisdom, be your guide.

I have been reading many of these texts off and on since 1939 when *The World I Breathe* suddenly brought Welsh glory here. I have read them alone and in the company of students, whose guesses were often more ingenious than mine. It was hard for some to go only so far as the text allows. Our principles, however, were close reading and comparison. To notice parts, to ask questions, and to scribble margins were our practice. Sometimes, defeated, we gave up for a while. Sometimes we found, like those Germans of Tacitus, that what baffled us by night became clear in the morning when the sleeping mind had done its work and the fumes of our confabulation had dissipated. More than my solitary speculations—though largely these—the readings here are in part a composite of what I have gathered through the years from many co-operating classes and seminars, with whose members I read about half of the poems and most of the stories. Reading in concert seems the surest way of getting at matters so difficult as these, the surest way of getting familiar with the text and reaching inconclusive conclusions about it of one's own.

I am grateful to all who have read Thomas with me, particularly to these: Lita Hornick, Hyman Kleinman, Annis Pratt, Donald A. Roberts, George Warner, Julia Weil, Maurice Wohlgelernter; and I am grateful too to those who have helped me in other ways: Elliott Dobbie, Hoxie Fairchild, S. F. Johnson, and John Unterecker.

Reading the poems through from first to last brought many connections among them to light, many similarities in word, image, and theme. Reading the prose brought out many connections with the poems. Whatever his apparent abundance, Thomas had a limited stock of images and themes. The reading of one poem helps with the reading of another, and a story may help with a poem. Such textual comparisons account for my clutter of parentheses, not there for diversion but for looking up. Not for sitting back with, this book is for holding in one hand while holding *The Collected Poems* in the other. In a word, this book in hand is a manual. Unless otherwise stated, the parenthetical numbers refer to pages in the American edition of *The Collected Poems*, published by New Directions.

My analyses follow the order of the poems in *The Collected Poems*, Thomas' own arrangement, which, as J. Alexander Rolph and Ralph N. Maud have shown, is far from chronological. Thomas developed in theme and method from the dark early poems of womb and tomb to the sunny poems of childhood and Laugharne, but conclusions about development must be cautious; for he took one step back for every step forward—and one step sideways. Some of the early poems are bright and some of the late, dark. To announce, as critics have, that this or that poem marks a change is incautiously to challenge chronology. To help keep it straight I provide for each poem the date of first publication and, when significant, the date of the manuscript. A date followed by a question mark indicates Mr. Maud's conjecture. For details of dating see J. Alexander Rolph, *Dylan Thomas: a Bibliography* (1956) and Ralph N. Maud, "Dylan Thomas' Collected Poems: Chronology of Composition," *PMLA*, LXXVI (June, 1961).

Author's Prologue (1952), *pp. xv-xviii*

To announce his collection and commend it to "strangers," Thomas echoed his later poems, those about Laugharne in partic-ular. "Poem on His Birthday" is the closest parallel to "Prologue," but, as my parenthetical cross references show, he raided many of the poems from "A Winter's Tale" to the end of the collection for image and theme. More than summary and parallel, however, "Prologue" stands by itself as an affirmation of nature and art, the destructive and creative fellows of his forked green fuse. Here, as in the following pages, time and death prove the triumph of life. Here, again, the glory of art proclaims nature's glory. The dying craftsman's gaiety emerges from his tricks. What more fitting preparation for what follows?

Though the newest of his completed lyrics, "Prologue" offers little that is new; for innovation is none of a prologue's business. Here, as in the earlier poems that follow, the old machinery turns again. Contending opposites—life and death, water and fire, sea and land, light and dark, country and city—circle, diverge, and unite as before; and metaphor provides the forward movement. As metaphorical God, Thomas creates the destructive flood. As metaphorical Noah, he builds an ark. Indeed, foxier than Noah, he builds "multitudes of arks," where, undeserted, his circus animals, two by two, are on display. More logical than the fabulous shipwright, Thomas hews his arks from the tree of words. Here, then —and what more fitting introduction to his poems?—is a poem about writing poems.

The hundred-and-two lines of "Prologue" fall into two parts of fifty-one lines each. The second part mirrors the first. In a letter to his publisher (*Adam*, 27-28) Thomas explains his metrical scheme: the second part, he says, "rhymes *backward* with the first. The first and last lines of the poem rhyme: the second and the last but one; and so on. . . . Why I acrosticked myself like this, don't ask me." Even for so crafty a poet, the formidable task he set himself required "a devil of a long time."

Thomas liked fiddling with words and shapes of words. "Vision and Prayer," rising or falling to centers, is an example. The not altogether dissimilar scheme he followed in "Prologue" is more accountable than he allowed. Good fun for him, it is an elaborate joke on the reader. But there are better reasons than this for that. Devotion to sound, however, is not one of them. His scheme is almost without aural value since, until their meeting in the middle (lines 51 and 52), the rhymes escape notice. What he was after here was not a shape of sounds but a shape for the idea of shape, something to suit creation, his theme; for creation is shaping. He calls the result of his serious play a "rumpus of shapes." So God's world, too.

Verbal displacements increase the fun. Internal sounds, especially alliteration (e.g. lines 34-36), atone for the displacement of rhyme. The rhythm, as in many of the later poems, is a free adaptation of Hopkins' sprung rhythm. Four, three, or, sometimes, two stresses lend variety and surprise to lines that look like equals.

Description of the seaside at Laugharne yields in the second part to description of the woods, whose beasts and birds replace the fish, shells, and birds of the shallows. Singing sunset at the summer's end, the boy of summer, seedy but tropical to the last, turns toward his nightfall with joy; for the shipyard is noisy as ever by "fox light."

I

A triumph of heavy rhythm and interwoven consonants, the first line establishes the idea and feeling of time. The clock of the seasons is "winding down" to "summer's end." "Now" and "end" acquire weight from terminal position. "God speeded" makes time's inexorable movement sinister by an implicit good-by. The setting sun of waning summer ascends the "torrent" like a salmon to spawn and die.

Dead starfish (cf. "the stars' seashore dead," 192) lie on the "scummed" sands along with empty shells; but shells still sing the seven seas, sandpipers still run, the gulls are cross as fishwives, and herons (cf. 187, 190) stab for fish. Against the brightness of the sky wading fishermen are black as crows. "Tackled" implies both fishing equipment and cloud-scraping rigging. The foot of the neighboring wood becomes a "dancing hoof" in honor of Pan; for nature is dancing and piping as it dies.

Laugharne's shore may be an image of death in life and life in death, but "the country is holy" (182). Not so the city of dreadful night ("of nine / Days' night") where Thomas was a nine-day wonder. Lines 19-22, a vision of London and New York as Sodom and Gomorrah, prepare us for "the bum city" (86), "Sodom To-morrow and London" (175), and "Prologue to an Adventure," three Biblical visions of the city, improved, no doubt, by Wordsworth, Bunyan, and T. S. Eliot. Here Thomas sees the destruction of New Sodom by the fiery, "religious wind" of his poetry.

Though back in his bucolic refuge (cf. "The Countryman's Return," Watkins, 87-90), he sings "at poor peace." (Compare "cloud quaking peace," 192. "Poor" implies domestic interruption as well as poverty.) The "strangers" to whom he sings, defined in his prefatory "Note" as "my readers," are the urban welcomers the old ram rod is "dying of" (196). Nevertheless, he sings to them out of the "seathumbed leaves" of this volume, "seathumbed" because composed by the hand of a "tide-tongued" poet. Like the leaves of autumn trees, his published pages will "fly and fall . . . Crumble and undie" in "the dogdayed night" that awaits all artists as young dogs and all the boys of summer. "Undie," a word from *Dracula*, means living death on library shelves. Poems are leaves (cf. "dry leaves," 96) because they come from the "tree of words." Thomas' association of tree and word (see 19, 83, for example) explains the metaphor of sawing and woodworking. "The world's turning wood," not only its "winding down," seasonal change, and diurnal rotation, suggests turning wood on a lathe—turning arks or poems out. "Sawn, splay sounds," though cut with care, are clumsy and infelicitous—among the "crudities, doubts, and confusions," maybe, that Thomas regrets in his prefatory "Note." To display the splay was his unhappy necessity. The parenthetical and happy definition of his poetry as the "burning and crested act" of a firebird, returning in the world's turning wood, implies fire to destroy Sodom and the fires of Lawrentian renewal. (For Thomas' Phoenix and his other firebirds see 120, 134-35, 187.)

Meanwhile the salmon sun sinks, "sucked"—exhausted by spawning or engulfed—into the dusk of the "dabbed" or birdpecked bay. That swans, which sing when dying, are "dumb" puts poetry off for a time in life's favor. Yet, undiscouraged, Thomas hacks his "shapes" that strangers may know how he glories and trumpets this bird-roared, sea-born, man-torn, bloodblest "star" or world. "Spinning," which seems to complicate wood turning by another craft, may mean winding down or turning with the world's wood.

The woodworker builds an ark, "bellowing" with beasts and

shapes of sound, as "the flood begins." In "Prologue to an Adventure," a story, the flood destroys the wicked city. More creative than destructive here, the molten flood spouts and erupts (cf. 146) from Thomas' fearing, raging, living "fountainhead," at once spring and volcano, to cover his beloved Welsh farms. Why these innocent "sheep white" farms (cf. 131) are "hollow" is beyond me unless they are ships. To him they were neither empty nor trivial. "Wound asleep" recalls "winding down" and "turning." "Hark" and "Look," which introduce the series of imperatives in Part II (cf. 134), prove flood, hollowness, and winding benign. "To the best of my love" assures us again that his poems "are written for the love of Man and in praise of God." Since Thomas created this flood, however, one wonders what god he had in mind—and what flood. This flood seems something to float arks in.

I I

"Arms" in the fifty-second line, agreeing with "farms" at the end of Part I, links the parts by a meeting of the rhymes. The rhyme of "asleep" in the fiftieth line with "keep" in the fifty-third indicates the widening pattern.

Clasped in his arms, Wales is plainly his darling, but "To Wales" seems to imply that the flood extends all the way to, but not including, Wales, that the flooded Welsh farms are unflooded or not Welsh, or that he hugs the unflooded area alone. If "To" means in order to, the line, elliptical now, means that the flooding of farms makes Wales huggable. This flood, I am afraid, must be included among the "confusions" that Thomas regrets in that prefatory "Note." But "To Wales in my arms," above reproach in sentiment, has a fine sound.

A catalogue or passenger list of beasts for the ark demands interjections: Hoo, Huloo, Ho, Hist, and the like. We have left the sunset shore of Laugharne for the moonlit woods of "the hooting, nearly dark." Internal rhyme and dissonance, symphonies of vowels, and insistent alliteration heighten romantic enthusiasm and thicken it. Edith Sitwell praises the "exquisite exactness" of "the woods' praise"—all that "Coo rooing." What denser example of "texture" could she have come upon? "Moonbeam" and "moons" are synesthetic verbs. The owls' "castle keep," not only the castle at Laugharne, is the "greenwood keep" of "In Country Sleep." "Dingle," balancing "cockle" (Part I), verbal concentrates of wood and shore, help unite the parts. "Deer," as Shakespeare knew, are small beasts of any kind. "Bryns" are Welsh hills; a "plumbed" bryn may imply a mine shaft or a well. The "Welsh and reverent rook" prepares us for a flock of priestly blackbirds and their rooking (e.g. 13, 19, 135, 184). Curlews and "gabbing capes" bring the seabirds of Part I back to mind.

"Hoo, there" (line 53) and "Heigh, on horseback hill, jack / Whisking hare!" (lines 67-68), echoes of Hopkins' "Windhover" (cf. 184), suitably serve to introduce Thomas' union of God and nature: "Hail to His beasthood!" Not the pun, but the pantheism would have displeased Father Hopkins, who, although he would have allowed "jack . . . hare" for its aural relationship with "Hears, there" and as a sign of God's grandeur, would have been displeased no less by the intrusion of Jack and Jill (cf. 199), which reduces holiness to the level of Mother Goose.

Thick beasts "sleep . . . thin" in the "Clangour" of Thomas' shipyard. (Compare busy Noah at the end of "A Prospect of the Sea," a story.) The hewing of his "flood ship" and the clashing of his anvils become the fiddling of a poem. "Fiddle" is a noun, parallel to "Hubbub" and, despite the comma, a verb governing "this tune." God and Satan, equally creative, "fiddled in the shaping-time" (46). Thomas' poetic ark, shaping up, becomes "a tongued puffball," spreading its spores abroad as the tree of the word spreads its flying leaves. The "fox light" by which the fungoid fiddler-shipwright works is the "owl-light" or twilight of "Altarwise" and the inner light of a poet whose "foxy tongue" is celebrated in "When, like a running grave." "Ahoy, old, sea-legged fox" (line 98) is Thomas hailing himself. Not only a young dog and the sea dog of a "sea-legged deck" (166), Thomas is a dog fox, like the burning fox (184) of D. H. Lawrence.

"Hogsback woods," the tops of haystacks, and the roofs of "hollow" farms, crowded with refugee hens and cocks, emerge from the "throng of waters." (Compare "haystacked" with "fishermanned," 166.) But Thomas' other "neighbors," the other romantically holy beasts, come for safety to his patchworked ark. Even "finned" neighbors or fish seek refuge there, along with the "felled" or furry. Thomas, the self-exposing captain of the ark.

drinks "moonshine," like Noah, his great original. Not only illicit spirits of the mountains, "moonshine" is also imagination. That Noah Thomas is drunk on both augurs imperfect navigation.

Although the flood leaves the roofs of barns dry, it covers the steeples of churches, whose sunken bells "noise" abroad the poet's "poor peace" as the sun, already set, sets. (Thomas liked sunken bells, e.g. 42, 167.) The dark "shoals every holy field," making it shallow—not too shallow, however, for floating a multitude of arks, "wooden islands," sailing from hill to hill, over "the water lidded lands." Crowded into arks, "we" or Thomas and his passengers "ride out alone." However shoal the water, their riding cannot be on horseback, still less on hogsback.

The "prowed dove with a flute," recalling Noah's dove and the fluting of Part I, is both figurehead and ark. That fluting arks are poems, which destroy wicked Sodom by fire and save holy nature from water, explains Thomas' salute to the "sea-legged fox," himself as poet-captain, both prowed and proud. It may be that this fox and the tomtit or titmouse (cf. the "telltale tit," 194) of the following line are bestial passengers in the arks, but Thomas' "beasthood," like God's has made him one with all the felled and the quilled. "Tom tit and Dai mouse" strengthens the identification; for as tomtit and titmouse become one—as, indeed, they are—so do Tom and Dai. Tom is short for Thomas, and Dai, short for David, evidently stands for Dylan, whose ark of poetry, still tropical, still sings in the setting sun at summer's end. "Now," the last word, is the first. The penultimate line, repeating the second line of the poem, also leaves him where he started, except for the flowering flood. A "flood flowers" by bringing fertility or by being transfigured. This uncertain flood is poetry, too. Away sails Thomas on his singing voyage to death (cf. 193), saved with his natural cargo by the arks of poetry from poetry's flood. But a flood, gushing from its source, is shapeless. Arks, the products of craft, are shaped—and in his trimmest craft are glory holes. There is more consistency than first appears in this sad, exuberant "rumpus of shapes."

Adam, 27-28. Edith Sitwell, *The Atlantic Book of British and American Poetry*, 1958. W. S. Merwin, in *Casebook*, 67. Stanford, 142-43.

18 Poems, 1934

All eighteen of these poems from Thomas' first volume reappear in their original order in *The Collected Poems*. Thomas wrote them in 1933 and 1934 when he was nineteen and twenty years old. Generally of what he agreed to call his "womb-tomb period," these poems concern creation, both physical and poetic, and the temporal process of birth, death, and rebirth, which he accepts with resignation and gaiety—verbal gaiety and the gaiety of naughtiness. Some of the poems are indelicate, some socialistic, and some, recounting dreams, dreamlike. Less hope in these than fear: fear of impending war, sexual experience, and literary failure. Less ecstasy here than horror. The rhythms are monotonous, the structures tight, and the textures rich. Some of his best poems are in this volume. Even the second best have fine lines and images. Most of these poems invite comparison with the early stories.

The Lockwood Memorial Library of The University of Buffalo has manuscripts (dated 1933 or 1934) of thirteen of these eighteen poems. The texts of nine of the poems in manuscript are substantially the same as the final texts; but these four manuscript texts differ considerably from the texts in *18 Poems*: "In the beginning," "I fellowed sleep," "When once the twilight locks," and "Our eunuch dreams."

I see the boys of summer (1934), *pp. 1-3*

We admire a dazzling surface first, a quarrel of images with no immediate sense. "Frozen loves," "cargoed apples," "boiling honey," and "jacks of frost" create a climate of extremes where "brawned womb's weathers" and "dogdayed pulse" seem more at ease than we; but monotony of rhythm and regularity of structure hint order within this disorder. The second line of each tidy stanza of Part I begins with a verb ("Stature," for example), each fourth line with "There," and each fifth line with "Of." "I see," says someone in all but one of the first lines. But imperfect rhymes (a a b c c b), quarreling with neatness, keep us awake by variety as we are put to sleep by monotony. Hardly rhymes at all, "hives" and "voids," "threads" and "nerves" are but ghosts of rhyme. Even dissonance and assonance are certain alongside these. (By dissonance I mean an approximate rhyme in which vowels disagree and consonants agree, e.g. goat-gate, thrash-flesh. By assonance I mean an approximate rhyme in which consonants disagree and vowels agree, e.g. rake-pain.) Yet this order of dis-agreements, we must agree, offers an experience like nothing else —and a good experience, too. Maybe, prizing that, we should take the dazzling thing as, if ignorant of music, we take some-thing by Bartók, without inquiry.

But poetry, made of words, is not music, whatever these arts have in common. Examination of this thing of words shows the element of sense that words must bear. Indeed, examination shows a rational theme that determines and orders what we have been struck by. To see how rhythm, rhyme, structure, and image serve this theme we must challenge the images and place the contenders in what seems a debate.

The speaker, taking a dim view of the boys in Part I, sees their ruin. Justifying themselves in Part II, the boys answer their critic. Part III, proving the structure dialectical, resolves this conflict of thesis and antithesis by a kind of synthesis. Of these debaters, the boys claim our notice first. Summer is the season of fulfillment; yet the boys of summer, like improvident grasshoppers, are doomed. Probably these boys are all men—in their aspects of sperm cells, embryos, and adolescents. That they are also Welshmen, driven from mine, factory, and home by the depression of 1931 (the year Thomas left school) and ruined in London, is not altogether unlikely. Plainly the speaker who sees these complex boys is one of them, sharing their fate. Since he is also a poet, the boys are poets, too. Poets, Welshmen, adolescents, sperm cells, and embryos—all of these at once—these boys are victims of time. Temporal process, suggested by sun and moon, is established in four stanzas by the four seasons, autumn, winter, spring, and summer in this order.

I

The first stanza, a contention among images of heat and cold, wet and dry, love and sterility, involves the autumnal game of bobbing for apples; but apple and flood, from Genesis, suggest conception. Yet the expected harvest will be frozen and the "gold tithings" (plots of ground) laid barren. As fertility and sterility, life and death, creation and destruction proceed together, each involves its opposite.

The second stanza, following conception and genesis in the first, concerns the development of the embryo in the dark hive or void of the womb, which, though feeding nerves, holds death's frost. "The signal moon" may be that of the ninth month. Womb and moon are "zero" by shape and promise. That the boys at this point are also adolescents "in the sun" is made almost plain by their activity. Playing with words (Jack Frost) and with themselves, they finger "jacks of frost." As the honey-boiling womb holds curdling, frosty death, so the penis.

Still "in their mothers" (or, as adolescents, attached to them), the summer children of the third stanza enjoy "the brawned womb's weathers" until obstetrical spring paints emerging skulls with light at birth and promises bony death. As embryos, they paint the "shades" (ghostly darkness) of the "quartered" (four, inhabited) seasons on the walls of their dams (mothers and retainers of amniotic fluid). As adolescents, they try "fairy thumbs" Such suggestions of masturbation and homosexuality.

noted by most commentators, serve the theme of sterility and death.

Grown up at last or fully statured, the boys of summer come to nothing in summer, leap as they will in amatory heat. Their hot pulse is frozen stiff; yet thaw is not impossible. As there is ice in summer, so there is summer in ice. This ambiguity, complicating doom by hope, is confirmed by "seedy," the key word, which includes fertility and decay. Our seedy boys "lame the air" as the pulse of "love and light bursts in their throats." Every dog has his day. Every poet as a throaty young dog, seeking love and light, responds to his "dogdayed pulse"; yet "bursts," including glory and destruction, is as ambiguous as "seedy."

I I

In Part II, these seedy "men of nothing," responding more to the nasty tone of their critic than to his ambiguities, cap them with ambiguities of their own; for nothing is simple in this debate. It may be, they say in their first stanza, that all men are victims of time; but making the most of time, let us "challenge" it before the clock strikes the "chiming quarter" of midnight or death. Aspiring, let us "ring the stars" while old man time ("the sleepy man of winter") rings out Tennyson's wild bells at year's end. Midnight may be irreversible, but blowing, however vain, is the activity of vital winds, poets, and whales; and ringing the bell of the stars could imply Tennyson's new year.

As "deniers," we may deny promise, they agree in the second stanza; and it may be true that begetting children brings death into the world, but even men of "straw" (Yeats' scarecrows? Eliot's hollow men?) are better than nothing. "Death" in the second line means birth. "Cramp" refers to embracing and death by water. "The fair dead who flush the sea" are embryos, pulling the chain of the amniotic cistern. "Davy's lamp," lighting the dark submarine or subterranean womb, seems Welsh, whether a miner's lamp or a lamp on Davy Jones' locker. The "bright-eyed worm," more than the glowing coil of this lamp, is both phallic and charnal, as the complex of birth and death demands.

In the third stanza, "four-winded spinning" (cf. "twelve-winded," 69, 145), "green" (life), "seaweed" (cf. "seaweedy," 55), and "iron" (metal in Thomas' world is flesh) present nature.

Holding the sea up to drop her birds is another image of birth, which flushes the wasteland, bringing momentary fertility. "Spinning," "ball," and "comb" complicate water by suggestion of the fatal sisters and their thread. The "wreath" suits death and poets alike.

"County gardens" have introduced the merry squires of Christmas—Mr. Pickwick's host at the Manor Farm, for example (cf. "burning gentry," 82). Nailing the squires of Christmas to the trees, we confuse Christmas with Good Friday, birth with death; yet Easter means rebirth. Drying "love's damp muscle" and breaking a kiss in "no love's quarry" mean love's end in sterility. The "poles" of the last line, not only cross and phallus, are all the antipodes that have obsessed the speakers. Pointing to life and death, "promise" is both ironic and literal. The boys of summer, as ambiguous as their critic, have said nothing more than he.

III

Part III, a quick interchange between the old boy and the ruined boys, speaking alternate lines, adds little but an air of finality to the established theme of life and death, creation and destruction. Nobody wins. The "maggot's barren," as doubtful in grammar as in sense, includes wormy womb and tomb, the double "pouch" in which all men are both "full and foreign." The old boy as the man their father was unites the living and the dead, fathers and sons. "Sons of flint and pitch" are sons of the "short spark" (80), not only sex but life itself. The last line, a geographical conceit, like Andrew Marvell's "planisphere," unites all contraries, ambiguously. No less double, exclamatory "O see" carries two attitudes. "Cross," implying union and crucifixion, includes sex, two generations, religion, death, poetry—in short, life, our general cross. (Compare "crossed sticks," 13, and "two poles kissed," in "A Prospect of the Sea.") From Genesis we have come to Calvary.

The danger of guessing the senses of a thing like this is that idea, replacing poem, will drive out marvel. If we can put the commonplace idea into its place among many elements, awareness of the idea may enrich the rest; but subordinating the idea is difficult. Better maybe, as I have suggested, to leave the thing what William James called a buzzing, blooming confusion. My first experience of this poem as something rich, strange, and mysterious, was, I think, better than my present experience, limited by awareness of the commonplace ambiguity that centers the parts. Useful as excitement and scaffolding to the poet, idea, distracting readers, may denude the poem.

Yet examination helps us to admire the poet's art. All the parts, we find, conspire. Conflicts among images, not there alone to dazzle us, present the conflicts of life. Rhythmic monotony and formal regularity give the feeling of eternal process, while dubious rhyme mixes our feelings. Man's condition and his fate emerge as theme; but verbal play and the gaiety of language prove life good, however bad. Whatever our fate, poetry is fun, and this poem proves it by example.

W. S. Merwin, in *Casebook*, 60. Fraser, 13. Olson, 43. Treece, 79. Stanford, 40-44. E. Glyn Lewis, in Tedlock, 17. Geoffrey Moore, in Tedlock, 252.

When once the twilight locks no longer (1934), pp. 4-5

"I sent my creature scouting on the globe," a great line in the grand manner, raises the main problems. Who is the speaker, who his creature, and what the globe? Plainly, the speaker is a creator: any father, God, the poet—probably all together. As in Joyce, the artist is God of creation, father of everything and everyone. His creature, therefore, can be Adam, a son, the Son, a poem, the creative instrument (word or phallus), or the projected self, his "ambassador."

Post-creative reminiscence detains the creator in the first stanza. His finger-worm-fist seems not only the phallus but the poet's hand; and "the mouth of time" is both womb and the vocal imagination. "Locks" could be those of a canal, a door, or hair in this context. "Twilight," recalling Yeats, anticipates "Love's twilit nation" (22). Dryness, though usually a sign of sterility, means weaning here. (Compare "the waters of the breast dried up; the nipples grew through the sand," "The Burning Baby.") "Damned," probably a misprint, is "dammed" in 18 *Poems*.

"Galactic" in the second stanza, a portmanteau word combining lactic with galaxy, unites mammal with the Milky Way according to the habit of Hopkins. ("The dry seabed," of course, is the womb after birth.) Like galactic, the globe of hair and bone (cf. 31) unites macrocosm or universe with microcosm or man—or, indeed, the poem itself, a rounded little world, as in the last stanza. "Rib," bringing Adam and Eve to mind, is at once skeletal and phallic. Glancing suggestions have embraced genesis of all kinds; and genesis, as Milton says, brought death into the world.

The imagery of fuse and powder looks forward to the destructive-creative "green fuse" (10). Replacing his creator in stanza three, the creature enjoys a post-creative "sabbath" on a sun-day. Light, sun, and stars seem at once God's properties and external reality, as in the final stanza. The creature, having become creative, replaces father's "magics" or art with magic of his own, a dream or vision that comes by chance—by drawing straws? Whether drowning is a reference to the womb of the imagination or to the wetness of this dream, "He drowned his father's magics in a dream" is as grand in manner as the other great line of this poem.

The creature's vision, occupying the next two stanzas, is a womb-tomb poem. "Redhaired cancer," "cataracted eyes" filming the shroud, and the "bushy jaws" of corpses, unable to shave, improve the horror of death; but "bags of blood" could refer to the womb and the male genitals—fly-lords both (cf. 69)—and the horror of life. "The Christ-cross row," referring to the alphabet in old primers, includes our Calvary and, since trees are both Word and words in Thomas (c. g. 19), the poem and the poet's awareness, such as it is. Clearly, still at school, he is learning his alphabet. "Issue," in the first line, works equally well as noun or verb. Armour, like any metal, means flesh (cf. 40). The "grave," in the first line, is also the womb.

The fifth stanza, continuing this morbid poet's vision, unites womb and tomb by images of water and dryness. The tomb "gives up its dead" (Revelation, 20:13; cf. 7) to the "working sea" of the womb, where submarine shades (souls and embryos) floating up toward rebirth and light, raising periscopes, are not unlike the sinking men of Rimbaud's "Bateau ivre," which, at this time, Thomas had not read. Another stanza, elaborating this one, follows it in *18 Poems*. Enough is enough, Thomas may have thought, suppressing that stanza here.

"The twilight screws" of the present sixth stanza seem at once marine propellers, sexual endeavors, and coffin-screws. This stanza, a recapitulation, adds little but a suitable pause before the hortatory briskness of the finale, which dim recapitulation makes brighter. Abandon your morbid concern with womb and tomb, the creator urges his creature at last. Come out into the sun, not for a sabbath but for working days in the town or on it—under Milk Wood maybe, in Llareggub. "Poppied pickthank" (meaning dreaming tell-tale) are words as archaic as the creature's old dream. New worlds for old (cf. "globe") or poems hang, like apples of knowledge, on the alphabet trees of Christ-cross row. Fall, leave the Garden, and face the poet's Calvary, says he to himself—we, his privileged overhearers.

The theme of this poem is creation. By the device of a poem within a poem Thomas limits creation to the making of a poem. His subject, as usual, is himself as boy and poet, at once creator, creature, and severest critic. The creature's poem is a parody of young Thomas by young Thomas; and the hortatory ending is advice to himself. His famous struggle towards the light began earlier than most think.

The stanza (a a b c c b) is that of "The boys of summer," but the rhymes, much less ghostly, are dissonant now in the manner of Yeats, Owen, and Auden. Rhythmic monotony is broken only by the troubled movement of the last line of the fifth stanza.

The Buffalo manuscript of November 11, 1933, extensively revised before printing, has a "violet fungus" in place of "the red-haired cancer."

Olson, 36. Stanford, 44-46.

A process in the weather of the heart (1934), *pp. 6-7*

This poem is parallel in theme to "The force that through the green fuse"; but most of the early poems show Thomas' obsessive concern with the natural process that, linking man and world, inner and outer, turns upon the axis of life and death. Not this ordinary theme but what the poet does with it is our concern.

Here monotonous rhythm suits monotonous recurrence more aptly than usual by means of periodic stops, indicated by semi-colons, in each second and fifth line, except the last. The usual stanza (a a b c c b) and the ghostly rhymes are augmented here by three additional lines that agree in rhyme with the preceding stanza. That these ghostly rhymes are the important words of this ghostly poem is not without importance. Favorite words ("weather," "fork," and "dry") connect this poem with its rivals.

Applying "weather," a word for outer climate, to inner climate joins two worlds. "Damp" and "dry," customary tags for life and death (cf. 3, 4, 12, 38), introduce a customary collocation of hot and cold: "golden" or molten shot (sperm) in the freezing tomb of the womb. Lawrence's thinking with the blood brings knowledge of death ("turns night to day") as the memory of suns in their blood darkly enlightens both "living" coffin-worm and penis. ("Blood in their suns," a playful reversal, looks forward to the Apocalyptic climax.) These parallels or correspondences fix the theme: awareness of death as part of life. Possessed by death and seeing the skull beneath each embryo's skin, Thomas is more than usually dismal here. Usually in his graveyard meditations the forces of life balance the forces of death.

Dark weather in the eye enables it to see the darkness of bones in the tomb; and the womb brings death with every birth "as life leaks out." Half the "light" or knowledge of the weathered eye is dark and of the dark. The "fathomed sea" of the womb breaks on "unangled" (unfished, unmeasured, dry) land. Seed becomes pubic forest in vain; for each tree there "forks" (cf. 14) or divides its fruit, half of which drops in death's wind.

"Damp and dry" remind the poet of "the quick and the dead" (from Acts 10:42 and The Book of Common Prayer). At this point the metaphysical ingenuity that distinguishes this poem begins. To the eye enlightened by darkness, both the quick and the dead are dead and both are ghosts. (That the quick are dead, more than a seventeenth-century paradox, is Joyce's contention in "The Dead.") Natural process, in the world as in the heart, ambiguously "turns ghost to ghost." This could mean that the quick ghost becomes a dead ghost, that these ghosts, meeting socially, confabulate, or that each ghost becomes more ghostly. Anyway, we sit in the "double shade" of these twin shades. Shades of shades are a fancy worthy of John Donne, also fascinated by more than ordinary nothings.

The final lines, hurrying along without semicolon, are Apocalyptic. Sun and moon meet like those shades, blood in their suns maybe; the curtains of the flesh, even the lids of our knowing eyes, fall on our shabby play; and the heart "gives up its dead." (Compare "the sea gave up the dead" at the last judgment, Rev. 20:13; *Collected Poems*, 5; "The Enemies.") Inner heart has become outer sea, and the two weathers unite in a general confusion that allows "gives up" to be read in more ways than one. The tone of this tight and logical structure of conflicting opposites, joining one another by correspondence and confusion, is resigned.

Awarding this processed poem a prize, the editor of the *Referee*, where the poem was first published, called it "a microscope-poem," in which each phrase, repaying "careful scrutiny," demands close and separate examination.

W. S. Merwin, in *Casebook*, 60. Stanford, 47. Runia Macleod, in *Adam*, 20.

Before I knocked (1934), pp. 8-9

The speaker is an undifferentiated, vital liquid before it has assumed shape as sperm cell; yet this blind mouth foresees. Foreknowledge of life and death and man's condition is the theme of this poem. (Compare the dark light of eye and vein in the previous poem.) Since Christ is all men in one sense, especially, according to poets, all poets, this liquid mouth identifies itself with Him. Not speaker, as some commentators affirm, Christ is no more than parallel here—as in Joyce's *Ulysses*, for example. The liquid's future as sperm, fertilized egg, and, after delivery, man alive will recapitulate Christ's past. Mary's womb and Christ's tomb are every man's extremes. The sufferings of Christ are general myth.

Before knocking (cf. "knocking head," "The Burning Baby") with liquid hand on the door of the womb, this pregenital liquid is as shapeless as shaping water in Christ's Jordan or in the jordan (chamberpot) under mamma's bed, a future home. The play is Joycean here. "Mnetha," puzzling William Empson, is from Blake's *Tiriel*, a prophetic book. An old nurse, Mnetha serves as mother to senile Heva. Being brother to Mnetha's "daughter" unites senility and youth. Since Mnetha seems a combination of Athena and Memory, her daughter could serve as Muse of poetry. That our speaking liquid is not only her brother but father's sister indicates the androgynous state of vital fluid before sperm fixes sex. The "fathering worm," more than papa's member, could be the serpent of Genesis, who also brought death into the world.

Although this liquid knows nothing of the outer world, although the "armour" (cf. 4, 40) of its flesh is still molten, it is aware of the sexual activities ("thud" of "rainy hammer") of father, who, as a smith at his forge, works from his starlit "dome" (head, Yeats' church; cf. 21, 22, 40). Father is like Vulcan, Thor, or God Himself.

This "ungotten" liquid or sap knows weathers, especially "the Eastern weather" of the Holy Land, and suffers the crucifixion ("rack," "gallow crosses," and the "lily bones" of Easter). Christ's "living cipher" could be chi rho, and "brambles" the crown of thorns. Like Jesus, the speaker thirsts on his cross; but, since the liquid throat or "well" will be a poet's, from his pierced side come "words and water." Smelling the maggot in his stool is foreknowing death and remembering the jordan. When conception makes this liquid a "mortal creature," the sap will sip at the Eucharistic "vine" of the umbilicus. The "hellborn dew," a problem, could mean the Fall (dew falls) in Eden's Eastern weather.

Born, like Christ, of "flesh and ghost," but, like man, a "mortal ghost," the shaped liquid will die. ("Death's feather," a favorite phrase, may imply an easeful Keatsian death or, as a commentator suggested, "You could have knocked me down with a feather.") The dying breath of the poet is that of "dying christ."

Since any man is Christ and God's flesh, pity every man and God, our general father, who, repeating the miracle of Incarnation endlessly, has "doublecrossed" every mother's womb. "Doublecrossed," the great word of the poem, was tried in an early version of "When once the twilight locks," suppressed, and reserved for better use, the climax here. More than climax, however, this word of many senses and tones, is probably the poem's origin and the point from which the rest exfoliated. To doublecross means deceive or betray (cf. Yeats' "honey of generation had betrayed"). God deceived Mary and denied her pleasure by ghostly begetting. Any father deceives any mother by engendering death. Two crossings of the maternal gate, one in and one out, two knockings at the gate, and the double crucifixion of birth and death, of man and poet, are also present in this condensation. As crowded as any word of *Finnegans Wake*, this great word, catching up the tone of "Jordan," qualifies the solemnity of man's fate with levity. The union of seriousness and levity, as T. S. Eliot observes in his essay on Marvell, is a mark of wit; and wit is a high and serious thing.

The stanza, more than usually adventurous in shape, complicates the rhythm with feminine rhymes (in the first, third, and fifth lines) on the same sound, "r," in each stanza. The three masculine endings of each stanza agree in one consonant, "m" in the first stanza, for example, and "n" in the fourth.

William Empson, in *Casebook*, 112. W. S. Merwin, in *Casebook*, 60. Marshall W. Stearns, in Tedlock, 117-18. Elizabeth Drew and John L. Sweeney, *Directions in Modern Poetry*, 111. Stanford, 47-49.

The force that through the green fuse drives the flower (1933), *p. 10*

This poem made Thomas famous. Immediate in appeal, communicating much to all, it yields, like most great poems, further glories to closer inspection—but never all. What other poet of that time, Yeats aside, could compose a thing so simple and rich, so dense and clear? "The green fuse" makes many of the early poems seem essays, working toward what would be impossible without them.

The theme is familiar. Life and death, the poet says, as he says in "A process in the weather of the heart," are parts of a natural process that links man with what surrounds him, inner with outer, above with below. That there are correspondences between macrocosm and microcosm is no news at all; nor is it news that time and eternity rule apparent contraries and parallels, that creation and destruction are our kissing poles. Clearly, this theme which failed to lift "A process" to greatness is not the cause of glory here, though familiar theme, putting us at ease as we exclaim, "True, true," may help—as any element may. But truth must work with rhythm, image, and all the other parts for effects like this. Their arrangement and happy interaction establish glory.

Inspection sorts the elements out, even the classical four (in fuse, water, wind, and sand) and an anatomical progression from vein, mouth, hand, lips, and womb to that ambiguous worm—all involved in the making of a poem. Veins, as Empson guesses, may also be veins of ore in a mine. Such ambiguities and juxtaposed or condensed opposites, along with paradox, oxymoron, and inner echoes assist the feeling of unity and duality that the theme demands. No collocation of inner and outer need surprise us in this anatomy of the world.

The structure, tidy but not logical, depends on statement and restatement in other terms, repetition with variation, a structure like that of nature itself, whose logic is not altogether ours. Oscillation between life and death, making and destroying, rising and falling affords the movement. Pause is afforded by momentary condensations of contraries. Conflict and union, as in other early poems, are the machinery here. Our sense of regular process is aided, as in "The boys of summer," by verbal repetition. First lines, except for that of the coda, begin with "The." Fourth lines begin with "And." Last lines, except for that of the first stanza, begin with "How."

The stanza, evolved after many experiments, is an expressive pattern. The caesura, marked by a semicolon, in the second line (cf. 6), the falling cadence of the short third line, and the free-running fourth and fifth lines (not a rhymed couplet, but involved by rhyme with the first lines) constitute the very form for falling and rising, a contention of opposites, and an agreement of parallels. After statement, counterstatement, and fall comes orotund triumph. The approximate rhymes, except for the feminine endings of the first stanza (cf. 8) are regular in their irregularity until the last line of the third stanza, where "lime" seems unattended—to be attended, however, by "time," an internal rhyme and the only true rhyme of the poem, in the first line of the fourth stanza. The pattern of a b a b a, broken by "lime," becomes a a b a b in the fourth stanza. Feelings of recurrence, variety, and surprise seem effects of this scheme.

But rhythm is what chiefly moves us. That rhythm of the metronome is not the only way to present temporal process is Thomas' discovery here. The more or less regular first line, establishing the beat, is counterpointed by the last two lines, which are as flexible, almost as "sprung," as those of Hopkins. Scansion depends on the reader's interpretation. Take "And I am dumb." Where do the accents fall on these four syllables? Reading the poem in a New York broadcasting studio, Thomas, as I recall— and I was sitting next to him in the capacity of commentator— placed equal stress upon each syllable. But the reader is at liberty to stress "I" and "dumb" or "dumb" alone. This flexibility within strict form is one of the values of a thing that calls for reading aloud, preferably by Thomas. A concert of rhythms and sounds, this poem makes it seem likely that, as early as this, he was Hopkins' schoolboy. Imagery of rope, sand, and water, supporting the clue of rhythm, recalls "The Wreck of the Deutschland."

Almost as allusive as something by Eliot, this poem also calls Blake, the Bible, and secular myth to mind. Thomas' crooked rose and worm point to Blake's "The Sick Rose," and most readers, expected to make this association, have made it. (Compare the cankered rose and taint-worm of Milton's "Lycidas" and the worm from Blake's *Thel*, quoted by Thomas in "The Visitor.") Exodus, Job, and John seem present, as Giovannini and Johnson have discovered. And the "shroud sail" of stanza three, an apparent reference to Theseus and Tristan, supports the thematic marriage of love and death.

1: The image of explosive force, both creative and destructive ("fuse," "blasts"), is like that in the third stanza of "When once the twilight locks." "Green age" (youth) wears the greenness of the fuse. "Crooked" means bent, deformed, aged, and wicked. The poet's youth is as "bent" as old age, with which it shares "wintry fever," a juxtaposition of hot and cold that refers to the sterility of love in age and adolescence alike. In "And I am dumb to tell" dumb means silent, inarticulate, incapable of telling or else, according to the American slang that Thomas loved, foolish: I should be foolish to try to tell or I should be inarticulate if I tried. Telling could mean writing a poem. Try scanning the last, sprung line.

2: Water in rocks and streams is parallel to blood in veins.

"Mouthing," which goes with "mouth," "spring," and "sucks," can imply the mouth of a river, its source, or the mouth of the poet. Since "wax" is what undertakers fill veins with, this waxing is waning. In Thomas, however, it never wanes but it soars.

3: "Quicksand," a brilliant condensation, unites the quick and the dead. A quicksand engulfs us as quick sand in an hourglass marks destructive time. Yet quick testifies to life in death. Blake's "eternity in a grain of sand" or Hopkins' "soft sift in an hourglass" would help, if implied here, to unite time with eternity. The "hanging man" is both an embryo, hanging from its umbilicus, and an executed criminal, Christ on the cross, maybe. "Hangman's lime," in which corpses are buried, is quicklime, another union of the quick and the dead. (Compare "The hanged who lever from the limes" in the suppressed stanza of "When one the twilight locks," *18 Poems*.)

4: The image of water and veins from stanzas two and three recurs. "Fallen blood" is that of death and birth. When the latter, it will calm mother's sores. Ubiquitous "weather" suggests time (introduced by "quicksand"), which now ticks like a clock. But the idea of heaven or eternity is a product of time, the above (heaven in the stars), a product of the below. Heaven, in the maternal context, could also be a child. "Leech," a noun used as a verb, means to act like a sucker.

The two-line coda, providing finality, catches up some of the themes. That of love-death is echoed in "lover's tomb." Tomb, as in *Romeo and Juliet*, remains love's tomb; but every tomb in Thomas is also womb, where dead men hang by living cords, and the end of love. The last line, packed with meanings, brings the senses of the poem together. If the "crooked worm" in Blake's "crooked rose" is a coffin-worm, confirming the idea of death, then the "sheet" is a winding sheet or a "shroud," like the sail in stanza three. If this worm is phallic, the sheet becomes a bedsheet. If this worm is the poet's finger, telling us dumbly as it writes, the sheet is a sheet of paper. Worm and rose, united by crookedness, are opposites, the one masculine, the other feminine. Yet rose is a traditional image of Christ, as worm, a traditional image of Satan.

Compare Hopkins' "residuary worm" and the worms, at once charnal and amatory, in Marvell's "Coy Mistress": "Worms shall try that long preserv'd virginity." Compare "the living worm" of "A process" and this worm from "The Enemies": "a crooked worm, disturbed by the probing fingers, wriggled blind in the sun. . . . Life would go on in the veins, in . . . the flesh of the green grass." The force that Thomas celebrates is the life force itself, however involved Eros may be with Thanatos—and the more the more appropriate. This double force, we must agree, remembering Lawrence and Freud, is one of the forces in modern British literature.

In the 1933 Notebook at Buffalo the last line of the poem served originally as the last line of the first stanza; but Thomas crossed the original first stanza out, and the text of the completed manuscript is substantially that of the printed version.

G. Giovannini, in *Explicator*, VIII (June, 1950). S. F. Johnson, in *Explicator*, VIII (June, 1950); X (February, 1952). William Empson, in *Casebook*, 113. W. S. Merwin, in *Casebook*, 60-61. Francis Scarfe, *Auden and After*, 114. David Daiches, *Poems in English*, 744. Fraser, 12. Treece, 134. Olson, 45. Stanford, 59.

My hero bares his nerves (1934), *p. 11*

Not only cosmic bard, young Thomas was naughty boy, out to dismay the decorous by indecorum. Masturbation, hinted in "The boys of summer," emerges here as a theme. For some, maybe, high spirits may redeem low theme; but to the outraged outrageous humor offers no atonement.

Identifying the hero is the problem. He may be the poet's ego, his hand, or his penis. Stanford, the only commentator to brave this indelicate poem, inclines to the last of these. Inclining this way or that on each rereading, I incline most often to hand, which, along with finger, seems one of Thomas' preoccupations. But that the hero may be a composite of his three or more possibilities, I cheerfully allow. Our hero is mock-heroic.

This hero "bares" nerves and heart. Baring, unpacking, stripping, and flushing, the actions of this poem, may be what Thomas called bringing more to light than Freud had done. The nervous system, central in this poem, includes nerves, spine, brain. Proceeding from the organic to the inorganic and reaffirming

Thomas' habitual confusion of metal with flesh, the nervous system becomes wires, box, and chain.

The "mortal ruler" of the first stanza is the spine, straight as a ruler, a measurer, and a boss. The nerves from head and spine, entering the wrist, control the poet's hand as he scrawls "all love hunger" on the page. Unlike the ruler, his scrawl is "unruly." His "empty ill," the matter of his poetry, seems the frustration of adolescence. "I hug to love" may mean I love to hug my paper or I hug my paper in order to express my love.

As the third stanza makes plain, writing adolescent poetry is parallel to the "secret heat" of masturbation, that strips the "loin of promise." The naked heart, a Venus emerging with "bloodred" hair from animal sea to fleshly beach (cf. 63), is a picture by Botticelli and Dali in unlikely co-operation. The brilliance of this pictured encounter of hero with hairy heart makes us forget their solipsistic purpose.

Since "holds," in the final stanza, could mean grasp or contain, the hero, still unidentified, could be hand or penis. As poet or poet's instrument, he praises the "mortal error" (cf. "empty ill") of life and death. ("Death from playing with yourself," says the adolescent hero of "A Prospect of the Sea.") He praises life while condemning sin—original sin? He also praises the two thieves on Calvary and "hunger's emperor" on his cross between them. These sad thieves, whether grammatically in apposition to life and death or further parts of a series, suggest the testicles, reservoirs of life and death and thieves of time. In this case, "hunger's emperor" between them must be Christ and penis, an irreverent collocation, theologically possible, however, since the Word is God's tool. ("Mortal ruler" and "head," in the first stanza, now seem equally ambiguous and no less phallic.) If the emperor is the penis, the hero, praising it, must be the poet's hand unless, as ego, he is praising himself. That hunger's emperor rules the "love hunger" of the adolescent poet in the second stanza is clear.

But the last line, one of Thomas' most dazzling concentrations, calls for unpacking. As the naughty shock to which the poem has been obscurely working, this line implying that masturbation is like pulling the chain of a toilet, also implies that masturbation, writing a poem, and defecation are parallel and of equal value. Flushing the toilet, however, gets rid of waste, making things clean. Flushing takes its place with stripping, baring, and exposing. Writing a poem like this is cleansing the adolescent head and maybe other and older heads as well. This poem cleans up darkness by bringing it to the light of ribald comedy. Exposing repressed things, as in the analyst's confessional, serves enlightenment and health. It may be that the obscurities, ambiguities, condensations, and displacements of this poem, like those of a Freudian dream, are efforts of the censorious ego to prevent its exposure. The identity of our hero would be clearer without this dreamworker's activities. But the images by which he hopes to conceal what he must reveal cannot altogether puzzle the patient analyst.

That moving "cistern" could serve as the poetic reservoir or "box." Compare "flush the sea," the genetic cistern of "The boys of summer."

The rhythm is as regular as the theme irregular. The stanza, as conventional as the theme is unconventional, alternates lines of five beats with lines of three. The approximate rhymes are what we expect. Expected form quarrels with unexpected matter.

In the manuscript at Buffalo (dated September 17, 1933) several crossed-out lines follow the present ending—crossed-out because they weaken it.

Stanford, 38, 56-57.

Where once the waters of your face (1934), *p.* 12

Here is one of Thomas' most beautiful lyrics. The glittering surface, pleasing and supporting us, makes diving unnecessary. God's plenty of music and magic and color is here on top, before us:

> There round about your stones the shades
> Of children go who, from their voids,
> Cry to the dolphined sea.

But for those who are not content with the abundantly given, these remarks: the theme, recalling "damp to dry" of "A process in the weather of the heart," reverses the process Now we pr∋

ceed from dry to damp. Acclaiming fertility, the poet celebrates
the triumph of life. The womb, dry and sterile after birth, will be
full again. The speaker is either a father or a child, and, since
father was child, probably both. This lyric is dramatic.

Like some of the poems of Donne and "The Blessed Virgin"
of Hopkins, this poem elaborates a single metaphor: the womb
is the sea. Hence boats, mermen, weeds, dolphins, serpents, and
tides. Hence sea-faith is our faith in life and genesis. Yet, simple
as this is, the original metaphor from which all proceeds is ob-
scured by fooling around. "The waters of your face" is a reversal
of "the face of the waters," the sea of Genesis. Once past this difficulty, we need fret no more.

The "screws" of the first stanza, suitably maritime, are propellers of ships on the genetic sea. Interpreted, this metaphor
yields father's endeavors or the kicking embryo. The "dead" and
the "mermen" are embryos alone. Delivery has left their precincts "dry" and open to sterile winds. "Ice" may represent a notion of sexual indifference during pregnancy. "Salt and root and
roe" are all fertility and our origins.

In the allegorical second stanza Thomas personifies sterility
as midwife or obstetrician, emptying the womb, laying the "wet
fruits low"; for birth is death. His deadly scissors and knives recur
in many of Thomas' poems and stories (e.g. 21, 24, "The Lemon,"
"The School for Witches"). For "lovebeds of the weeds" try
weedbeds of the loves. (Reversal is a trick Thomas took from
Finnegans Wake, which he was reading occasionally in *transition.*)
Green seaweed is a recurrent image of maternal fertility (cf. "seaweedy," 55; "deadweed," 83; "Adventure from a Work in Progress"). The shades of children in their voids cry for actualization
by mamma and papa. The dolphin-crowded sea is a happy allusion here; for Yeats' dolphins carry shades to heavenly Byzantium,
and Milton's dolphins carry Edward King or his shade across the
Irish Sea to Wales.

The "coloured lids" of the last stanza, at once the lids of eyes
and Egyptian coffins, will not shut while "magic" or creation,
including poetry, is "sage"—green, wise, and pungent. Tomb will
become womb again. Corals in the lovebeds of the weeds, alluding to *The Tempest,* imply the transformation of bones. Tone,
movement, and rhyme are triumphant. True rhyme (glides-tides,

sky-die) emerges into light, assuring us after many uneasy disa-greements.

Olson, 59. *Adam*, 20.

If I were tickled by the rub of love (1934), pp. 13-15

Adjustment to reality seems the theme of this adult poem about not being an adult poet or, for that matter, an adult. A voice from the darkness, fearing what it wants, reviews frustration and desire. Adjustment to reality, the ultimate rub, must be that of man as well as poet.

Fine lines, striking images, and shrewd insights show the poet has the power he wants and all the words. That he can control an intricate stanza (dissonant yet regular in beat until the short spark at the end) is no less apparent. Structure is firm. The first part, consisting of four parallel conditions, is rhetorical in the grand manner. The three meditations of the second part, no less rhetorical, compose a sequence of statements, questions, and a single exhortation, reserved dramatically for climax and end. Passion, as in Hopkins, not only survives rhetorical play, but feeds on it.

Thomas calls upon the several meanings of "tickle" and "rub" to pack the great opening line. "Tickled" means both stimulated by gentle friction and amused. "Rub" includes friction, impediment, roughness, annoyance, and difficulty. The condition is contrary to fact; for the speaker, a ghost or a pre-natal virus, knows neither the delights nor the troubles of love, its rub in short. Not altogether alive, he is like the liquid voice of "Before I knocked." If he were a young man, a baby, an adolescent, or an old man (the four ages?) he would fear nothing. Fear keeps him from the delights and troubles he yearns for. More than nothing, however, he is a fearful nothing with a voice—a metaphysical notion worthy of Donne and all his worthies.

1: "Rooking" means thieving, cheating. The "straws," a favorite word with several meanings, may be those of the girl's nest or rookery here. The "bandaged string" is the young man's broken connection with his mother. "Red tickle" seems a noun, and "set" could mean *could*. If he could laugh at calving, he would not fear the apple (sin in Eden) or the Flood (punishment for sin). "The bad blood of spring" may be that of adolescence, of Genesis, or of the crucifixion.

2: The cells, after determining sex, drop a child like a plum, an unforbidden fruit. If he were a baby with "hatching hair," "winging bone" (the heels of Hermes or of anyone are the last things out at birth), and itching thigh, the speaker would not fear death. The "crossed sticks" of threatening war imply crucifixion again—like the crossing poles of "The boys of summer." Life, love, death, and poetry were crucifixions for Thomas as for Lawrence.

3: If like his "hero" (11), he were even a naughty boy playing with himself, "rehearsing heat upon a raw-edged nerve," he would not fear sex: the phallic "devil in the loin" and "the outspoken grave" of the womb.

4: The friction of love may not bring youth back to age, but if the speaker could love, he would not fear time. "Lock" and "jaws" (composing lockjaw or poetic silence) and "butter . . . flies," not only playful dissociations, may signify dissolution. "Crabs" (from *Hamlet* II, ii, 205?) may mean the crablike walk of an old man. "The sweethearting crib," a greater difficulty, can hardly mean a baby's crib in this context. Affected by "crab," the bed of love becomes "crib," according to the rule of dissonance. The last two lines are magnificent:

> The sea of scums could drown me as it broke
> Dead on the sweethearts' toes.

"Dead" and "sea," another dislocation in this stanza of dislocations, imply the sea of life and death. Sweethearts, wading now like crabs, have risen from their cribs.

5: The second part, abandoning conditions contrary to fact, begins with ambiguous statement. "Half the devil's and my own" can mean two things: half the devil's and half mine or all mine. Plainly the speaker, having abandoned mask, is now himself, a yearning adolescent, "daft with the drug that's smoking in a girl" —another splendid line. "Forks," a favorite word of many senses (cf. 26), means fixes, impales, or pierces here: her eye is fixed upon the male "bud" that preoccupies him, too. At once an impotent adolescent and an impotent old man, he watches the worm of his finger (cf. 10, 11) wearing "the quick" or life away. While he sits with Onan on the shore, the sea of life with all its scums is crowded with Yeatsian fish—with "all the herrings smelling in the sea." "Smelling," the ambiguous word of this grand line, means stinking in death or sniffing for roe. Death and life proceed in this herring-crowded sea, while Onan sits and plays.

6: That "rub" comes from *Hamlet* becomes clear. Onanism is the only rub that tickles Onan as he "swings along his sex," immature, apelike, not far removed from the dark womb's dampness and the nursing midwife's attentions. "The midnight of a chuckle" means the slightest and darkest laugh. He is not tickled to laughter by mother or lover or even by his "six feet in the rubbing dust." This amazing image could mean a six-foot grave (tomb-womb; flesh-dust) or else, calling upon Kafka, it could mean that Onan is insect as well as ape.

7: A series of unanswerable questions prepares for the hortatory conclusion. "Rub," changing with each appearance, now means reality. What is the reality that he must adjust to before becoming man and poet? What can he write poems about? About "Death's feather" (cf. 9, 36), the tickle of adolescent masturbation? About a beloved whose kiss, like a thistle, prickles rather than tickles? About Hopkins' "Jack of Christ" with crown of thorns on cross? (Thorns, less tickling than thistles, prick.) The "wordy wounds" of poetry are the wounds of Christ's agony, but I have no idea why the poems of the crucified poet "are printed with your hair." (Who is you?) But the ending is almost certain: "I would be tickled by the rub that is," by adult reality, that is.

"Man be my metaphor." From this condensation meanings leak out. Since man is the microcosm or little world and correspondences connect microcosm with macrocosm or big world, man can serve the poet as analogy for all things in heaven and earth. Indeed, man's head contains them: "Within his head revolved a little world," as Thomas announced in the *New English Weekly* (January 25, 1934). If in "Man be my metaphor" the emphatic word is "my," this great line can also mean, let the speaker be like a man, not like the urchin or ape with which he has compared himself. If he must compare himself with something, let it be with man, whose estate he has not yet attained to. True to his gift in this final line, Thomas is both final and ambiguous, a combination as pleasing to twentieth-century ears as to those of the seventeenth century.

Olson, 37-41, 98, 100-101. Treece, 98. Stanford, 55-56. Marshall Stearns, in Tedlock, 116. Thomas recorded this poem: Caedmon, 1018.

Our eunuch dreams (1934), *pp. 16-18*

"Our eunuch dreams" consists of four "curtal" sonnets, based formally on Hopkins' "Pied Beauty." Having fewer than fourteen lines, this kind of sonnet is called curtal because cut short or curtailed. "Pied Beauty," Hopkins' curtal sonnet, has ten lines with a little tail or coda: "Praise him." Thomas' fourth sonnet, with a longer coda of one and a half lines, ends "Praise to our faring hearts." "Pied Beauty" is divided into an "octave" (if we can call it that) of six lines and a "sestet" of four lines: a b c a b c —d b c d, plus the tail in c. Thomas' second sonnet, also divided into six and four, rhymes a b c a b c—b c b c. The other sonnets are variously rhymed. Hopkins was so much on Thomas' mind, during the writing of these sonnets, that even the word "eunuch" may have come from Hopkins' "Time's eunuch."

That Hopkins devoted "Tom's Garland" to social and economic matters provides a convenient transition to what may appear a surprising theme in Thomas' garland of four sonnets. Hopkins was a religious poet and Thomas a solipsistic poet; but it is hard to be entirely religious and harder, in a society like ours, to be entirely solipsistic. That Hopkins and Thomas left their chosen areas for a look at society is less surprising than it seems at first.

Thomas came from the lower middle class, as his English critics like to point out. What is worse, Swansea Grammar School is not a public school. But Thomas did not allow his origin to disqualify him from proletarian concerns that seemed, in the early 1930's, the playing fields of public school boys from the upper class. He was a product of the depression years, severe in Wales, and these years were the Spender period when poets, loudly committed, were joining the Party at the drop of a hat. Thomas told me (in 1952) that he was a Communist. My disbelief was shaken, however, at a party a few days later. Here Thomas suddenly arose, kicked the cat which turned and bit me, and, to the embarrassment of our hostess, called a distinguished and once radical American novelist, who was also a guest, both "renegade" and "prick." The shade of the Party, becoming the death of the party, broke it up. Augustus John says that Thomas said he joined the Party but left it when directed to convert his verses of womb and tomb to propaganda. He did attend a convention of Pinks in Prague. Whatever his color, pink or red or green of the seaweed's iron, it is plain that his sympathies lay with the disestablished.

These sympathies, commonly kept dark in his poetry, come to light in the third and fourth of his curtal sonnets. Pack off "the Welshing rich," he urges, and raise the "red-eyed earth." "Blowing the old dead back; our shots shall smack. . . ." Nicely ambiguous, "blowing" and "shots" include violent revolution among their meanings. No less ambiguous, "red-eyed" refers as much to vampires from *Dracula* as to revolutionists. But for "fellows" we safely read comrades, shouting in the dawn like Stephen Spender. Too obscure for the uses of the Party, these calls to revolutionary awakening prove Thomas less of a maverick among poets of the early 1930's than he has been thought to be.

This social theme, not the only one, falls into place in the four sonnets as part of a larger theme: dream or fake versus waking or reality. Fake consists of erotic fantasy, the movies, and bourgeois society.

I

Although the syntax of the opening lines is obscure, the sense is clear enough. Boys' eunuch or impotent dreams of love prove "seedless" in the light of day. Dreams as schoolmasters whack or train their little victims. The girls they dream about are sheeted ghosts. "Winding-footed," referring to winding sheets, also looks forward to the footage of movie reels in the second sonnet. These ghostly girls, separated from all reality (of worm, bone, and sickness) are hoisted by pulleys (cf. reels) from the tomb, their proper house.

I I

The erotic fancies of boys are no worse than movies about "the gunman and his moll." (Thomas as a boy in Swansea was devoted to American movies.) Flat figures on the screen are "one-dimensioned ghosts," who hurry back to their "yard" (graveyard) when the projector stops and the light of Saturday afternoon returns. More than ghosts, these figments (as III makes plain) are sucking vampires from *Dracula.* "Arclamps," "shots," and "celluloid" produce a "show of shadows" to "give love the lie." Love and light are the enemies of erotic fantasy.

I I I

These two sleepings, day geared and "night-geared," must give way to waking reality. Shadows have sucked our faith that the shrouded dead may be reborn, that dry bones, flying from the grave, will "marrow" again. The society of "Welshing rich" is as much a fake as movie and erotic dream. Fallen asleep, we must "fall awake."

I V

"This is the world" answers "Which is the world?" in the third sonnet. Repeated at the end of the "octave," "This is the world" has another meaning. Here, losing its original irony, it means the "quick" and quick social reality, not the dream world of "trash" and fake, buried in sleeping-sack or shroud. "Have faith" is suitably hortatory. Let us rise like Lawrence's cock to a new dawn. "Shots," more than revolutionary bullets, refer back to the fake of photographic plates. Flowering in love, like the flowering flood of "Prologue," seems more Lawrentian than socialistic; but all the young conspirators adored their Lawrence.

Olson, 56, 93. Stanford, 38, 57-59. W. S. Merwin, in *Casebook,* 61. Augustus John, in *Casebook,* 277.

Especially when the October wind (1934), *pp. 19-20*

Thomas had many masks, each of which, hiding little, revealed a side of his many-sided personality and improved its appropriate voice. Neither socialist nor naughty boy in this great poem, he has his mask of druid on—of druid bard, casting spells on "the loud hill of Wales." These "autumnal spells" call for reading aloud with "hwyl," the orotund and enthusiastic delivery of the Welsh preacher that Thomas made his own for public recitation. (Consider the sermon by Gwilym in "The Peaches.") If not by free-hwyling Thomas himself, his incantation must be repeated by "dark-voweled birds." This necessity makes some of his critics uneasy.

The theme of this poem (as of many of his poems) is poetry and the writing of a poem. Making a poem, a defiance of death, is part of the creativity that Thomas celebrates. The important verbs are make, tell, and spell. Tower, tree, sea, and bird are images for the word, time's enemy. But bare, windy October, heralding death, is the time of Thomas' birth. This birthday poem is first of a series that includes "Poem in October" and "Poem on His Birthday."

1: The October blast (an allusion to Yeats?) is cold as the bard walks beside the sea in the "crabbing sun." Crabbing in the sense of catching crabs, the sun catches Thomas, who, since his shadow is a crab, is a crab. A creature of the living sea, a crab is as articulated as a poem. Articulate Thomas listens now to ill-omened ravens coughing in bare trees. Shuddering at the approach of deathly winter, his female heart (cf. his heart as Venus, 11), big with poems, "sheds the syllabic blood and drains her words." Some, enamored of the zodiac, may think the crabbing sun a reference to Cancer, the celestial crab, but in October the sun, having left Cancer, is on his way to Capricorn. One critic thinks crabbing means red. Cooked lobsters are red. Hard-shelled crabs, to be sure, become a kind of pink.

2: Walking the shore, Thomas is also shut in "a tower of words." Towers, abounding in his poems and prose (e.g. 40, 67, "The Tree," "The Lemon"), carry many meanings. In "The Orchards" the poet's pencil is a tower. Ivory tower, the Freudian tower, and the towers of Joyce and Yeats come to mind, all of them more or less relevant. But here the tower of words, confining the poet, keeps him from participating in the life around it. The poet's dilemma is that the words he must work with (and as Yeats says, "Words alone are certain good") get between him and what is there. The young poet of "The Orchards" says, "The word is too much with us"; and in "One Warm Saturday" words come between the poet and the girl he tries to see without making sentences about her.

Shut in his tower, this poet, trying to see, changes actual women into trees and "wordy shapes." Even the "rows" (a nice ambiguity) of children are confused with stars. But these "star-gestured" children playing in Cwmdonkin Park (cf. 72, 98, 123, "Reminiscences of Childhood") mark Thomas' discovery of the innocence and glamor of childhood, its naughtiness forgotten. Women as wordy trees and the trees of the park remind him, perhaps, of the ancient Welsh association of tree and word to which Robert Graves devotes a chapter of *The White Goddess.* "Vowelled beeches," "oaken voices," and "thorny shires" remind us that the tree of Calvary carried the Word, which created the trees of Eden. (Compare "In the beginning was the tree," "The Tree"; "tree of words," "The Visitor." As product of the chapel, Thomas was obsessed with the Wordy trees of scripture, and as spelling druid, he responded to the "ancient woods of my blood" (104). The "water's speeches" are parallel to those of trees; for he was as much a poet of the tides as of the woods. In "Some let me make you," the outstanding phrase, "make" is the important word. Hardly English, the order of these words, possibly Welsh, suggests druid speaking. Some he is making of his water-speeches and tree-talks; but his ears are for the birds.

3: The third stanza is devoted to time and the signs of approaching winter. "Pot of ferns" (cf. 96), "wagging clock," and yellow meadows confirm the message of October winds, but not to the exclusion of fun. "Windy weather in the cock," a witty play on weathercock, means death in the life-giving cock. Possessed by death, Thomas "tells" us of that black, ominous bird again—in Macbeth's "rooky wood," maybe. Telling and making are the words for creating in time and of time something beyond it.

4: The fourth stanza recapitulates the first as rhyming proves: "Wind" and "land" echo the dissonant rhymes of the opening; "words" and "birds" reverse the true rhymes of the first stanza. Words drained from his heart (in the first stanza) are necessarily "heartless." No longer a crab, the poet is a spider now; but spider is closely related to crab. Spinning webs in darkness is creative, but not of sweetness and light. There are no bees in this autumnal landscape. The wind, with turnips as fingers, clenches them and whacks the frozen land—one of Hardy's turnip fields, where birds as "dark-vowelled" as Hardy's darkling thrush sing in gloom; for poems are of life and death, especially in October. "Chemic blood" (cf. "The Holy Six") is probably alchemic, suitable for magicians transforming things by spells. This druid seems Yeats' magus from "Rosa Alchemica." "The coming fury" (of death) is a Miltonic confusion of the third fate (Atropos and her "abhorred shears") with the third fury, Megaera. Thomas, who knew of Aeschylus (see "The Mouse and the Woman"), was fascinated with furies (e.g. 80), but liked to think them seven. Wordsworthian multiplication makes them more furious to suit modern requirements maybe, or maybe, as Milton says in "Lycidas," this multiplication is but

> . . . playing on the steep
> Where your old *Bards*, the famous *Druids* ly.

W. S. Merwin, in *Casebook*, 61. Stanford, 51-55.

When, like a running grave (1934), pp. 21-23

Druid no more, adolescent again, Thomas devotes this complaint to frustration and desire, both of which mean death. At once "chaste" and a "chaser," he is time's victim and victim of head and heart, his incompatible masters. The speaker, like the boys of "If I were tickled" and "A Prospect of the Sea," fears the love he wants. The failure he confronts is in poetry as well as sex. Desperate acceptance of his condition is relieved by wit, humor, and all but surrealist imagery.

1: Time as a "running grave" establishes a race track here and the cinder path of the last stanza. A grave getting up to run him down is odd and, since "running" also means liquid corruption, gruesome. Since, for Thomas, grave also meant womb, he is being pursued round his track by the idea of woman, agent of death. However "calm and cuddled," a girl (or a penis; for both seem intended here) is "a scythe of hairs," like the scythe of Father Time (cf. 150; "The Visitor"; "The Burning Baby"). This scythe, composed of hair, cuts hair off. But passive now and allegorical, Love-death, a turtle dove in a hearse as slow as a turtle, is hauled up the Freudian stairs of a tower to the "dome"—sex in the head? phallus? womb? Yeats' symbol of art? Love's "gear" is both her finery and low gear or night-gear (cf. 17, 33). All kinds of affairs from masturbation and heterosexual love to the writing of love poems seem involved. This strange picture, beyond power of Dali, opens a long and very complex sentence that extends through the first five stanzas.

2: Tailor age comes like a pair of scissors (cf. "scythe" and 12, 24, 147, "The Lemon") to cut life short, his tape measure (used by undertaker as well as tailor) lacking "the bone inch" of phallic death. The main clause, "Deliver me," is a prayer—of a "timid" boy, who, despite sly, "foxy tongue," is barer of love than "Cadaver's trap," here tomb more than womb. Mouth as well as snare, "trap" includes the poetry of his foxy tongue. This fox, sitting for his portrait by "fox light" (xvii), is a young dog fox. Poetry and love, the instruments of creation, serve death.

3: "Deliver me," he calls to his twin masters, "head and heart," deliver me from "maid and head," a play on maidenhead that includes feminine heart, masculine dome, and deathly love. Cadaver's phallic candle waxes as it wanes when "spade-handed" instinct and time (like gravediggers) dig up children, bruising father's thumb on spade.

4: "Sunday faced," this foxy product of the chapel (cf. 194) wears knuckle-dusters under his glove. His "cockshut eye" is at once cocksure and frustrated, necessarily "chaste" as it roves or peeps (cf. the peepers in "The Followers"). His fear is that he will never enjoy the sexual experience he chastely chases. The "straight grave" is the vagina; and the "virgin o" is a female button for death's icy coat. The "o" signifies the zeroine our hero, more of a zero than she, wants and fears. Except for awareness of death as consequence of love, his condition is that of any inexperienced youth.

5: As [I] stride through life (Death's country) in my green "force," [I] halt among eunuchs (cf. 16), marked with the acid stain of sin and shame on "fork" (crotch) and face. No wonder. His fingers or "pickbrain masters morsing" or tapping in Morse code have destroyed his faith in self and in "maiden's slime" or normal sex. Not only masturbating, morsing can mean writing a poem (cf. 11). This one is in a kind of code; but a welcome period brings the obscurity and complexity of his first telegram to an end.

6: Short statements after long complexity bring dramatic relief. Time is no fool, he tells his skull (head and penis). The hammer of sex (cf. the "hammer swung by my father from his dome," 8) destroys what it creates. Shifting his metaphor to airplanes, he tells his "hero" (cf. 11) that Cadaver in his "hangar" (womb, tomb) "tells the stick, 'fail.' " The airman's "stick" is penis and poet's pencil (cf. "the long stick," 80). Flying, like climbing in the first stanza, is Freudian.

7: He tells "sir and madam" (head and heart) that joy does not knock for admission (cf. "knocked," 8, and Henry Vaughan's "knocking time," quoted by Thomas in his essay "Welsh Poets"). Disease and death's feather (cf. 15) keep joy out. Streets and subways (both Freudian) are not there to "foster" (help) man through "macadam," at once tar and our condition as sons of Adam (cf. "macadam" and "cinder track," "The Orchards").

8: This thought dims the waxing candles in "your tower dome" (cf. stanzas 1 and 3). Repeated "your" and "you" refer to himself rather than to us; for he is talking to himself. Joy, both sex and death or "the knock of dust," is mixed. "Cadaver's shoot of bud" of MacAdam is phallic and deathly, he says, never weary of saying the same thing. "Boxy shift" means boxing (cf. "boxed into love," 64), shroud, coffin, and womb. Sir, he tells his head, your doom is death and the light and dark of love's twilight. ("Cockshut," according to the dictionary means twilight.)

9: Both love and poetry must end: the tower of love and words and the house of wind (poetry and womb). All must fall from the tower like a masterbuilder, his feet up as down he comes (cf. 31, 105). "Cemented skin" (of "cancer's fusion" and the tomb) is warning. Let "summer" of the boys of summer "give over" or make way for winter.

10: These "madmen" seem head and heart or Shakespeare's lovers and poets. "Whistler's cough," the effect of October wind, is disease and poetry. Returning to the cinder track of the first stanza proves life an endless cycle—of cinders. But there is also a game of cards in progress. For his "trick" love takes "Cadaver's hunger" or the sex and death that drive us round the track, as the speaker, still talking to himself, takes "the kissproof world" for his. This tricky concentration of tones and sense embodies the poem, which is probably an elaboration of the pun. "Kissproof" includes desire and frustration. As a brand of lipstick, it includes Freudian lip and stick, death's agents and lovers' delights. Joyce had a hand in such doublin talk. The images of race and fall from tower and the desperate gaiety owe something to him, too.

Olson, 57, 93-95. Stanford, 59.

From love's first fever to her plague (1934), pp. 24-25

The young dog was always composing little portraits of the artist in prose and verse. The example before us, one of his simpler poems, is in irregular blank verse—some lines too long, some too short, and the whole falling into irregular strophes. Through them, he pursues the poet's life from creation to creation, from conception to art. As the child is conceived, so the poem. Each proceeds from unity to diversity and back to unity. The one and the many and the above and the below, lending a philosophical air, attend this narrative. All poetry, said Thomas, who sometimes heeded what he said, should be narrative in movement.

The poet's conception, birth, and infancy concern us first. "Fever" and "soft second," the heat and pleasure of love, are followed by love's "plague," a child, who, after sojourn in the hollow womb, is scissored (cf. 12) by midwife and fed his milk until weaning or "hanging famine." "One," the important word, carries the idea. To an infant all is one. Parental sun and moon, radiating or reflecting seven colors, are "one white light." Whiteness, the effect of optical union, is also a sign of innocence.

Warned by heart and flesh, the child now discriminates. One at first, sun and moon separate and wear particular colors. One hill in the first strophe becomes two mountains, which, although meeting, remain distinct. These mountains, parents as well as earth and sky, are all a child knows of above and below. First person singular, commencing here with "my," is a sign of identity and singularity, but elsewhere one becomes many. One wind becomes four. The "grains" of sand (at once fertile, sterile, and temporal), acquiring color, multiply (cf. 91, 143, "The Enemies"). But the green and golden childhood of "Fern Hill," anticipated here, is complicated by synesthesia. Confusing his senses, this strange child of a "singing house," hears the "light of sound" and sees the "sound of light," as poets will if anything like young Rimbaud. "We are all metaphors of the sound of shape of the shape of sound," says the young adventurer of "Prologue to an Adventure." But the younger poet here has not proceeded beyond sensation to shape. His confusion of the senses, moreover, sets back his progress from the one to the many by making two one.

The plum (cf. 13), dropped by mother's dark womb into the many-sided "lap of light," gets "wise to" American slang and the itch or tickle of sex, which, as Freud remarks, is not unlike hunger.

A metaphor of grammar carries this scholar through life's school. The "first declension of the flesh," like that of Latin, is feminine; but this decline is followed in the next strophe by conjugation. The "verbs of will" are rising. Twisting "the shapes of thoughts" shows discovery of concept and abstraction. Increasingly aware of words, he shades and knits (gardener and tailor at once) "the patch of words" left him by great poets of the past, now "moonless" or deprived of imagination and light in their graveyards. Even the tongues of poets must come to a name on a headstone. Anonymous worms mark the spot with an illiterate's X.

The boy's "secret" may be knowledge of self. "The code of night," tapping on his tongue (compare the Morse code of "When, like a running grave"), is the poetry he is writing in a kind of cipher to conceal and reveal his dark unconscious. The oneness of infancy now gone, this poetry is "many sounding minded."

Oneness has produced this manyness. From learning that sky is distinct from earth, above from below, he has learned "double" talk. But the "two-framed globe" becomes a "score" of worlds. The "million minds" of the past have suckled the "bud" that "forks" his compound eye (cf. 14, 22). Here, bud, sometimes phallic, may be tongue or mouth about to flower. "Forks," sometimes piercing or fixing, also means dividing here. His eye sees double as his forked tongue tries double talk. But "score" and "forks" together, bringing tuning forks to mind, could imply the music of poetry.

Art is unity from diversity. The poet, having discovered the many, makes it one. "Youth did condense," like poet's gas, after a "hundred seasons." The last line, which celebrates oneness again, unites infancy with poetic maturity. Sunlight and manna, both falling from above, like rain or condensed "tears of spring," are gifts to us, below. As there is condensation above, so below; and each has its appropriate precipitation.

Elizabeth Drew and John L. Sweeney, *Directions in Modern Poetry*, 110. Sam Hynes, in *Explicator*, IX (December, 1950). Stanford, 50.

In the beginning (1934), pp. 27-28

Genesis was the book for Thomas, in love with creation, whether of world, child, or poem, the three analogous creatures of the Word. "The legend of Adam and Eve," he says (145), "is never . . . silent in my service"—always of service to him, that is, in the ceremonies of his art.

Genesis includes most of Thomas' concerns: life and death, darkness and light, chaos and shape, sin, fall, and hope, not to mention worm. Opposite and twin to the Gospels, Genesis brings them to the chapel-nurtured mind. The trees of Genesis become the tree of Calvary. The face of the waters becomes something for walking on by the new Adam. Over Genesis and the Gospels brood the Word and the Trinity, patron of triple talk.

In this poem about the Word, the word "word" is central. Not spoken until the fourth stanza, it appears under the disguises of cipher, signature, sign, imprint, characters, letters, breath, and star. Used by God, it is Christ and world. Used by poet, it is poem and, if by father, child. It may be, as the poet Marlais says in "The Orchards," that the word was too much with him—too much, that is, for the simple reader of this dense, metaphysical, and excellent poem.

Metaphysical in substance and method, this poem is an elaborate analogy of things above and below, a "conceit" made of conceits. Conceits, as used by Donne, Marvell, and Crashaw, are correspondences or analogies, preferably odd, original, and surprising. There is Donne's plenty of concordant discord here. Parallel beginnings establish the idea of parallels and connect the stanzas. Monotonous rhythm carries the feeling of creative repetition; and a quarrel of rhyme with ghosts of rhyme accompanies the concordant discord of theme with concordant discord.

1: "In the beginning" begins the Gospel of St. John. But for his "Word" that was with God and was God, Thomas substitutes "the three-pointed star" to point three creative beams. This star, as star of Bethlehem, is Christ the child. Three points suggest the Trinity, according to Christians, and the male creative principle, according to Freud. As poem, this star has three points or meanings. But triple God is one God, whose "one smile" across the empty face of the waters is the moment of genesis. "One bough of bone" in the "rooting," genetic climate seems to combine the tree of knowledge, the cross, the rib, and the phallus. The punning repetition of "across" unites Genesis and Calvary. One "substance," the underlying essence of God, "forked" or divided to produce the sun of Genesis and the Son or Jesus. The "burning ciphers on the round of space" must be the signs of the zodiac, put there as the world began to turn. Blake's "heaven and hell," above and below, "spun" in the original mixture of chaos as they spin, co-operating, in the new world.

"Marrowed," a favorite word (e.g. 14), suggests life within the bone of death. "Forked," a greater favorite, that we have also met before (e.g. 14, 26), is a word of many meanings, as Webster, the Oxford Dictionary, and Shakespeare agree. As verb, fork can mean pierce, hold, divide, pitch, or throw. As noun it applies to tree, river, road, and music. As adjective, applying to words, it can mean ambiguous, equivocal, or polysemous. Enamored of words, Thomas could not resist one that also includes the opposites of union and division. An added value is that a fork may have two prongs or three or more. "Forked" and "forking," important words in this poem, unite the "three-pointed star," the "three-syllabled" signature, and the "three-eyed" spark. The prongs of this poem are three.

2: The triple "signature," an equivalent for St. John's Word, Thomas' star, and the creative "smile of light," is from Jacob Boehme (by way of Joyce?) or some other occultist. "Substance," "signature," "sign," and "letters of the void" imply some acquaintance with occult tradition, Hermetic or Kabalistic. The "imprints" on the water are Christ's footprints on the Sea of Galilee (cf. 141) and God's signature on the waters of Genesis. God's stamping the moon's face as if minting a coin could be getting the Virgin with Child. This conceit, based on the traditional association of Virgin with moon, is not unlike many of Donne's. "Blood," "grail," and "crosstree" (a word from Joyce) refer to Christ's agony; and touching the cloud to leave a sign is the Ascension. Forked language has made Genesis one with Gospel. But Thomas' Biblical fork has more than these two prongs; for it also divides to transfix any child or, as "imprints" and similar words make clear, any poem. As God is making and redeeming the world, poet and father are making worlds of their own for our redeeming.

3: From creative water we pass to creative fire, already accosted in star and sun. This "three-eyed" spark, blunt as a gamekeeper's flower or Thomas' bud, sparks all creation. (In the 1933 manuscript at Buffalo the creative instrument, neither spark nor Word, is the three-eyed "prick.") Whale spouting in the sea and oil pumping up to drive the grass are parallel images of gushing life. (Compare "Jonah's Moby," 82. For oil as the force that drives the green machine see 29, 39, 42, "The Mouse and the Woman"; for the confusion of the organic with metal and machine see 33.)

4: After three beginnings, St. John's very "word" sounds out, climactically, replacing star, signature, and fire, its predecessors. Light is God, creating from nothing (the "void"), abstracting letters from it as a poet does. (The letters of the Word are probably God's ineffable name, YHWH or Jahweh. Compare "The Mouse and the Woman": "There were a million stars spelling the same word.") The creative "breath" (cf. Hopkins' "arch and original breath") utters the word, which, like one of Thomas' poems, translates "first characters of birth and death" to the heart. "Flowed up" joins "spouted" and other verbs of ascension in this vision of making and springing. The discordant rhyme of "word" with "void" is concordant in Brooklyn alone.

5: Thought of "secret brain" is "celled and soldered" before it manifests itself in organ and metal. Hot solder, that puts things together, introduces hot, black "pitch," the chaos from which bright sun emerged. "Pitch was forking to the sun" is forked language for devil, Christ, and the act of pitchforking or dishing creation out. Veins shaking, like spaghetti in a sieve, are the very image for our forked body, anxious and holy. "Blood shot" forks blood of the Word and the red eye of stanza three. The movement of this stanza from dark to light is that of all creation, God's, the father's, and the poet's. Blood scattered to the winds of light could be poem, child, or world. Confirming this, the "ribbed original" of creative love is Adam, bough of bone, child, and lines of type. "Love," the last word, was the first word of creation.

Edmund Wilson wrote a book about "triple thinkers." Certainly Thomas is of this company. Discussing the previous poem, I called him a double talker—double not in the customary sense of saying nothing but in the sense of saying two things at once. Triple would be better; for he was as "trivial" as Joyce and almost as "quadrivial." From the beginning the forked word of Thomas was three-pointed, and this word created a world, which lies all before us—to sweat in.

W. S. Merwin, in *Casebook*, 61-62. E. Glyn Jones, in Tedlock, 174-75. Stanford, 50-51.

Light breaks where no sun shines (1934), *pp. 29-30*

Before putting or trying to answer unanswerable questions about this dark poem on light, let us see what is certain here. First: in place of the usual dissonance and rhyme, there is new assonance (shines, tides, light) interwoven with tenuous consonance of "s" in the first stanza. Later stanzas return to habitual dissonance and its shades. Second: the stanza is a variation upon that of the "green fuse"—almost identical if you lengthen the first line, omit the fifth, and loosen the rhythm. Similarity of form may imply similarity of subject. Certainly the images are familiar. We have met wax, oil, worm, water, poles, globe, light, and the others in poems preceding this in *The Collected Poems*, though not necessarily preceding this in date of composition. The quarrel of opposites is familiar. Here we have another series of contradictions and paradoxes, conflicts among the old antagonists of dark and light, inner and outer, above and below, microcosm and macrocosm. The monotony of rhythm, the recurrence of verbal patterns, the repetition with variation in place of detectable forward movement are equally familiar. Monotony of word and theme and repetition of pattern struck an early reviewer (in *New Verse*, February, 1935) as tiresome—not functional as they could be if the theme is regular process. But the theme is a puzzle.

Though plainly a war between darkness and light, in which light may be the winner, this poem leaves us in the dark about the nature of light, which appears as glowworm, candle, day, spring, and dawn. Is this a progression from small lights to big? Is light literal or metaphorical or now one, now the other? If metaphorical, does it mean creative power (like the "smile of light," 27) or enlightenment? The dawning of awareness or the coming of knowledge seems as likely a theme as any. But whose knowledge and when? Is the poem about individual development from fertilized egg to maturity and the coming of knowledge proper to each stage? Or is the poem an abstract arrangement like a recent painting?

1: "Light breaks" certainly states the uncertain theme. "Breaks," connecting this light with dawn, agrees with "push in" and "file through," the other verbs of intrusion; yet "breaks" can mean ending as well as beginning. No sun, no sea, no flesh in this place, yet, paradoxically, there are light, waters, and flesh. Light without sun suggests the first day of Genesis or, if light is life, a cell's first night in the womb. Outer sea and inner waters recall the "green fuse." The "things of light" as "broken" as light itself, are "ghosts with glow-worms in their heads," like those charnal and phallic worms of "the boys of summer." Since they file flesh in its absence, these wormy ghosts, which make womb seem tomb, may be the knowledge of life and death that instinct furnishes a cell or what precedes a cell. No amniotic water, no flesh here, maybe, because this is so long before conception that the knower is hardly there at all. Compare the thinking, metaphysical virus of "the rub of love," enlightened by foreknowledge.

2: General light and particular glowworm become phallic candle here, a candle without wax, exposing pubic hairs. Seed or sperm warms youth, burns age. Fruit of such seed could be a baby or a sublimation of the frustrated. An unwrinkled fig is ripe, but why does fruit from below shine among stars above? Are children starry in our eyes (cf. 19) or only such ideas? Is the fruit, taking wax from the neighboring, waxless candle, a wax fruit? This stanza could mean that knowledge of sex, frustration, and sublimation is present in child, embryo, cell, or thinking virus.

3: Dawn, replacing general light, breaks in the head, "behind the eyes." Enlightenment is localized in the brain. Meanwhile our blood flows like a sea between the poles of head and toe (cf. "skull of toes," 81). Possibly adding a little to the sea of stanza one, this sea is "windy." The external world seems more nearly with us. If the first stanzas are about conception, could this one suggest birth? The "gushers" spouting oil recall those of "In the beginning." But the gushers are in the sky with stars, not below where they belong. The divining rod that locates them may be the divine rod of The Twenty-third Psalm, Aaron's rod (see 63), the fisherman's divining rod (174), or the "old ram rod." Oil is the energy of life (27), and life brings tears and smiles. Are these celestial gushers further sublimations of sex? Whose moment of intellectual awareness can this be?

4: The dark "sockets" are those of candles and eyes. Moon and globes continue celestial and geographical metaphors. A "pitch moon" is dark as a socket. The "globes" are also eyes since vision is as necessary as candle for enlightenment. But after dark night, "Day lights the bone." This could be birth or resurrection from the tomb. The knower knows the "skinning gales"—not October winds but those of spring—that strip old winter's snowy robes off. Film, another covering to strip off, is also photographic film for light. The "lids" to be removed are those of eyes and coffins (cf. 12). We have had something to do with day and spring, womb or tomb, birth or rebirth, without knowing precisely what. Someone's vision is opening wider to some windy light; yet the "limit" of the eye is known to this visionary.

5: Light breaks over a wasteland of "secret [hidden, dark] lots," "waste allotments," and stinking "tips" or dumps. (There is a "rubbish tip" in "The Peaches.") The "secret" of this "soil" strikes our unlidded eye. Is this enlightenment social, moral, or religious, like that of Eliot's *Waste Land*, apparently alluded to? Is blood jumping in the sun that of a socialist at red dawn? But dawn ambiguously "halts" over the waste. Does halt mean that dawn pauses to increase the light on dark places or does it mean that dawn stops dead, depriving dark places of further light? But more than social or moral, the lots and tips are intellectual, like the dawn of stanza three. The "tips" are those of thought, dumps for dead and stinking "logics." Jumping blood (the sea of stanza three), replacing dead thought, may be Lawrence's thinking with the blood. Enlightenment now occurs below the neck rather than behind the eyes. If "tips of thought" alludes to Eliot's intellect "immediately at the tips" of the senses, the discordant concord of Eliot and Lawrence is a conceit. Anyway, Eliot and Lawrence seem present here, the one by virtue of tips and vacant lots, the other by virtue of blood.

What exactly is this bloody enlightenment and whose? Is it social, moral, philosophical, or literary? Is it that of the individual growing up or still the foreknowledge of child, embryo, cell, or sap? Does the dawn stop or proceed? Has light broken for us or, as broken as those ghosts, are we exploring the unknowable with dark lanterns? All we know for sure is that many paradoxes and contraries, uneasily side by side, agreeing and disagreeing, produce a confusion that may be that of life and so intended. As John Wain said, looking at an abstraction on my wall, "There's a lot going on there."

The critics listed on p. 66, while not entirely sure of what is going on here, are far surer than I. We have experienced a quarrel between tight shape and loose matter. Is this confusion, however like that of life, shapely enough to delight? Maybe the best a critic can do under these trying conditions is call attention to as many of the parts as he can and ask questions, more profitable in a case like this than limiting answers.

Marshall W. Stearns, in Treece, 151-54; in Tedlock, 125-29. W. S. Merwin, in *Casebook*, 62. Bernard Knieger, in *Explicator*, XV (February, 1957). William T. Moynihan, in *Explicator*, XVI (February, 1958). Thomas recorded this poem, Caedmon, 1043.

I fellowed sleep (1934), *pp. 31-32*

Many of Thomas' poems and stories rework myth, especially that of Genesis. More are dreams: "I dreamed my genesis," for example, "When once the twilight locks," "The Mouse and the Woman," "The Orchards," and "The Visitor." His approaches to womb and tomb were cluttered with the debris of myth, dream, madness, and fantasy. Ghosts and angels, *Doppelgängers*, madmen, vampires, and witches crowd these early poems and stories. Such characters owe more to Walter de la Mare, Arthur Machen, and Bram Stoker than to Llareggub. No cobbles here or cockled shore. Landscapes, often above land or under it or all at sea, are as strange as the impersonal personae of these personal fancies. Even when identifiable with Thomas, the dreamer or madman is not all there.

Freud, co-operating with the Bible and Bram Stoker, complicates scenery and action. The theme of the poem before us seems to be the resolution of the Oedipus complex—growing up, in short, and forgiving father. That this Freudian success has dream for setting is fitting, and fitting a cloudscape with ladder—what Joyce would call a cloudescape.

1: The dreamer's ego is accompanied by Sleep, a *Doppelgänger* or fellow. ("Fellowed" came to rival "marrowed" and "weathers" among words Thomas could not avoid.) Kissing Thomas "in the brain," Sleep puts him to sleep. Sleep's eye, reflecting the "light" of paternal sun, is a moon, maternal and lunatic. Like wing-heeled Mercury and an airplane, the dreamer flies "along" or alongside his fellow. "Dropped" and "upward" introduce falling and rising, the main actions of this poem, as of *Finnegans Wake*, a greater dream.

2: The dreamer and his "ghostly other" or maternal double leave solid earth for the intermediate clouds—above earth but below stars—whence their tears fall on the trees below. Climbing the "weather" is not the same as climbing the solid ladder of the last stanza. That the moony ghost is maternal is made plain by "mothers-eyed" or all mothers keeping an eye on all boys. Hence those tears. The last line is Yeatsian.

3: The third stanza is a dialogue of self and Sleep about fatherland and maternal cloud. That father's "globe" has a "nave" to knock on while it sings is odd; but a globe's nave could imply the holiness of earth, and father's globe could be mother, too. (Compare the globe of "When once the twilight locks.") Father once controlled maternal clouds or gangs of angels. Breathe on such figments of dream, says the fellow, and they disappear. Breath is life; and all ghosts are as unreal as mother's cloudscape.

4: So instructed by the ghost at his elbow, the dreamer blows these angelic fictions back to bed. There they lie where the sleeper lays them, ignorant of their ghostly betrayer. These fictions are "grave-gabbing" because, as talkative as women, they talk in their sleep of maternal womb and tomb, the dark places we must escape. Darkness and cloudy dream become unreal as the sleeper, freed from angels, approaches paternal reality.

5: In this fine stanza, the sleeper writes a poem to celebrate his vision of reality. "Climbing" on the words of nature, he spells this vision out by hand. "Hair" seems metonymy. His poem, like any of Thomas', crosses opposites: "soily star" with "worlded clouds," "light" with "deep," and "sleeping" with "waking." (The figure is chiasmus—a good one for synthesis.) Sleeping should be deep, perhaps, and waking should be light; but deep waking, the point of the experience and the poem, is waking to the light of reality, to which his poem is a "climbing." This climbing, the important action, is adult, and, according to Freud, an image of sexual endeavor. According to the Bible, Jacob's dream-ladder is an image of aspiration: "And he dreamed, and behold a ladder, set up on the earth, and the top of it reached to heaven," Genesis 28:12.

6: This ladder to the light is in time, not out of it like those fictions. Rungs of this aspiring ladder, which, like Jacob's, unites below with above, are "love" and "losing to the last" or life and death. "Inches" of the slow ascent have been "monkeyed" or fiddled with by the evolutionary blood of climbers. Becoming the ghost or successor of his climbing fathers and taking his place on the monkey ladder with his particular father, that mad, old man, the boy, once fellowed by the "mothers-eyed," climbs through dark, maternal rain toward the light of the paternal sun. (Hamlet and his ghostly father may be around. Cf. 48.) That when approaching reality the composite climber is a ghost and that his sunny father is mad or lunatic prove that reality is a confusion of opposites. The ghost within, unlike the "elbow ghost," is man's spirit. The struggle of mother and father for possession of the unconscious self of the son has been won by father. The waking sleeper fellows father now. But there is a long way to climb before reaching the light of full consciousness and maturity. (For climbing and ladders see 40, 41, 43, 80: "Star-set at Jacob's angle"; "Jacob to the stars." For the sun see 30, 34: "I seek the sun"; "blood jumps in the sun.") A similar contest between father and mother for their son takes place in the sonnets of "Altarwise."

I dreamed my genesis (1934), *pp. 33-34*

Far from extraordinary in theme and image, this poem commends itself mainly as an experiment in rhythm and sound. The terminal "rhymes" (a a a b until a a a a in the last stanza) agree only in a single consonant or vowel, "n" in the first stanza, "l" in the second, and "y" or "I" in the third. Internal sound effects are occasionally impressive. "Hold love's drop, costly," for example, is a little concert in "o." Rhythm is rocked in the third stanza by the rhyme of feminine endings with a masculine ending, after the manner of Hopkins. But a happier rhythm is provided by the caesura before a final participle or feminine noun, "breaking" or "harvest." This trick, borrowed from the opening of *The Waste Land*, recalls death and rebirth, the theme of Eliot's poem, in order, perhaps, to bring forward the similar theme of this.

Thomas' images for birth, death, and rebirth or nature's cycle center upon a customary identification of the organic with the mineral (cf. 8, 40). Nerves are "girdered." Sometimes there are "irons in the grass," and sometimes, according to a convention of the seventeenth century, grass is flesh. Animal, vegetable, and mineral, thoroughly confused, obey nature's force, figured here as drill, file, and gear (cf. 22, 27). We have encountered "night-geared" in "Our eunuch dreams"—dreams no worse than this one. This identification of love and death with machine would have displeased Lawrence, who preferred flowers in the hair to wheel chairs. But if nature's force can be figured suitably for readers in the age of machine and explosion by a green fuse, why not as airplane, screw, cog, pump, and oil-driven wheel? (At a banquet at the Waldorf of The National Association of Manufacturers I, a guest of The Minster Machine Company, met the president of The York Worm and Screw Company.) A poet should try to live where he lives and to communicate. Moreover, enamored of science fiction, Thomas was unable or unwilling to escape its apparatus.

The motor-muscled drill in the first stanza proves this dream sexual. "Through," significantly but ambiguously repeated, conveys the impression of a power great enough to penetrate a "rotating shell," either of a female world or a psychic obstacle. The dreamer, rounding his "globe of heritage," is both shaping it as a poet and journeying upon it in "bottom gear." "Man-melting night" is womb and tomb as furnace or forge. Suns melted there may be sons. "Shuffled off" is an intrusion from Hamlet on dreams (cf. 32, 48). "Creasing flesh" increases in the womb and wrinkles with shuffling age.

A dream "in sweat of sleep" must be a nightmare. "Genesis," the substance of this dream, is at once his own nocturnal activity (of which the less the better), his begetting by father, and Adam's creation by his. Allusion to the Bible leads to "From limbs that had the measure of the worm." Not double talk or triple talk, this splendid dream condensation is quadruple talk or better. Five worms, greener than those of the "green fuse" and more crooked, seem active here: Limbs begotten by father's worm acquire hereditary shape in the womb. Limbs in the tomb acquire the dimensions of the worms that eat them. Adam's limbs, succumbing to the worm of Genesis, are measured by original sin. Christ, the second Adam, had, in the sense of took, the measure of the worm of Genesis by conquering him. Since the dreamer is a poet, as "through vision" implies, maybe his limbs respond to his writing finger.

This dreamer has two deaths and two rebirths, both connected with war. Every birth was a death to Thomas; but his birth in 1914 coincided with general death in the First World War (cf. 36). The second war that the Hitler of 1933 made inevitable will be Thomas' second death. The images of war—shrapnel, blade, and gas—are obvious in this first poem of the second war. "Hemlock" (cf. 81) imported from Plato's Socrates, is inharmonious in all but death with the other images. The poet's "second struggling from the grass" of tomb and womb will be more manly, he hopes, and more enlightened than the first. "Power" tools have given power to his rerobed skeleton and ghost. "Spat up," an ejaculation, follows resurrection or erection in the solitary night. Thomas was always confusing resurrection with erection; and for him, as for Elizabethans "die" was a sexual pun. The two deaths of this poem make us wonder what precisely he was about. To the analyst, however, dreams reveal what they conceal.

Anyhow, he will climb out of the "feeding sea," whether amniotic or that of Genetic Adam, and, like the sleeper of the preceding poem, seek the sun. If sun is a pun on son, he will seek not only enlightenment and light of morning after a bad night but Christ and his own identity as risen son. The young poet never tires of saying in song that he must put on the light; but he is singing in the dark.

Stanford, 50.

My world is pyramid (1934), *pp. 35-37*

Sun sought in vain, apparently, the poet is back in womb and tomb—deep within a pyramid this time. But, as we shall see, a pyramid, though dark inside and heavy enough to hold the gaudiest Pharaoh down, is not so sunless as it seems. This long, dark poem is divided into two parts, the first a meditation on the mystery of division, the second the meditation of a divided embryo. Although the stanza of Part I differs from that of Part II, the parts are equal and more or less parallel, as if to illustrate doubling. The words to mark in this doubling talk are "fellow" (cf. 31, 40), "half," "cloven," "bisected," and "fork," which we have heard before. But, since parents become halves as they divide to create a halved embryo, the double halves are confusing, and so is the syntax. Bad syntax is good fun for poets, if not readers; and to play four halves against one another, two by two, is good metaphysical fun. Plainer syntax could impair the gaiety, which, like the theme, requires a little darkness and something more than grotesque double rhymes: "doubles . . . dabbles," for instance, and "bubbled . . . babbled."

I

1: The first stanza states the sense: Creating a "sea-sucked Adam in the hollow hulk" of the womb, father and mother divide to multiply. Milk to be sucked by tomorrow's child is "horny" for many reasons: Slang for sexy and in accord with "diver," "horny" suggests cows, bone-making, and the horn of abundance. "Bisected shadows" are the spirits or ghosts of dividing parents. "Thunder's bone" and "bolt" suggest the "short spark" (80) of begetting, and with "salt," the prow of a ship at sea. "The salt unborn" is the sea-sucked, thunder-bolted embryo, as double as its creators.

2: Juxtapositions of heat and cold, seed and shade, recall the boys of summer in their pouch. Some seed is "planted" to produce "the iceberg's crop" (life from death), and some lost—on barren ground no doubt. That milk swinging in breast and "pap" (teat, nipple) is "tufted" (cf. 69) suggests many things. As noun, tuft means top, clump, bunch; as verb, concentrate, cap; and as adjective, it includes all these meanings. "Ghost," or soul, goes with "shadow." A seeded embryo is both flesh and ghost.

3: "The broken halves" seem parents. But the crutched "cripple" that unites them could be either the embryo or the penis. "Marrow" (life and bone) taps on the same door in either case; both are "limp in the street of sea" (vagina-womb); and both are "tide-tongued heads and bladders of the deep." Since the name Dylan means tide or wave, since Dylan, admirably tongued, sang the womb's tides, and since bladders are a fool's equipment, this could be a portrait of Dylan in the womb. The syntax of the last two lines is unclear. "Sleepers" may be parents or the double, sleeping embryo. "Broken halves" could be the subject of "stake" (cf. crutch); "that" is either a relative pronoun or a conjunctive adverb. "Grave" and "vampire" from *Dracula* seem womb and embryo, sucking life out of parents. Staking is the approved way of getting rid of vampires, but who is being staked here, the vampire or the stakers? Whatever the syntax, a vampire suits a poem of the graveyard school.

4: "Patchwork," from tailoring (cf. 25, 147), is the union of two stuffs. The drill (cf. 33), rotated by parental halves and as "horny" as milk, is "horning" to suggest sound and piercing. "Wild pigs" and "slime" are images of the disgust, as "cyanide" and "adders" are images of the danger, of sex. Braided adders in the hair recall Medusa or the furies, probably the latter; for Thomas was always attentive to Tisiphone and her sisters. (See 80, "In the Direction of the Beginning," "The Mouse and the Woman." Like Yeats', Thomas' furies were "bitter furies of complexity.") For Thomas, no vampire or fury was so awful as sex; yet sex produces "the arterial angel." This double of flesh and spirit, of below and above, condenses the theme in one shining phrase. Like the "mortal ghost" (9) and the "double angel" (43), the arterial angel is both Jesus and any child—and maybe the poet, who also horns. But horn and drill, as applicable to war as to commerce, introduce images of war and death in the next stanza and in the second part.

5: These unanswerable questions, to be reversed in stanza five of the second part, are of glory, martial colors, and the white feather of cowardice. (For "death's feather" see 9, 15, 73). But glory and feathers belong to angels, who, traditionally, dance on a "pin's point in the air." Pin, needle, thimble, and piercing go back to drilling patchworkers. All this piercing and sewing produces a "thumb-stained" angel, fleshly ghost, or child, who, "in the straw" like Jesus in the manger, stammers though "dumb" (cf. 10) and recently "tide-tongued." "Dumb," reversing "tide-tongued," makes it tongue-tied. "Havoc," both destruction and hawk, is future flight and its result, anxiously watched by the "cloud-tracking" eyes of parents, blinded by the poetic brightness of their son; for angels, got rid of in "I fellowed sleep," are back. Angelic Thomas has looked homeward, as home, upward. His autobiography, like the biography of Tristram Shandy, Gent., commences before birth.

II

1: Thomas, who must have read a book on Egypt, was fascinated with pyramids and mummies. (See 44, 72, 84, 88, "A Prospect of the Sea," "The Mouse and the Woman." One of his schoolboy poems, dated April 27, 1930, concerns Osiris, Isis, Horus, and Serapis.) The "padded mummer" (with his fool's "bladders"), "Egypt's armour," and winding "sheet" make embryo in womb a mummy swathed in tomb, wound in mummy-cloth like something in Yeats. Scraping through "resin" combines embalmer's resin with musician's rosin, appropriate for fiddling around if not for "horning." "Parhelion" (cf. "The Mouse and the Woman"), a ghost of the sun, becomes, when united with "blood," son and ghost or "arterial angel" again. "Starry bone," another union of above and below, could mean that Pharoah's tomb was also an astrological pointer. For Egyptians the pyramid was a symbol of the sun and of aspiration to it. Four triangular faces are female, their apex, male. Uniting time with eternity, a pyramid keeps the dead for rebirth. That the womb-like chambers within this tomb are covered with hieroglyphs was an additional value for Thomas, whose ciphers, as readers know, are hieroglyphs. More than womb and tomb, his pyramid is a poet's place, and his mummy, not only an embryo, is a poem (see 84-85). Both mummy and poem are in sheets (cf. 10). The proper world for this embryonic poet, playing in the womb, is a hieroglyphic, mummy-crowded pyramid. But world is sphere. That a sphere equals a pyramid is the non-Euclidian conceit of an embryo not yet in Swansea Grammar School or else devoted too soon to paradox.

"Buckling," in connection with "armour" and the hawk of the preceding stanza, may be an echo of Hopkins' "Windhover," more appropriate there than here.

2: The "tide-tongued" embryo has exchanged his pyramid for a country churchyard. Fonder of graveyards and cypresses than Gray or Beddoes, Thomas once posed for his picture, knee-deep in the weeds of the graveyard at Laugharne; and if, like Donne, he had found a shroud, he would have posed in that. The "yards" in this stanza are at once graveyards, the playing fields of Swansea, and the yards of a ship, which are not unlike the cross. The "Austrian volley" recalls the First World War and Thomas' birth in 1914 (cf. 33). Heavy alliteration in "d" and "b" and internal echoes ("rattled . . . riddled," "bowels . . . bones") suit the "hill of bones," which unites pyramid with Golgotha. "Eloi," a variant of Eli ("My God"), is Christ's cry on the cross, repeated by A. E. Housman's "riddled lads."

3: "Crossing Jordan" seems to combine Allenby's campaign in Palestine, the life of Christ, mother's chamberpot (cf. 8), and water for the desert around the pyramid. As "dead house garden," the grave is womb, Eden, Gethsemane, and prison. Four directions (Arctic, South, Asia, Atlantic), like four faces of a pyramid, surround his little world and connect it with the world outside. ("Scut" may be the tail-end of the world.) "Straws of Asia" in his dumb mouth are from the manger; and "Atlantic corn" is what comes of seed planted in Wales.

4: "Fellow halves" are parents and embryo again. Thomas in the womb is an "unborn devil" with hot pitchfork and precocious crotch. Parents "beard" him in two senses. Yet, combining opposites, the double child is also an angel. Parents smell his heels at the moment of birth, as he runs away from home for skin trade, or, like an angel, glides. In any case he will be a subject for gossip.

5: The fifth stanza recalls the first and fifth stanzas of the first part to round the world out. The "salt unborn," the sea, and sucking echo the first stanza; the reversed questions and tracking echo the fifth. Questions raised there are answered here and new ones raised. Blowing "death's feather" away with the breath of life (cf. 31), he asserts life—as he asserts it by changing aristocratic blue blood of veins to the "stammel" red of low-class underwear. "The loin is glory in a working pallor" answers the question of glory in words that Lawrence's gamekeeper might have used; but in connection with stammel red, "working" may be working-class (cf. 17, 38). Still alone in the womb, this social embryo is "dry," a paradox. "Half-tracked," which echoes "cloud-tracking," makes the womb a kind of truck or lorry delivering life. But "half-tracked" could also mean that gestation is incomplete. Not only womb, "thigh" could be the child's own equipment. Is this "secret child" waterproof or sterile? Does "dry in" mean inside or in respect of? Dryness, recalling "A process in the weather" and "Where once the waters," introduces the next poem, "All all and all."

Olson, 36. Stanford, 49.

All all and all the dry worlds lever (1934), *pp. 38-39*

Relief of drought in wasteland and womb by love and politics seems the theme of this poem, which belongs with "Our eunuch dreams" and a few scattered hints of a "red-eyed" view. Syntactical obscurity and ambiguous image conceal the message and reveal its duality; for the revolution Thomas proposes is as much Lawrentian as Marxist. Clearly hortatory, he darkly exhorts himself alone. The three parts of his message are less dialectical than they should be. "Fusion" or synthesis occupies the third part, but confusion of thesis and antithesis occupies the first two parts. Love and politics call in vain for consecutive statement. As if to reveal premature synthesis, the dissonance of "lover . . . lever" at the end of the first part becomes "lever . . . lover" at the end of the second. To the discordant end of the poem rhymes qualify concord with discord. As if to reveal this agitator's condition, the regular rhythm of inevitable process is agitated here and there by an anapaest.

I

Is "lever" a verb or a noun? Is "worlds" a plural or a possessive, minus apostrophe? The agency of renewal depends on your interpretation. Either the dry worlds restore themselves or they are restored by an external lever, phallic or political. Paired phrases, beyond syntax, are further impediments. Maybe it is best neglecting syntax, to approach Thomas' syntactical enigmas through image and allusion. "Ice" and ashes go with "dry." "Oil," "lava," "spring," and "flower" go with the idea of revival. In the second stanza "my naked fellow," "the glanded morrow," "the corpse's lover," and "the foaming marrow" hint phallic renewal; but political renewal is hinted by "city" and "governed flower" in the first stanza. "Ashen towns" (cf. xv) may be cities of the plain awaiting reconstruction. "Staked and fallow" land may imply unused private property. "Oil" and "lava" show the usual identification of the mineral and the organic, as "lever" and "wheel" the usual identification of organ with machine. But "Dug of the sea" in a phallic context seems a confusion of sexes. "Pound of lava" recalls Shylock as "wheel of fire" recalls Lear. (The turning of this wheel means transforming.) Shakespeare, so invoked, may imply poetry as another agent of renewal. "All all and all" and "How now" have a fine Shakespearean sound. (For flesh as metal and machine see 11, 33, 40, 44; for dryness see 6, 12; for oil see 27.)

I I

The fears of doubtful Thomas, centered now upon the double agents of salvation, are social and sexual. "Fear not," he exhorts his timid self ("my mortal"), fear not "the working world," at once fermenting, copulating, and proletarian. "Synthetic blood," recalling the blue blood of the previous poem, may be that of capitalists, in contrast to heart's blood "in the ribbing metal" of the revolutionary breast. "Tread" and "milling," composing a treadmill, seem sexual and social, as do "trigger," "scythe," and "blade." For scythe read penis or hammer and sickle. "Trigger," "flint," and steel, though adequate for loving sparks, make Thomas' revolutionary weapons antiques. The "flesh's lock and vice" and the "cage" for deathly raven could do for womb and social oppression.

But that broken "jawbone" is less customary. Samson's weapon for smiting the Philistines is also the poet's instrument; but unlike Shakespeare's, this jawbone is "riven" (cf. "lock . . . jaws," 14). Fear neither the failure of poetic power, Thomas tells his bone, nor the power of conformity. As the photograph stands for mechanical reproduction and fake in "Our eunuch dreams," so the phonograph here, suggested by "jointed lever" or tone arm (alien to the phallic lever of the lover or to the revolutionist's crowbar) and by "the screws that turn the voice" on the "face" of a record. Here, too, there are sexual suggestions.) The "driven" voice on the record, an image of convention, is in the groove. (For phonographs see 42-43, 139.) "O my bone" is lover's tool and poet's jawbone. Even a riven jawbone is better than a driven record.

III

Whatever the grammatical ambiguity of "worlds couple," it is clear that renewal of coupled worlds is the issue. A "contagious man" is one in contact with the still "shapeless people," infecting them. Squaring the circle, a geometrical conceit, not unlike Donne's conceit of compasses, implies the impossibility of love and revolution. "Mechanical flesh" is that of lovers, wielders of compasses, and workers, united in "the people's fusion." The image of flowering, which also ends "Our eunuch dreams," unites the worlds of Lawrence and Marx. Flame, oil, and light on high, opening the "coupled bud," should encourage "the governed flower" of the first part. "All all and all" at the end, an attempt at squaring the aesthetic circle, may square the "mortal circle"; but the terminal discord of "oil" and "all" has a nasty sound.

Stanford, 61-62.

Twenty-Five Poems, 1936

Some of the poems in Thomas' second volume were written in 1935 and 1936, but more are contemporary with those of *18 Poems*, and some are earlier. The first date after each title is that of first publication. When the date of the manuscript is significantly earlier, I append that to the publication date. Thomas filled the volume out with poems from his 1930-33 notebooks, now at the University of Buffalo. But before publication he revised many of them. Of the sixteen of these twenty-five poems in the notebooks eight are substantially the same as the present texts, and eight are radically different. *Twenty-five Poems* shows little development in theme or method; but three or four of the poems are excellent. The arrangement of this section of *The Collected Poems* is that of *Twenty-five Poems*.

I, in my intricate image (1935), *pp. 40-44*

Doubles and fellows are at it again in this narrative of poet, poem, and their making. After climb and fall, his intricate images rise and roar, doubly, from heaven's hill. "Heaven may understand," said a commentator, "but I do not." Obscure to be sure, this history, nevertheless, yields a little to those who, having read *18 Poems*, are familiar with Thomas and his ways.

This formidable poem is in three parts of six stanzas. Terminal sound, as Thomas told Vernon Watkins, is remarkable for liquid "l," which, occurring twenty-four times in each part, comes to a total of seventy-two. Whether meant for ear or eye, these liquids, apt to escape both, show Thomas up to new tricks. But the rhythm with its fixed caesuras, balanced phrasing, and dying falls is customary.

I

1: "I," the first and most important word, adequately introduces the hero of this lyrical history and states the subject. The "intricate image" in which he strides, treads, and sidles like a crab, is double, at once his persona and his poetry. Both are metallic coverings and masks for their sensitive creator, who is active on "two levels" by virtue of his double façade. As "brassy orator" or young poet with a lot of brass, he lays his ghost or spirit in the metal of a printer's form. Like Stephen Dedalus, he is a forger or a smith and a fake. The "scales" of this double world are balances and hard surfaces, that he treads "on the double"—double talk for the quickness of a double-dealer and nimble balancer. (Thomas was born under the zodiacal sign of the Balances.) Half his ghost seems behind the "armour" of his persona and the other half behind type. Both shields are the "man-iron" of his indirect approaches. "Death's corridor" is life, and "I" seems the subject of "hold." (For doubles and fellows see 7, 31, 35; for ghost see 7, 31-32; for crab see 14, 19; for metal, armour, forging see 4, 8, 33, 36, 38. Metal is flesh and poem.)

2-3: The second and third stanzas, which are parallel to each other, restate Thomas' conviction that birth is death, dooming "bulb" and "ghost," seeded flesh and spirit. A shift of metaphor from metal to spinning and vegetable spring may dazzle the reader, who looks in vain for metaphorical consistency until "metal phantom" and "bronze root" bring the first stanza back. The inconsistency of the second stanza is superficial, however, rather than fundamental. Careless of metaphorical agreement, here, Thomas was careful of logical agreement. The inconsistent images refer to unstated ideas which are as consistent as the metaphors through which we must approach them are inconsistent. To interpret the poem we must leave dazzling surface for logical interior and return to the surface with what we guess. This poem is an interaction less of image with image than of images with ideas, which came first.

Spring and "the colic season" indicate the poet's immaturity behind those masks. Like a spinner (Clotho and her colleagues, maybe), spring "unravels," "threads," and "casts" her sap and petals. "Man like a mountain" is the distant prospect of maturity. The "metal phantom" or "twin miracle" emerging from creative earth is both persona and poem, which, like all art, seems "mortal, unmortal," in time and out of it. The poet's double creation of mask and poem seems a sexual "fusion" of female, immortal "rose" with male, mortal motion. "Image of images," a good description of the poem, means a significant form composed of significant parts as well as ultimate image. "Image," "miracle," and "phantom" (shade) are probably allusions to Yeats' "Byzantium," a similar vision of the work of art. Thomas' images for the miracle of creation would do as well for the creation of a child.

4: Manhood, alluded to in the second stanza, becomes the goal of this creative adolescent; but the adult world, as dangerous as climbing a tower, makes him fear what he wants. The fears and troubles of adolescence (cf. 21) belie those brassy masks. "Bone-railed" implies sex, insecurity, and death. "Masterless" seems an allusion to Ibsen's Master Builder, who fell, like Finnegan, from a tower (cf. 23). Climbing a tower is a good dream image of sexual experience. The alternative to the perils of adult sex is committing a solitary nuisance in the service of death. This sedentary death, though parallel to the climber's death, is less to be esteemed. "Shadowless man" (a vampire), an "ox" (infertile), and the "pictured devil" (a fiction) serve death alone. Not only a

Freudian adventure, climbing a tower is writing a poem; for to Thomas towers were towers of words. (For towers and climbing see 19, 22, 32, 54, 67, 95, "The Lemon," "The Tree.")

5: The poet's twin images or masks brave the perils of ascent, their "tread" less confident, however, than that of the balancer in stanza one. Tower is tree and tree, like tower, is word (cf. 19). Poems, forced up like sap through a green fuse, mount on the green steps of predecessors, among whom Yeats with his tower and winding stair must be included. Ascending a "spire," a more than sexual or verbal enterprise, is aspiring. The twin images climb, but the secret self who made them timidly remains below, shut in his "glass bed," apparently a kind of greenhouse or bottle, together with fruit, beast, and flower. Glass protects him from the "weather" outdoors. "I with the wooden insect in the tree of nettles," Watkins says, was Thomas' favorite line. Wood, like tree, could be cross or word. An insect (cf. 47) is an articulated thing, like a poem; and a "wooden insect" is as artificial as a poem. "Tree of nettles" suggests Christ on cross with crown of thorns (cf. 15). The poet, embottled in his "glass bed of grapes," could be Eucharistic wine or Christ Himself—and the poet as holy wino.

6: "Intricate manhood," uniting "image" of the first stanza with "manhood" of the fourth, is the hoped-for fusion of mask, poem, and maturity. But living means dying. "Ending," "final," and "harbour" imply the death that awaits all men, masks, and poems. "Voyaging clockwise" is in time. Meanwhile, "the invalid rivals" (himself and his images), waving farewell, greeting "seablown" successors, and crossing the bar, put out to sea—"on the level" (cf. "on the double," another example of his enhancement and complication of cliché). "The consumptives' terrace" sounds like Auden, who wheeled Death anywhere "in his invalid chair."

The shifting images of Part I correspond, as we have noticed, to implicit ideas. The surface, which is all we certainly have, is "image, all image," as the poet Marlais cries to his "fallen tower" in "The Orchards." This poem on "intricate image" illustrates its theme by example.

II

1: While Thomas himself, under glass with his flowers and snails, thinks of death, his projected doubles continue their ascent of the

"windy spiral," out in the "weathers" of the "twelve winds."
(Thomas' winds, commonly twelve, combine the months and the
principal points of the compass. See 63, 69, 145, "The Lemon.")
The winding stair affords a view of dying animals and clouds,
"the white host at pasture." ("Mounted," which refers to the
horses of the "corral," is a transferred epithet.) But those climbers, out in the weathers, can see through the glass of Thomas'
retreat, where the snail mimics their giddy spiralling. A "haring
snail" is a composite of fast and slow.

2: Diving from the tower, those climbers bite the dust and
land in water. This descent into matter is an image of begetting;
but sidling Thomas doubles and redoubles metaphor. As diving
here is a metaphor for dying and dying a metaphor for begetting
a child, so begetting a child is a metaphor for making a poem.
The waters of regression and birth are a metaphor for the gestation of a poem after its conception. Double masks hide constant
theme. But back to metaphor: "the highroad of water," the
"channel," or "the long sea" of the womb is made "arterial" by
the embryo, the "riderless dead" (cf. 108). His "petrol face" is as
shapeless as the oil of life that drives him (cf. 8, 38, 39). The
waters of genesis are crowded with seabears (seals) and Yeats'
mackerel. Death by water is birth.

3-4: These stanzas are a gloomy parenthesis on death; for
womb is tomb. Sharp instruments, surgical operations, dissections,
anatomies, and war combine suggestions of sex, death, and,
maybe, analysis. The "long eye," split open to increase or de-
crease vision of the "long sea," anticipates "the slash of vision" in
Part III. The "spiral turnkey" (from the "windy spiral"?) is a
suitable warder for the "corkscrew grave" of the womb or the
corkscrew grave of the tomb that Thomas knew awaited him in
what he called "the drinking dark." "Antiseptic funeral," like
other phrases in this poem, is authentic Auden. After surgery and
war (cf. 33, 36), the dunghill-cock who summons Lazarus forth
summons the poet to death. His saviour is dust and the soil of his
graveyard, however "conjured" by common prayer, is dust and
ashes. "Dust be your saviour under the conjured soil," grandly
symphonic, brings us back to poetry.

5: Those divers into mother (cf. 35) hear sunken bells as
they drown (cf. 167). Bells "clapped in water" ringing out

the "Dead Sea scale," are gestating poems. Triton "dangling" (cf. 148) from the "hangman's raft" by rope of "whale-weed" (cf. 10) is the embryo gestating. "Salt glass breakers" are complex. Salt breakers are waves of the genetic sea; but glass breakers could threaten that glasshouse or bottle, a womb on shore. Bell towers of "spindrift" are as poetic as "spindrift pages" (142); and "the tongues of burial" are poems of womb and tomb. That the submarine and subterranean preoccupation of Thomas' "tide-tongued" images is not altogether agreeable to Thomas becomes clear in the self-critical parenthesis that concludes Part II. Light breaks through glass to enlighten its occupant. Seeing, he "hears" weathers fall outside (I, 5) while his sunken images, seeing nothing, "hear" divers' bells. Hearing and seeing are the senses of the second part; and hearing, as we shall see, brings us to the phonograph.

6: This parenthesis, a second interruption of forward movement, hints Thomas' displeasure with the poems of womb and tomb that his aquatic images insist upon. Since his phonographs are disagreeable (cf. 39, 139), to call his poetic record a phonograph record is dispraise. His world has been the "circular world" of a "wax disk," which, going round and round, "stands still." He must jump from his groove, leave womb, tomb, and low-vaulted past, come forth to light. Meanwhile that "face of voices" remains his world. Land turns on a "moon-turned table" around the spindle of the amniotic sea. The electrical pickup ("stylus"), like Thomas' imagery, dazzles; but there is no veritable lightning as the record scrapes out all the "shames and damp dishonours" of adolescence. The tone is bitter, the exhortation ironic.

Part II, however obscure, is plain compared to Part III. Plainly, to bring things to light you must keep them dark—as in a Freudian dream. Moreover, as Wilde's Lord Darlington observes, "Now-a-days to be intelligible is to be found out." Maybe Thomas, who had found himself out (e.g. 22-23), was dazzling and damping readers to keep them from finding out what he had found.

III

Hortatory rather than narrative until the last line, Part III appears to be Thomas' sermon to his images, now at their lowest point. The preacher urges uniting, rising, and exchanging **water** and earth for air and fire, the higher elements. By his exemplum of the crocodile, he condemns tomb and womb. So instructed and deeply moved, those images rise and shine. If they rise apart from the preacher, the triumph is that of art. If they rise with him, the triumph is that of maturity. Part III in this case would be the synthesis in a dialectical process, which may have been intended. But images going several ways at once get in the way of straightforward process. At its end, however, it is clear that the exhorted images find the preacher's images clear enough to act upon. Nor is this odd; for an intricate image should feel at home with intricate images.

1: The images "suffer" (in two senses) their sunken condition. "Undead," a word from *Dracula*, refers to the condition of vampires—embryos here in the womb's scenery. From "sea-stuck towers" ring sunken bells; but, in connection with male "skull" and female "thimble," these towers are phallic as well as poetic. "At the fibre scaling," nicely intricate, includes climbing, surface, interior, and deep decay. Exhortation begins with the second and less ambiguous "Suffer." The Aran Islands are barren ground. Let a tree sprout there. "A double angel" (cf. "arterial angel," 35, and "double shade," 7) implies unity, upward flight, and, in connection with "locker," a gold coin, which, like any coin, is a single thing with two faces. As "topsy-turvies," the images, having fallen head over heels, are in no position to rise; yet let them come forth from the womb like twins.

2: Syntactical confusion seems incompatible with exhortation, yet it proceeds. The preacher commends unity and ascension to "Brass and bodiless image," the persona and poem of the first stanza. Skewer yourselves, he says, on a single stick: your common ghost, a fool's bauble, and Jacob's ladder (cf. 32, 80), which, angled at the stars, will bring you from the valley of dopes ("smoke" and "hophead") and from the sea. "Five-fathomed Hamlet on his father's coral," a mixture of *Hamlet* and *The Tempest* that Joyce would have enjoyed, may be a way of implying that the early poems are deathly, submarine, allusive, derivative, and confused. (Yet father's bones, transformed, are coral now.) Ironic self-criticism continues in the last line. "Tom Thumb" was a dwarf and an early steam engine. A "tom-thumb vision" is a small one; and however much a small locomotive puffs, an "iron mile" is a short track. That metal and machine are flesh improves the Freudian possibilities.

3: "Suffer" is now ironic. Stay drowned, blind, and ship-wrecked in the womb if you must, says the preacher. Continue the downward voyage of death. "Give over" or abandon the "seawax struggle" of love's candle and all hope of love's "fire." No lovers "lock" (cf. 4) in your stony "lockers" or damp "bed of eels." "The slash of vision," which recalls "splitting the long eye open" (II, 3), seems blinding here rather than penetrating. "The man-string," like the "flaxen whale-weed" (II, 5), is the umbilicus by which the hopeless embryo is anchored.

4: The preacher's claims for his own condition come by way of contrast. His circle is "boiling." His instrument is "nicked in the locks of time"; for in the nick of time he has discovered adult sex. His Lawrentian blood is "single," not double; and he is out in the weathers of "the pouring town"—Swansea or London in the rain. But his elements, as a poet's should be, are air and fire. "Wind on fire" is a poem, "a burning and crested act" (xv). So, like a sidling crab (cf. 19) with "pincers," he claws the croco-dile out of Eden to serve as object lesson. More than crab-bing preacher, he is magus, spelling by images. Association with "scales" (I, 1) may account for the crocodile's presence here. Compare "green Adam's cradle" with "green genesis" (47).

5: Like Lewis Carroll's Isaac Watts, the preacher, improving the crocodile as it improves its scales, draws a lesson from it. Egyp-tian crocodile means death. Man as crocodile is tail, snout, and enameled "scales," which, no longer balances, are surfaces now, like the metallic coverings of the first stanza. (Birds of the Nile sit on crocodiles to pick their teeth.) How man as crocodile saddles Moses' bulrushes escapes me—unless saddling the wind among the reeds is making papyrus from them. "The hourless houses" are pyramids with mummies embalmed in oils, ointments, and wind-ing sheets—poems, in short. A "sea-hatched skull" unites tomb, womb, and man's condition. "All-hollowed man," a pun, com-bines mummy, eviscerated for embalming, and saint. His white apparel is winding sheet and innocence, both to be wept for. Ointment on a "flying grail" prevents ascension. (For Egypt see 36, 72, 84.)

6: As scaly crocodile, man is a mask or mantle for death.

(For Cadaver see 21-22.) "The rotten fathom," umbilicus again, is the windy master of a womb-tomb poet. The ghost in forged metal marks a return to the first stanza. A "metal neptune" seems a suitable diving suit for a dangling triton (II, 5).

The ending is a little abrupt. Although his poetic genesis was the "intricate seawhirl" of the womb, the preacher appears to have climbed above his origins—or so, at least, he tells his congregation of two sunken images. Climbing out in their turn, they ascend heaven's hill to light and love. "Roared and rose," an example of hysteron proteron, means rose and roared. Those images sound like good poet and poem now. But their triumph is less actual than resolved upon and prayed for. There they are on heaven's hill; but the poet's "thirtieth year to heaven" is not here yet—not by a long shot.

Watkins, 15. Stanford, 71-72. Olson, 36.

This bread I break (1936; *ms. 1933*), *p. 45*

Like Sir John Denham's classical Thames, this poem is "deep, yet clear . . . without o'erflowing full." Yet "This bread I break," however classical its depth and clarity, celebrates romantic pantheism in romantic triple talk. What seems immediately clear becomes, on re-examination, dense. Although self-subsistent and suitable for anthologies, the poem gains richness from the obscure neighbors it brightly emerges from.

Bread and wine of the Eucharist, the ostensible subject, serve as analogy for the holiness of nature—of all green force from sap to sperm—and for the holiness of poetry. Every simple word is loaded. Forked language, uniting the three themes of religion, nature, and poetry, divides them. Of the three prongs on this fork poetry is the longest. Nature and Eucharist become its parallels. The green force of nature and poetry is sacramental, but natural force, as Thomas has said before, is no more creative than destructive. We destroy what we enjoy and break the holy bread of life to receive it. Plays on the word "break" carry both meanings.

1: The unnatural bread and wine of the Eucharist come from natural oat and grape—as the poem, another example of transubstantiation, from the poet's flesh and blood. "Plunged," whether past participle or active verb, adds sexual connotations to tree and fruit. The "foreign tree," however, is primarily the grapevine, the cross, and the fruit-bearing tree of Eden. But natural man and nature's wind destroy oat and wine. "Broke the grape's joy" combines the breaking of bread with the taking of wine, and natural force with the fall of man and the crucifixion. The joy of creation becomes the joy of destruction. Parallel structure and symmetry support these paradoxes and parallels.

2: "Wind" in the first line of the first printing of the American *Collected Poems* is a misprint for "wine," correctly printed in the second American printing and in the English edition. "Knocked" (cf. 8) is a favorite word for sex, birth, and heart. Here "Knocked in" goes with "broke." Unscrambled, lines three and four read: Once the oat in this bread was merry. "Summer blood," which implies Christ's blood or the wine of the Eucharist, leads to "Man broke the sun." For punning Thomas, as we have noticed in earlier poems, sun becomes Son. Man destroyed Jesus by crucifixion on a foreign tree. "Wind," more than natural here, is the divine breath and the breath of poets, who, like Jesus, are destroyed by man. (Wind is destroyer, creator, and victim of destruction.) The Word, whether Jesus or poet, is sacrificed. Receiving the Eucharist and reading the poem destroy creation for creation's sake.

3: "This," the Yeatsian demonstrative of the first stanza, refers particularly to this poem, sacramentally consumed by reading. (The language offers genetic parallels.) The poem's blood, like elements of the Eucharist, came from "sensual root and sap"; for man is one with vegetable. Reading Thomas you empty his veins of vegetable love.

"Sap" and "snap," the only true rhymes of the poem, make a snappy ending. Not the artist but the reader is the young dog now, and so is the communicant. Dog, according to Joyce, is opposite to God—according to Thomas, too. The stanza, appropriately recalling that of "the green fuse," is a variation upon it. Rhythm is regular enough, but the rhyme, except for the final couplet, is ghostly.

Hopkins devoted "The Half-way House" to "the breaking of the bread." Thomas read Hopkins and Hopkins was holy. Thomas broke bread in chapel as a youth or saw it broken. But his use of the sacrament here does not constitute holiness or signify belief. Less like Hopkins than Joyce, who was fascinated with the Eucharist, Thomas used it for analogy. Holy analogy, however secular its application, preserves and lends a holy air to brighten, in this happy union of clarity and density, the diffused romantic holiness of nature and art.

Stanford, 73-75.

Incarnate devil (1935; ms. 1933), p. 46

His heart was in the Garden. "In the beginning" and references in many other poems celebrate other visits. Place of fall as well as creation, the Garden, like nature's green force, has two aspects, evil as well as good. Their double auspices appeal in this poem, originally called "Poem for Sunday," to a poet of two minds, whose religious position, if any, seems Manichaean. But Thomas, like his God and Satan, was only fiddling around.

1: The devil incarnate in the snake stung the "circle" of God's creative compasses awake. The snake's garden is either in the plains of Asia or else includes them. It is the "shaping-time" of Genesis. As good a shaper as God, the devil "forked out" (by pitchfork and forked tongue) the "bearded apple," at once Eve's forbidden fruit and bearded Jesus as fruit of that fruit. Meanwhile, God, having described his circle, is walking in the cool of the evening and "fiddling." "Fiddling," the important word, suggests tinkering with, playing with, standing idly by, fooling around, or scraping out music, like Nero, while the Garden burns (cf. 36). Fiddling as making music accords with "shaping" to suggest poetry, as much an aspect of creation as making a world or a child. Playing down pardon from "the heavens' hill," where images roar (44), God is announcing salvation on Calvary or minimizing it. For the moment, this "fiddling warden" seems less of a creator than Satan, and, off on a hill perhaps, less responsible.

2: "Wisemen" (magi or philosophers but certainly not Sunday-school teachers) tell us what went on in the Garden before our creation—before the face of the waters was "guided" by tide or the waters of the womb by time. The "handmade moon," someday to rule the tides, was still in a cloud. "Handmade" means created by God's hand to be a handmaid to Adam and the sun. The moon as Eve, also made by Satan, is "half holy" and half evil, like everything else under the sun, especially in the Garden. The "garden gods" are God and Satan, combined with the gods who presided over Roman gardens. Equal creators, God and Satan "Twined good and evil on an eastern tree," at once the tree of knowledge and the cross or the "foreign tree" of "This bread I break"—and maybe "the sole Arabian tree" of phoenix and poet. When fully created and able to guide the seas, the moon, as windy as a woman, is half the devil's and half Christ's. Eve was black as Satan and white as Christ, but why she was "paler" I have no idea—unless she was pallid through terror and guilt. Anyway, the conflict and union of black and white suits co-operative creation, and so do the other conflicts and unions. Heaven and hell (cf. 27) are mixed.

3: When in the womb, our particular Eden, we had fore-knowledge of good and evil—like that of the liquid, shapeless being of "Before I knocked." Warm waters and "mighty mornings" refer to Eden, womb, and birth. "The cloven myth," not only that of Satan and Eve, is the myth of divided creation. In our Edens we knew light and dark, heaven and the midnight of the Son (the fall of man?), which a serpent, as good a fiddler as God, gave shape to. "Shaping-time," the final word, unites Eden, womb, and poetic creation. Fiddling around is the creative act.

The 1933 manuscript, entitled "Before We Sinned," lacks fiddling and all other merits.

Stanford, 66. Runia Macleod, in *Adam*, 22.

To-day, this insect (1936; *ms.* 1930), *pp. 47-48*

Again and again during twenty years and more, alone and in company with alert readers, I have accosted "the insect certain." Still uncertain, it still invites guesses—as it would not do were the poem not so fine an arrangement of sounds and rhythms. We are on familiar ground, however. Insect and crocodile figure in "I, in my intricate image." Genesis and the circle figure in "Incarnate devil." As these images detained Thomas, so his constant theme: the parallel creation of world, child, and poem—here especially the last of these. My latest guess, that is, is that here is another poem about the poem, a fresh enigma about enigma.

The stanza of eight lines, variously rhymed, suggests Yeats' ottava rima. The couplet that magnificently ends the first stanza is a monument of Yeatsian magnificence. So, too, the ending of the poem. The two statements that separate the stanzas are, in the manner of the Delphic oracle, oracular. "Adam I love, my madmen's love is endless" interweaves liquids and nasals in the manner of Hopkins and the Welsh.

1: This insect is the problem. Thomas' "wooden insect" (41), "timeless insect" (53), and "sorcerer's insect" (93) suggest that insect is poem; for wood is word, poetry is beyond time, and the poet is a magician. Like the crab (19), the insect is an intricate image, articulated, segmented, covered with shell or scales, and the result of metamorphosis. Fabulists, including La Fontaine, Joyce, Kafka, and Lawrence, have celebrated ant, grasshopper, cockroach, and ladybird or scarab. That "this insect" serves as poem here is confirmed by the immediate context of "symbol" and "sense." That it is also a literal insect and the poem's occasion is no less likely. The time is the present, the place, any city, Swansea or London, at whose "spectacles" countrymen gape. Seeing an insect (in the sink perhaps), Thomas makes insect his metaphor.

The poet's "symbols," like all art, have pushed time ("Today") and space ("the world I breathe") aside, though they have only half-escaped their origin in "daft" craft or nudging the sentence. When analyzed, the poem, as double as its creator, reveals two parts, "trust and tale," which correspond to the "head and tail" of the divided insect. (That the word insect means "cut in" or almost divided may have decided this insect's fate.) Literally, Thomas may have cut his insect in two with a bottle-opener or anything equally handy. Metaphorically, this division implies the analysis of a unified thing that destroys wholeness and origin. Thomas' head, dividing his poem into "broken halves" (35) of meaning and form, maybe, has destroyed its green genesis in imagination and the innocence of creation. "Trust" is innocent belief and "tale" is fable. "Guillotine" and "blood-red" may hint the poem's social sense. "Witnesses" from the Apocalypse (11:3), observing fall in Genesis, unite and separate the two ends of the Bible.

"The insect certain is the plague of fables." In this oracular pronouncement every important word has at least two senses. "Insect" is either literal insect or intricate image, either whole or divided. "Certain" is either a noun, an adjective, or an adverb. "Plague" is either a multitude, a destroyer, or an annoyer. "Fables" are either lies or fictions in Wallace Stevens' sense: created things. The sense of the oracle depends on your arrangement of these possibilities: The insect, for example, is the Biblical plague of locusts; the poem destroys lies or consists of multiple fictions; reality is myth or fatal to it. Certainly the oracle is talking about insects or poems, insects and poems, fact and imagination, truth and falsehood, and about art as fiction in two senses. If the insect is Christ (see 41) or a child, other interpretations of creator, creature, reality, and myth are possible.

2: "This story" is either the story of Eden or this poem or both Eden, the origin of fictions, is a fiction. Satan as serpent coils round the blazing circle of the "shaping-time" (46). "The last shocked beginning" is fall and birth. ("Scrams" seems misused American slang.) The crocodile (cf. 44) is a likely result of the unlikely mating of serpent and insect. "Chrysalis" refers to the metamorphosis of insects; "shell" refers to insects and crocodiles; but "caul" to the embryo, begotten by phallic guillotine and now in the Eden of the womb "Before" ambiguously combines time and space, as "from" in "the fall from love" combines cause and separation. The "heartbone," flying before Adam's fall, is Jesus, Adam's misplaced rib, and phallus—as falling from love and "children's piece" imply. (Compare "the flying grail," 44, "heart bone," 160. Heart and bone unite life and death.) The "sabbath ass" (Christ's on Palm Sunday and maybe Thomas in Sunday school) is part of a children's tale or fable that destroys the fable of Eden, as the Gospels blow Jericho on Genesis, as birth destroys the embryo's Eden, and as the poem, without receiving credit, destroys old fable by new. An example of fable and analysis of fable, this stanza certainly unites poetry, religion, and obstetrics.

The second oracle, rearranging elements of the first, adds "promise," a new ambiguity, at once hopeful and discouraging. The promise of the "insect fable," depending on your preference, can be Christian, obstetrical, or literary. Each seems certain. But as the next stanza shows, this promise, however you take it, means death. Paradox: art destroys fable, yet art is fable, hence doomed to die with religion and child. What is certain about all is certain death.

3: That "Death," the certain promise, includes fable is shown by a catalogue: Hamlet's death and that of all "nightmare madmen" (dreamt by daft poets), Don Quixote's windmill, the wooden horse of Troy, John's apostolic beast (the eagle), and Job's boils. "Air-drawn" means moved by air and sketched by imagination (cf. "wind-drawn," "In the Direction of the Beginning," and Hopkins' "dapple-dawn-drawn"). Dying Hamlet and his peers are "fibs" or fictions of "vision" or the imagination. "Greek in the Irish sea the ageless voice" may be that of Jesus, Edward King's Milton, or James Joyce. ("Greek" could mean classical or incomprehensible.) The timeless Greek, loving Adam and all madmen or poets, is a "tell-tale lover" or a poet himself. His "end" is certain death and the artist's intention. Like any poet, he is Christ, but his crucifixion is a crucifiction. Less tree of knowledge than cross, his "tree of stories" is hidden from readers by the "fabulous curtain" of the poem. Nobody knew how Thomas, the creator, suffered on his tree of words, "all legends' sweethearts" on the trees beside him.

The 1930 manuscript, nothing like the final version, lacks "this insect," the crocodile, the city spectacles, the guillotine, the cross of tales, all the Biblical allusions and all those to secular literature; but there are a butterfly's chrysalis, a creature measuring his length along a wall, and a division of "sense into sight and trust." From "The certain is a fable" enigma was to develop. Rewriting made a poem out of nothing much.

Olson, 55. Bill Casey, in *Explicator*, XVII (March 1959). Gene Montague, in *Explicator*, XIX (December 1960).

The seed-at-zero (1936; ms. 1933), *pp. 49-51*

After that fine poem, this mediocre poem—here, maybe, to fill the volume up. Good poet, as Wordsworth proves, cannot be good poet always. These verses of seed and egg are remarkable chiefly for paired stanzas, the second of each pair an echo (with variations) of the first. Hopkins' use of echo, a possible source, is golden. Here, however, pairing with leaden variation suits the theme of one plus one or begetting and conceiving. Creation above is like creation below. Virgin, child, and star are alike, whether divine or human. The metaphor of storming a citadel, consistently elaborated, helps us conceive assault and uncertain victory.

"The seed-at-zero" is seed as nothing, or safely in its "virgin o" (21) and "green nought" (79), or, according to the military metaphor, at zero hour, about to storm the "manwaging" or "warbearing line" of the "manwaged" womb. "God-in-hero" seems to combine pagan divinities, Christ, and any man, especially Thomas. The assault of male zero upon female zero comes to nothing, according to sublunary arithmetic and what Sir Thomas Browne calls the "mystical mathematics of the city of heaven."

But assault from above is successful in the second pairing. "Star-flanked seed," muscular and divine, falls like "manna" to take and quicken the "virgin stronghold" of the Virgin. "Riddled," if taken to mean shot full of holes as the military metaphor demands, is misleading. Here it must mean fabled or told as a mystery.

The third pair plays question against answer, small against big: village against continent, hemisphere against "green inch," planet against village green. Drunken sailors in the "harbour" hide the seeded egg from Herod?

The fourth pairing unites human and divine, above and below, creation from nothing and zero hour, in one heroic seeding. The "hero-in-tomorrow" or the embryo will not range his "cannons" on "the sky-scraping place" (new world, heavenly city, and womb) or on "the grave-groping place," the womb alone.

"Shall" and "shall not," the insistent verbs, seem more demanding than the poetic circumstances demand.

Stanford, 68-69.

Shall gods be said to thump the clouds (1936; *ms. 1933*), *p. 52*

Almost a sonnet, this slight, agreeable thing of fourteen lines is oddly rhymed and divided oddly. Short imperatives follow long interrogatives with an air of finality. What seems a dismissal of old, anthropomorphic gods becomes another celebration of the intricate image or work of art. "Be said" and "stones" are the telling words.

When it rains is Jove around with his thunders and his watering can or Venus with her dugs? Those gods are stony images. But talking stones or works of art are all we can know of divinity. They are "shapes of sound."

Here in this spring (1936; *ms. 1933*), *p. 53*

Quatrains are violated by a stanza of five lines in this pretty poem of the four seasons and their signs. Time's sermon, not in stones or running brooks, is in birds and worms. As the poet, a bird and worm-watcher, tells time by the seasons, so bird and worm tell him of time. Worm or slug, telling destruction better than bird, is a calendar, somehow related to the "timeless insect." Whether worms are charnal, phallic, or rural, they are recurrent and, in this sense, timeless, too. Insects commonly serve Thomas as images of Jesus and poem (see 41, 47) or the Word. Jesus and poem, both as timeless and vital as the worm, afford the most telling intimations of mortality, and, as the Yeatsian question that inconclusively concludes the poem allows, of immortality. The 1933 manuscript differs in most respects from the 1936 revision.

Do you not father me (1935), *pp. 54-55*

Uncertain syntax is all but successful in concealing the simple theme: As poet, Thomas is one with father, brother, sister—maybe with all but mother, who seems to serve as oracle or Muse. The elaborated metaphor of house and tower by the weedy sea carries the meaning. Retaining part of their Freudian significance, these images are enriched by other systems. This tower is also the tower of Babel, the "tower of words" (19), and the ivory tower (67). This house is built on sands. Erection and fall of tower are man's metaphor.

1: The "fellow father" (35) fathers the poet. That is clear; but neither "nor" nor "cast" is clear—nor the scrambled phrasing. "Nor" seems a condensation of "is not?" or "does not?" "Cast," taken with "arm" seems an active verb; but with "tower" it can mean cemented. Anyway, father is building Dylan's tower out of mother's material. But Dylan as "lovers' house" (made by parents) suffers from or accepts his "stain": perhaps any sin, all guilt, or original sin. The second "nor" could mean "do I not?" Do you not, he asks sister, share guilt for the crime of erecting my turreted house? Brother, climbing the tower (cf. 21-22, 32, 40-41), sees "summer," the happy season for its boys, from the windows. Questions here and those in the next stanza will be answered in the last two stanzas, along with more questions.

2: Not only his own father, like the Shakespeare of Stephen Dedalus, the poet is also his climbing, peeping brother. The poet's sister as himself and his "saviour" completes the confusion of identities. "Am I not all of you?" asks this romantic concentrate of all things and all men—all members of one another. The sea beside him is "directed" by moon or womb's time (cf. "guided sea," 46). The "babbling" of bird and shell in the seaside tower makes it the "tower of words" or poem as well as poet. The roof, made by the "towering tiler," is of sand, and, as we shall see, the tower is built on sand. The poet as father is his own master builder. "Wanton starer" and "towering tiler" sound like early Auden.

3: Mother and father agree that the poet is "all these." More than builder, father is destroyer, sacking and hacking all he has made, an "Abraham-man" intent on sacrificing Isaac. (Remember that the force through its green fuse is as destructive as creative.) The tower of words, speaking now, tells how it is "razed" by him who raised it. "Timeless stroke" seems an act of God the father, aghast at His act. Once of stone and sand, the tower is now a "wooden folly" (cf. 58) or pretentious structure. Since "wooden" in other poems (e.g. 41) suggests both word and cross, God's destruction of His Son, more successful than Abraham's, seems implied. Destruction of a tower recalls that of Babel, anticipated perhaps by "babbling" in the second stanza. That tower's razing caused a confusion of tongues. This tower's raising is attended by a confusion of syntax.

"Dry-as-paste" and "ringed-sea ghost" recall the sterile womb of "Where once the waters of your face." But "man-begetters" or creators rise from the "wrack." An important word, to be developed in the last stanza, "wrack" means wreck, ruin, rack or cross, and marine weeds. As ruin, it fits the fallen tower. As seaweed, it suits mother.

4: The fourth stanza returns to the beginning. "Destroying sand," on which house and tower are built, is time. "Seaweedy," proceeding from "wrack," is a wonderful word for mother. (Compare "seaweed," 2, "lovebeds of the weeds," 12, "deadweed," 83, and the weeds in "Adventure from a Work in Progress.") Seaweedy, "the salt sucked dam" of the weedy sea, repeats herself. She may be speaking together with "the darlings of the land/ Who play the proper gentleman and lady," the Welshing rich maybe; or she and her lower-middle-class husband may be aspiring to gentility.

Question: will the poet continue to be "love's house" (cf. "lovers' house") in "widdershin" or topsy-turvy society? ("Woe to the windy masons," who built him, may predict parental dismay.) However proper, the gentleman and lady know life. Love's house and death's tower, they say, must fall, though unaware of their fate (cf. "the tower ending" and "the house of wind," 23). "The grave sin-eater," punning on "grave," refers to an old custom. A sin-eater is one who, for a fee, assumes the sins of a dead man. This sepulchral rite recalls the "sin," "stain," and "crime" of the first stanza. The sin-eater may be grave, Christ, and the poet.

Using words for all they are worth, Thomas was a dictionary-eater. Pity about the syntax, we say. But poetry may be an arrangement of disarrangements—as Rimbaud, who systematically deranged his senses, would agree. Like derangement, disarrangement may help renew the language of the tribe. The Mallarmé of Glamorganshire, Thomas was also, as he said, "the Rimbaud of Cwmdonkin Drive."

Out of the sighs (1936; *ms.* 1932), *pp.* 56-57

Something too painful for fiddling gave this poem bare words for bare feelings, which free verse, Thomas' first published experiment in the form, fits. (Most of his schoolboy poems, still in manuscript, are written in free verse.) Though relatively unimagistic, the poem is not without images, simple images now: that of the wounded soldier in the second strophe and that of the dog in the fourth. Only the latter shows signs of fiddling.

The sense of the first strophe is immediately clear. From the three stages of pain (sighs, grief, and agony), "a little comes" from the first alone. "A little comes, is tasted and found good" has the classical bareness of the later Wallace Stevens, for whom Thomas had little use. "If not of loving well, then not" has the leanness of Gertrude Stein, for whom Thomas had no use. "Be praised," an ellipsis in accord with the concision of "then not," means "God be praised."

Fruitful barrenness, interrupted by the conventional image of the soldier's wound, returns in the third strophe. In the second, that wound, spilling words, defines the trouble, as much poetic as amatory. (Compare "the wound in the throat," 153.) The "sweet lies" (cf. "fibs of vision," 48), the "vagueness" (ambiguity?), and the "hollow words" of poetry are no longer a cure for what ails this poet.

Were poetry enough, the young dog would be "cured of distemper." The fine image of the dog, suddenly emerging from bareness and commonplace image, is masterly. Poetry is no cure, but the dog gropes for matter under his dish in order to offer what he can for what it is worth. "Bone, blood, and sinew," the "twisted brain," and "fair-formed loin" have produced poetry, which seems nothing better now than "crumbs" found under a dog-dish in the "barn." (Doghouse? The "halter" must be a leash.) The verse of this strophe suddenly tightens into an approximation of stanzaic form. Ambiguity returns with "For all there is to give," which can mean "What there is," "For what it is worth," "Instead of," or "Because of." This last strophe, bitter and moving, is not unlike the last stanza of "The Circus Animals'

Desertion" by Yeats. Nor does Thomas' tightening strophe lack all the glory of that great stanza. Beneath the manuscript of this poem, which concludes the 1930-32 notebook, Thomas wrote, "This has taken a hell of a time."

Most of his poems must have taken him, as they now give his readers, that

Hold hard, these ancient minutes in the cuckoo's month (1936), *p. 58*

Welsh bard again, Thomas chose flexible blank verse (a little sprung) for this excellent poem in his grandest manner. Some lines exceed the limit of five beats. Occasional assonance ("tales . . . game") and dissonance ("lands . . . descends") relieve the blankness, and there are other, more tenuous, disagreements. The arrangement of sounds and rhythms calls for reading aloud—by Thomas, with "hwyl."

The theme is time again and the four seasons, which ruined the boys of summer. There the speaker sneers at those boys. Here Thomas shouts encouragement to the children of spring. Summer is coming—then, December. Make much, or as much as you can, of time, personified as hunter and racer. As this poem recalls "the boys of summer," so it anticipates "In Country Sleep" and "Over Sir John's hill." Emergence of the later Thomas is heralded as much by feeling, tone, and attitude as by theme and subtleties of rhythm and sound.

As usual there are problems. Which, precisely, is "the cuckoo's month," April or May? No British bird-watcher, I cannot be sure. Of little help, Thomas puts "bone-breaking April" in one stanza and "this fifth month" in another. No bird-watcher, I fall back on Spenser's "merry Cuckow, messenger of Spring," whether of Eliot's "cruelest month" or of Hopkins' juicy May. I incline to April, which, beginning with fools, seems more cuckoo than May. Temporal confusion also attends the huntsman and steeplechaser —for me at least, never in the pink or at the track. Surely fox hunting is a sport of autumn or winter; and the steeplechase, ac- cording to *Whitaker's Almanac*, replaces "flat" racing from September 25 to the end of March. Hunting and chasing for the steeple in April seem equivalent to nuts and may. Maybe confusion of seasons is the point. Always in season, time is out of season. But there is also the problem of "folly," which we have met in "Do you not father me." There it is plainly a costly, unfinished building. Not so plainly here, where it is "lank" and ridden by a fox hunter in his pink. ("Tantivy," as Samuel Bennet says in *Adventures in the Skin Trade*: "Always the right word in the right place.") "The lank folly's hunter" takes a spill. According to *The Oxford Dictionary*, a folly can also be a clump of trees on a hill, and this "lank" folly, the fourth one (in sequence or side by side?) is "on Glamorgan's hill." (Maybe the hills of Swansea display follies of one kind or another—but the guidebook is of no help here.) For Elder Olson's attractive notion that a folly is a hurdle in a steeplechase my dictionaries offer no corroboration. Hurdle or clump, "the lank fourth folly" and its rider seem metaphors for April, the fourth month, ridden by time. In respect of temporal process April is a costly, unfinished structure, somehow "lank" in respect of vegetation. Foolish as a cuckoo, April is careless of time. Meaning time, cuckoo is a word of fear—even to unmarried men.

1: Minutes, even of April or May, are as "ancient" as time himself, who drives the "green blooms" through the fuse. "Green" and "bloom" combine bud and flower. "Ride" and "drive," the chief words, support the image of hunting. "The vault of ridings" is a concentration of jumping, tomb, and trees overarching a "riding" or a forest pathway. "Hanging" means impending, in abeyance, sloping, or deathly. "The hanging south" could be impending spring, which forebodes death, like a hanging judge. "Under" the folly on the hill, implying domination and location, could make "hanging" a hanging wood to the south. "In a folly's rider" may mean in the likeness of. Time is riding the folly of a cuckoo month. "My children," in apposition to "men" and directly exhorted to "hold hard," are driven by the hounds of spring. Children are hunter's quarry, and since the hunter is "a county man," victims, maybe, of the better sort. Anyway, hold hard, my children, to these minutes, however menacing.

2: The "sport" of country, like that of the children in the

final stanza, is summer. "Sport" is pleasure or games or, if country is also a hunter, quarry or game. "Crane and water-tower" are the industrial scenery of Glamorganshire (cf. "crane-hills" in "The Orchards"). The trees near Swansea are "seedy" in two senses —like the boys of summer. But "December's pools" (connected with summer by an illogical "and") lying "this fifth month unskated," are puzzling. There is no skating in May, to be sure, or in April, the fifth month from December, counting December. Certainly those pools have not been unskated for each of those five months unless it was a warm winter. "And the birds have flown" could be birds gone south in December or gone from the nest in May. Children "in the world of tales" of Robin Hood's "greenwood" anticipate the little girl preparing for country sleep (181). Robin Hood hunted deer at any season, but this is "the first and steepled season," a confusion of spring with winter's steeplechasing and nature's holiness. "The summer's game," going back to summer's "sport," combines pleasure with quarry again. Not only time's quarry, children must become hunters—or else, one with the game that summer hunts, must clasp it and hold hard. Summer is the time for boys of summer to play games.

3: The "horns of England" are those of Robin Hood, of county men across the border, and of English poetry, especially, it may be, those of elfland, faintly blowing. (Elves are like fairies, and Thomas thought himself "a dog among the fairies," 80.) That these horns include poetry is established by "the sound of shape" (cf. 84), which, like "the shape of sound," is a good definition of poetry. ("We are all metaphors of the sound of shape of the shape of sound," "Prologue to an Adventure," Cf. "the light of sound . . . the sound of light," 24.) Poetry, like spring, summons the Apocalyptic "snowy horsemen" of death (cf. "The Horse's Ha"). Now a harp, Glamorgan's hill, crowned by the fourth folly, has four strings; and the "sea-gut" or gully by the sea is musical catgut. Like the lyre of Orpheus, this instrument of nature sets rocks heaving. (Orpheus, plainly alluded to, could imply orphic, esoteric, oracular, entrancing—words that fit Welsh bards and Organ Morgan.) Hurdles, guns, and railings of steeplechase and hunt, crack to the music, spilling "folly's hunter" and "the hard-held hope" of the children. Spring, associated with this intolerable music of death and life, breaks and is broken; for spring is also a steel strip in a vise, and metal is flesh and bone (40).

4: "Four padding weathers" (a bestial composite of the four seasons) become the hunter now. Lands are his "scarlet" coat, and valleys are "harnessed" for his riding. Like the spilled hunter of the third stanza, the hunting weathers fall, but not down. They fall upon the children's faces; for weathers are wrinkling time. "A tail of blood," once trophy of the fox hunt and used to "blood" young riders, is quarry's tail no longer but that of the hunting beast, also a hawk, falling upon falling birds. (Compare the hanging hawk and falling birds of "Over Sir John's hill" and Hopkins' riding hawk as horseman in "The Windhover.") Does straightening Glamorgan stiffen in death or direct the swoop?

The proper sport of children (like that of country in the second stanza) is summer, their time of games and game for such "county darlings." But, whether angry spring runs after them or away, let children hold its minutes hard; for spring is the "hard-held hope" of summer.

A dense thing, in which each thing belongs with other things within the arrangement and without. Specific gravity may be a sign of merit, and intricate arrangement another—and still another an agreeable conspiracy of solution and puzzle.

Olson, 97.

Was there a time (1936; *ms. 1933*), *p. 59*

No especial merit here. "Time," the villain again, has those children down. Once they could find distraction in fiddle, circus, and book. Now "time has set its maggot on their track." (Compare the "calendar" worm or slug, 53, the "track" for the "running grave," 21, and "Time tracks," 84.) The dancers with fiddles recall early Yeats and Hardy. The rhythm of the third line is as troubled as the sense.

"Arc," which belongs with sky and "skysigns," is both the arch of the sky and an arc-lamp for a sign—in Piccadilly Circus, maybe (cf. "arc-lamped," 82). But "skysigns" are also the stars, astrologically portentous. (See Empson's note on "sky-sign.")

The last four lines are the *sententiae* of a cynical boy who knew all about dirty hands. His epigrammatic and desolating truths are as true as worldly wisdom. We see all, but the blind man, seeing nothing, sees best.

Now (1936), pp. 60-61

How now? A poem of "unwarrantable obscurity," said Vernon Watkins, who urged Thomas to suppress it. "Verbal doodling," said Henry Treece. We too, on first looking into this poem, must agree it is obscure and, if curious, must ask the reason. Was obscurity a protective device, as Thomas hints in a letter to Watkins? If so, why was similar protection unnecessary in other poems of similar import? Does dislocation of word and phrase, freeing them from the death of language, renew them? Is obscurity a disguise for commonplace matter or an activity of the Freudian censor? Does value lie in sound, shape, and glancing image? Thomas told Watkins that the poem has "no meaning at all." If that is so, why did he insist on including it? To baffle the reader? As verbal arabesque? But a fifth or sixth return to the text proves it more than that. Thomas was a joker, but his poems are always more than jokes. One can never believe what critics say about Thomas or what Thomas said about Thomas. Let the text before us be our guide.

A good way to approach this dazzle of images is, ignoring syntax, to fix on images, which other poems have made us familiar with. Another good way is to notice pattern, which, proceeding from a simple word, becomes more and more complex. Is this pattern a significant form? In short, to find a needle in the haystack, find the haystack.

Question encourages hypothesis. Since Biblical Thomas was fascinated by Genesis, Gospel, and Apocalypse, it is possible that "Now" is the creative Word of Genesis from which all proceeds. The last stanza is a kind of Apocalypse, and the middle stanza concerns Jesus. The poem may be a Bible in miniature, and each stanza may mimic creative process. The stanzas are of seven lines. Seven, according to "The Mouse and the Woman," is a magical number, suitable, according to occult tradition, for unions of above and below and for magicians busy uniting them. The poem is esoteric, lean, elliptical, intense, and suggestive, but so are things in nature, as the physicists, in search of elegance, assure us. My fiddlings are hypothetical.

1: In the beginning was the word, and the word is "Now." Dryness, rock, dust, and anger serve sterility and death (cf. 6, 38, 54); but the "flowered anchor" introduces wetness, flowering, and hope (cf. the sexual anchor in "The Long-legged Bait"). This flowered anchor, a curious affair of sea and land, must be blown from the "deadrock" or death's bedrock by laying a mine. ("Mine" is a verb.) Only explosion (cf. 10) can let life out. Hopping in the dust, an affair of life and death, is sexual, and "centre" seems womb. "Fool" and "hardiness" are dislocated foolhardiness. Anger, creative love's opposite, says "nay," as dry men do. Not God's word, "nay" is the devil's. The poem, like Joyce's *Ulysses,* is to become a contention of blooming "yes" and sterile "no."

2: Enter "yes." Unscrambled, the first lines mean: Sir, do not say "nay" or death to "yes"—or, by chiasmus, "yes to death." "The yesman" (American slang) says "no," and death responds. The last two lines are a pretty kettle of fish; but one man's fish is another man's *poisson.* Splitting children must be by "handsaw," probably King Solomon's here. But is sister a dope on the "cure"? However this may be, death is around. "Cure," however, could promise renewal. If this poem is a little Bible, we are with Solomon now in the Old Testament.

3: The "dead stir." Jesus enters with promise of resurrection for the "shade" of the "landed" or buried crow, a black bird of ill omen. But since the crow is acquisitive, like the raven, he may be a landed proprietor, one of the "Welshing rich." The dead man lying low with ruin in his ear suggests Hamlet, senior, now deaf to cockcrow. "The cockerel's tide upcasting from the fire" is a brilliant concentrate of Lawrence's escaped cock (Christian and phallic), the phoenix, and the water of life. Firebird and waterbird are nothing like old crow, whatever his association with firewater.

4: The sequence of "fall," "ball," and "fail" shows dislocation for the sake of sound, in the manner of Hopkins. "Star," burning "ball," "sun," and "light," Thomas' goals, appear after resurrection from the tomb. The "mystic sun" may be Lawrence's sun behind the sun. Male sun fertilizing female "nought" (cf. "virgin o," 21, and "zero," 49) comes a cropper on the petals of the unanchored flower he rides. (Compare the spilled rider, 58.) Fall follows riding of this sort, but, as Milton maintains, the fall of Adam was happy and creative.

5: "The seal of fire," uniting the seals of the "mystic" Apocalypse with Lear's "wheel of fire" (cf. 38), keeps the four creative elements in mind. We have had earth, water, and fire. "Arm of air" and "cloud" will complete the tally. "Hairy-heeled" death seems phallic and "the tapped ghost in wood," female or poetic. But a spirit in wood is either in the coffin or in the keg, which, when tapped, yields firewater. "We" may be the male and female creators who made the poet. "The two-a-vein, the foreskin, and the cloud" seems very good to William Empson, who has no theory about the meaning of this splendid line. There is something here, he feels, with no idea what. The line, however, is not all that difficult. "Two-a-vein," going back to "we," could be parents, blood to blood. The "foreskin" is father's; and the "cloud" (cf. 31) is mother's. As foreskin below, so cloud above. But difficulties remain. Why just the foreskin, for example? Synecdoche, or the part for the whole, maybe.

Watkins, 16. Treece, 132-33. Empson, in *Casebook*, 112.

Why east wind chills (1936; ms. 1933), *p. 62*

The unequal strophes of four and three beats are unrhymed, but the terminal words of the second strophe have "s" in common and, occasionally, there are assonance and alliteration. Rhythm is moderately flexible. The discouraging limits of knowledge and the certainty of death are the theme. Children's questions (cf. 81), like all questions, receive a reply that is both uncertain and certain. Two of the three poems preceding this in *The Collected Poems* are about children, to be a major concern of Thomas' last years.

Children's questions about the nature of things will receive a "black" or a "white" reply—in death. "Shall they clasp a comet in their fists?" Their question recalls John Donne's "Go and catch a falling star." "From high and low" the same answer echoes from the rooftops. Perhaps Jack Frost "cometh," as O'Neill's Iceman was to, in order to show the likeness of folklore and the King James Bible. (Compare "jacks of frost," 1.)

Ironic "All things are known" introduces astrology, the science of high and low that brings certainty to Jack Frost and comets. The stars of the zodiac "round" the "towers" ("houses" in the first version) of the sky. Houses are the stations of the zodiac. Astrological certainty calls or attracts some who are "content" with easy knowledge. That Thomas is one of these is proved by the repetition of "content" in "I hear content." In the corridors of school or life itself, he hears wise words that fail to inform him or to answer those children. (Verbal play of "content" with "content" and "Know" with "know" forms a pattern.)

The last two lines, returning to the first two and the last of the second strophe, summarize our predicament. "Of" in "Of echo's answer" could mean concerning or about or I know of. Now "the man of frost," no longer plain Jack Frost, is plainly death. Fists, clenched and raised in frustration, have failed to catch the falling star.

Could fist and star be Russian? The east wind, "a white answer," unhappy children, and "Be content" have political possibilities, as uncertain as the politics of the poet.

Jack Frost, comets, and raised fists are present in the 1933 manuscript, otherwise different from the 1936 revision. A question (in 1933) about the color of glory was to find place in "My world is pyramid." The unanswerable cry of the children is "ghastly" in 1933—to match the "ghostly" comets.

Stanford, 78-80.

A grief ago (1935), *pp. 63-64*

Back to the womb again in this poem of embryo speaking of mother. "A miraculous concentration," said Edith Sitwell, discovering Thomas. But concentration brings obscurities along.

These she deplored, while admiring internal sounds and the fugitive pattern of terminal dissonance, assonance, and rhyme. All in all, "a beautiful poem," said Dame Edith.

1: Since "grief" seems time's equivalent (cf. 76), it was a long time ago that the important she, whom the speaker holds (maintains and possesses) to be the abundant "fats and flower" of life, was "lammed," as if an American, by amniotic water and the "scythe-sided thorn" of the deathly, life-giving phallus. "Hell wind and sea" or male and female are connected by chiasmus with "Rose maid and male" (cf. "rose and male motion," 40). Dante's hell is married here to his heavenly flower by Blake's service. The "cementing" stem wrestling up the tower (cf. 21-22, 54) goes with obstetrical water, phallic thorn, and all green fuses. She who is who sails like Venus toward the light through the "paddler's bowl" of lammed water. (Compare Yeats' "every paddler's heritage.") "Masted venus" is upright as a mast in Botticelli's shell. As Dame Edith observed, this syntactical mess is rich and pretty strange.

2: By syntax alone, it is hard to tell whether he or she is the "chrysalis" (cf. 47) "unwrinkling" (cf. 29) on "iron" or flesh (cf. 40). But "chrysalis" must be embryo; and "iron," jumping from the frying pan to the firearm, begets an elaborate metaphor. The "fingerman" (misused American slang for pointer-out) has his finger on the trigger of his shooting iron. The "leaden bud," both bullet and vegetable, "shot through the leaf." Aaron's "rod" becomes a gun, while maintaining connection with Biblical water-making and father's tool, enfolded by mother. "The rod the aaron/Rose cast to plague," as baffling as it is suggestive, is double talk in two senses. Is "aaron" an adjective with the noun "Rose" or is "Rose" a verb with phallic rod? "Cast" goes with iron, but its grammatical function is unclear. Did the rod rise in order to cast a "plague" (cf. 47), which, belonging with Aaron, Moses, and Egypt, may refer to mother's plague, the embryonic frog housed in her side? "Horn" and "ball of water" combine father, mother, powder horn, and bullet. But a confusion of parts may be the very form for presenting the general sense, which emerges somehow.

3: Her Exodus, a chapter after Genesis, seems giving birth. "Ring" refers to marriage and womb, branded by the lily as

punishment for original sin. This "lily," the Joycean flower of
funerals and Easter, is Jesus, bringing "pardon." According to
Freud's system, the lily is male, bringing "heritage." "Tugged"
may imply sweat of brow and painful labor, the curses of Adam
and Eve. "The twelve triangles of the cherub wind," standing
for external weathers after birth, engrave signs as they blow on
fertile "field" and sterile "sand." We have encountered the twelve
winds that correspond to the twelve principal points of the compass and to the triangles of the ornamental compass rose on maps.
The cherubs, on old maps, blow winds from each corner. (See
41, 145, the "two cornered cherubs" of "The Map of Love," and
the cherubs who blow from the "four map corners," "In the Direction of the Beginning.") Thomas' cornered cherubs may
owe something to John Donne's seventh "Holy Sonnet":

> At the round earths imagin'd corners, blow
> Your trumpets, Angells, and arise, arise
> From death, you numberless infinities. . . .

Donne's imagined corners are from Mercator's projection, as
Thomas' could be, too.

4: The opening question is a good one for those bothered by
Thomas' syntactical habit. Definition of mother follows. "The
people's sea," which may be Aaron's Red Sea or Spender's pink
one, is general womb. "The caesared camp" includes father's
occupation of mother's camp and imperial obstetrics. Her shaping
dens "Shape all her whelps with the long voice of water"—a line
that captures water's long voice. "That she I have" ("hold") may
"rise before dark," like a full moon, is a possible unscrambling
of what follows. "Dark" is also death.

"The country-handed grave boxed into love" seemed to Dame
Edith a pleasing rural picture of a farmer growing flowers and
corn. No farmer this, said Thomas, ungraciously rebuking his most
generous critic. The "country-handed grave," he said, is the grave
in the likeness of a tough boxer with fists as large as countries
(cf. "boxy shift," 22). But Thomas had the mistaken idea that
intention limits meaning. Dame Edith saw a possibility which,
even if unintended, the text allows. Also there, unnoticed by
Thomas and his critic, is the image of the undertaker and his box.

(Compare "spade-handed," 21.) The image, which also includes father and womb, seems richer than Thomas knew or, at least, allowed.

5: The dark is rising, and the dark is acid death, leaping mother, like father. (For acid see 4, 22, and "The Lemon.") Let mother draw her "dead" or children to her before the "suncock" of dawn casts her bone upon the phoenix pyre, bringing resurrection. Let children, therefore, cross her palm with "their grave gipsy eyes," telling her fortune as she tells theirs. "Grave" is what each gravely tells the other. "Gipsy" means Egyptian, which in Thomas' iconography (e.g. 36) means grave. Compare the closed fist at the end of "Why east wind chills." There the fist is empty, here full. Hence this grief.

Watkins, 15-16. Edith Sitwell, in *London Mercury*, XXXIII (February 1936); in *Casebook*, 126; in Treece, 146. W. S. Merwin, in *Casebook*, 63.

How soon the servant sun (1935), *pp. 65-66*

Vernon Watkins found this poem the rival of "Now" among poems unwarrantably obscure. To Geoffrey Grigson it made "no sense at all." Yet, to those familiar with Thomas' tricks and habits, it makes plenty of sense. The theme, a habitual one, is Thomas' poetic development in terms of embryonic development. Not a theme, embryo is parallel. Thomas as poet, says self-critical Thomas, is embryonic; but he hopes to clamber out to light. The metaphor of the embryo, however, is complicated by metaphors of dog, mouse, and trumpet, and by verbal play.

1: The obstacles here are "cupboard stone" and two parentheses that interrupt what syntax there is. "Stone" and "Fog," evidently specimens of the rhyming argot of Cockneys, are to be interpreted as bone and dog—foggy young dog, who finds Mother Hubbard's cupboard bare as a stone (cf. 199). The comma at the end of the first line and the missing comma in the second also get in the way of sense. "Sir morrow" is the future, and his "servant sun" is both sun and son or embryo. Thomas seems to be saying this: How soon can Oedipal time solve the riddle of the sun or son who serves him? This son is a young dog who, unshelving the bony stone of the cupboard, will trumpet it into meat. As trumpeter, one with the cherubs of the preceding poem, he is poet (cf. "bugle," 149). Seeking meat, he is an embryo, fleshing —but still a naked egg, which must stand up and put a "gown" of flesh on his "gristles." Standing up straight is the moral, phallic, obstetrical, and poetic necessity of the dog-poet embryo. Examination proves some of Thomas' obscurest poems his easiest. The easiest are obscure.

2: "Sir morrow" or tomorrow becomes a nurse, surgeon or obstetrician now. This elaborate metaphor proceeds through "sponge," "wound," "records" (cf. Eliot's fever charts), "cut," "basin," and "sewing." The whole womb is a hospital. The scrambled third line seems to imply nursing future giants from the basin of the womb, where we still float with the embryo. Still a foggy dog, the embryonic poet, at his "spring" or source, soaks up the amniotic tides that sew him together. Sir morrow tells us this as his "Man morrow" (future man servant or servant son) "blows through food" like a whale in the sea or an imperfect trumpeter or a poet feeding as he blows. Poetry so produced has to be foggy, immature, and, since blown through food, obscure. Here is Thomas' opinion of his early poems, still in the dark of the womb. Obstetrical Tomorrow confronts a difficult birth.

3: Now serving the son, nerves, coming to light at birth, must serve the sun of external reality. Tomorrow's poems must become servers in "The rite of light"—someday to assist at a "Ceremony After a Fire Raid." Metaphor, always shifting, shifts now to mouse, which emerges from its dark hole as an embryo must. "Mouse's bone" is a misprint for "banc." This "long-tailed stone" is as sterile as dog's bone. Trapping the mouse or conquest of self is by "coil" (complexity, trouble, trap) and by "sheet," the poet's sheet of paper and a bedsheet; for the phallic mouse, coming out, must go to lovers' bed. (Note the internal rhyme of "coil" and "soil" or origin.) Is he a "biting man," as he hopes, or a clawing, squealing mouse? Let "the velvet dead inch out." Mice are "velvet" and embryos are dead. (Compare the mouse in "The Mouse and the Woman," where there is also a buried dog. This suppressed mouse with "velvet paws . . . inched into light." Cf. "foul mousehole," 195.) Dylan, says Caitlin, had a horror of mice.

4: His "lord" seems time. Sir morrow, stamping his watery

heels on "the floor of seed," is still an embryo, kicking. How soon will the embryo-poet, leaving his present "level," "raise a lamp," "spirit up a cloud," or walk "erect"? Does "cloud" imply that his elevated poetry will still be foggy? "Erect" recalls "stand straight" in the first stanza. The "shroud," another "sheet" (stanza three), combines caul, winding sheet, mask, and paper. Walking erect and going up are the necessary actions for this horizontal child.

5: On his present "stump" he must grow a long leg for walking. Since "leg" and "stump" figure in cricket, it may be that he must also play outdoors—with others. But "This inward sir" or introspective poet, supine in the dark, is still "womb-eyed." Someday "all sweet hell" or external reality will echo the blast of his trumpet. (Remember the images that roared on "heaven's hill," 44.) The "hour's ear," deaf to the blast, is time and the reader.

Watkins, 16. Geoffrey Grigson, in *Casebook*, 121. Caitlin Thomas, *Leftover Life to Kill*, London, 1957, p. 68.

Ears in the turrets hear (1936; ms. 1933), *pp. 67-68*

The "inward sir" of the preceding poem wants to get out again. Turreted house and womblike island insulate him from the mainland, which sends menacing intruders. Going out, for this egregious man, is as frightening as staying home. This hesitant renewal of a resolve to abandon womb for light (e.g. 32, 34, 44, 66, 98) is more interesting as plain statement of dilemma than as poem.

Not unlike early Auden, "Ears in the turrets" shows the allegorical tendency that Thomas shared with the master. We have encountered allegorical tower, house, and citadel in "The seed-at-zero" and "Do you not father me." Many of the stories are allegorical journeys, like the one proposed and feared here. "Prologue to an Adventure," which begins with the opening words of *Pilgrim's Progress*, makes Bunyan's Vanity Fair of Thomas' frightening London. "The Map of Love" is a geographical and cartographical allegory of a kind with the poem before us. The manner of Auden is appropriate for a social resolve, but the hesitancy and fear are peculiar to young Thomas.

Hands of intruders knocking on the door or fumbling with the locks may hold either "poison or grapes," death or the wine of life. "The white house" combines the executive mansion of rugged individualism with innocence. "Locks" (cf. 4) and "door" help prove this house a womb and the poet its occupant. The towers and houses of Thomas are as various as their meanings (e.g. 19, 22, 40, 54, 93). He may have meant a tower of another variety in a letter of 1936 to Watkins. Your own "private four-walled world," Thomas said, "isn't escapism . . . it isn't the Ivory Tower."

The turreted house of this poem is either on an island or becomes an island—of flesh and bone, far from the mainland (cf. "mansouled . . . islands," 193). But if nothing "disturbs this island's rest," what about that sinister knocking on the door? Island and mainland recall John Donne, who, commending the "mainland" in his *Devotions*, says "No man is an island." Island and mainland also recall young Yeats, who wanted to abandon the pavements of London for the peace of an island. Young Yeats was as uneasy on the mainland as young Thomas on his island, and neither was easy where he went. Here is the great question: shall Thomas stay or run to the ships with the "wind"? This wind is the weathers' wind or external reality.

The last stanza and the coda recapitulate the preceding stanzas. All is neat and clear. Assonance, dissonance, and internal rhyme provide a little relief. But Thomas is better when rich and strange.

Watkins, 23. Stanford, 80-81. E. Glyn Lewis, in Tedlock, 181.

Foster the light (1934), pp. 69-70

"Foster the light" amid encircling womb, but do not altogether "veil the manshaped moon"; for genesis is the "shaping-time" (46), the womb a den of "shape" (64). This hortatory poem, that becomes a prayer, praises created light, creative darkness, and the creator's "circle" (46). "Shape" and "circle" are the telling words of a poem laudable for density and shape or shaped density.

1: "Foster" means cherish or encourage. "Nor" (cf. 54) seems to mean "yet do not." "Manshaped," a reference to the man in the womb, anticipates the "merry manshape" of the last stanza and introduces the idea of shaping. The poet's journey toward the light is interrupted by an affectionate backward look. "Nor" marks the balancing point of the forward and backward looks that provide matter for a structure of checks and balances. "Foster the light" yet do not dismiss the dark "weather winds" of external reality that do not blow the bone down but serve to free the "twelve-winded marrow" or life from its bony circle. These twelve winds are those of time and the world's weathers (cf. 41, 63). More than bone, the circle is all creation, made by God's compasses. "Master" the darkness, but do not serve icy death, Wallace Stevens' "snowman," who "shapes" the bushiest life into icicles. The frigid polestar, pointing our inevitable direction, rules the circle of our compass. In plainer words, cherish light and master darkness without neglecting the realities of womb, wind, and ice.

2: Except for "cockerel's eggs," stanza two concerns vegetable nature, seed, blossom, and fruit. A young cock's egg is either an unnatural egg or a natural one, fertilized. The "four-fruited ridings" (cf. 58) are the paths of the four seasons, bringing heat and cold, snow and blossom, and each its fruit to Andrew Marvell's "vegetable" time. "Red-eyed," confined to blossoms here, suggests neither the "red-eyed" communists of "Our eunuch dreams" nor the "red-eyed elders" of Wallace Stevens; nor does the grafting "Farmer" seem related to the "country-handed grave" of "A grief ago." Sowing the "seeds of snow" (cf. 133) is making tomb of womb. Compare the "burning leagues" of these orchards with the burning orchards of "The Orchards."

3: Beelzebub, the Lord of the Flies (insects or poems, 47), shares with God the responsibility for creation, as "Incarnate devil" makes plain. The Fly Lord's "acre" is Eden or the world. Father forth like God and Satan or be a maker, the Manichaean poet exhorts himself. Do not be a "goblin-sucker" (vampire, parasite, embryo) raised on the "owl-seed" of wisdom in the dark, but be a "wizard" (poet-magician) railing with "ribs" (of a poem?) the "heart-shaped" world. "High lord esquire," the poet prays his fly-lord or his lord, aid my song and that of all poets. Raise the "singing cloud" of "mortal voices" to the level of "the ninnies' choir"—of angels, that is, or, ironically, of poetical fairies. Pluck or help me pluck music from the mandrake root or root of life's marrow. (Compare the "Twelve-winded marrow" of the first stanza.) To Thomas, as to Donne, the mandrake is man's image (e.g. 80 and "The School for Witches"). In plainer words, let me become a good maker and sing elevated songs about life, birth and death. According to tradition, the mandrake root shrieks when plucked from the ground by a dog—a young dog here. Maybe it sings when plucked by God, dog's identical opposite. Let mandrake be this maker's metaphor.

4: "O ring of seas," he prays, addressing mother as creator now. The "unmanly" lady of the tides, who appears as moon in the first stanza, is "manshaped" because she takes the shape of the man or mandrake she is shaping. Metaphor becomes suitably nautical: Do not sorrow as I love and leave the girls (cf. 194) with "a starboard smile" (the right, green, sideways smile of the young ram rod as navigator?) or when one of them lies in "the crossboned drift" of piracy, love, and death. "Cross-boned" and "marrowroot," marrying, seem to have produced cross-bow, arrow, and the killing of cock robin. Since mother is "unmanly," she cannot turn "cockwise." Turning clockwise on an axle suggests the world, as turning cockwise suggests sex. But what is "this turning tuft"? (Compare "tufted in the pap," 35.) Is it the "bushy item" of the first stanza? A tuft at sea could be an embryo or phallus, and the tufted axle, the womb or phallus.

5: The God of Genesis, creating the seas, gave them shape and colour (cf. "sound of shape," 58). Playing with clay, God shaped "my clayfellow," Adam, and sent the "coloured doubles" two by two into Noah's ark. Since the maps of our voyage in the ark (cf. xviii) are "shapeless" and the seas have "shape," these maps seem inadequate. Yet the shaper's glory abides in the shapeless and the shaped, in bad copy as in good thing. "Make the world of me," the poet prays to "glory in the shapeless maps." This prayer, at once ambiguous and plain, means: think the world of me, make me into the world or make the world out of me. Macrocosm, microcosm, and ego seem equally involved. Do by him, the poet prays, as he has done by himself. A maker himself, he has made a "merry manshape" of God's walking circle," which includes all creation from zodiac to womb. Whether the poet has made a man of himself, begotten a child or made a poem, God's original circle is model, matter, and source.

Images of this poem (voyage, crossbones, owl, mandrake) reappear in "Altarwise." That is a creator's story, this a creator's prayer. Repetition of imagery, however, means only that, like most poets, Thomas had a limited stock of images and used them again and again for a limited number of themes. The manuscript, dated February 23, 1934, differs in most respects from the present version.

Olson, 95-96.

The hand that signed the paper (1935; ms. 1933), p. 71

These tidy quatrains in the Augustan manner are odd for two reasons. First, they are comparatively clear. Second, they seem unconcerned with self. Political without party, they condemn all tyranny from that of contemporary dictator to that of God. Can it be that obscurity, there to protect, attends poems of self alone and that excellence is their other attendant? Thomas' heart was in himself, and density, his proper medium, is our proper study.

Thomas was fascinated with hands, fists, fingers, and their uses (e.g. 4, 8, 10, 11, 19-20, 62, 64, 67, 84, 90). Here, private hand becomes public. Writing, whether the handiwork of poet or dictator, is power.

"Five sovereign fingers taxed the breath" wittily combines kingship, money, and the ultimate tax on air or life and poetry. To tax the breath is also to exceed its normal capacity. Balanced opposites in the third and fourth lines of the first stanza recapture Pope's pithy way, which rhymed couplets would have suited better than these semi-dissonant quatrains.

Joints "cramped with chalk" combine arthritis with writer's cramp. "That" in the fourth line of the second stanza, referring ambiguously to "quill" or "murder," serves clarity less than the neatness demands. Has the tyrant, ending murder, become benign for a moment or does he combine benignity with the suppression of free speech? Fever, famine, and a plague of locusts (cf. 47) are more in a tyrant's line.

These "five kings" or "sovereign fingers," like the king of heaven, lack tenderness or pity. That "Hands have no tears to flow" is at once an evident truth and a conceit of blind hands, which, like Milton's "blind mouths," lack vision.

Fraser, 14. Stanford, 81-82.

Should lanterns shine (1935; *ms.* 1932-33?), *p.* 72

Time, stasis, and change, light and darkness, two boys, a mummy and a ball are the matter of this lyrical composition.

Our world is pyramid again. A boy with lantern inspects a chamber, but the boy is not there; for his visit to the tomb is conditional. Should he visit, he would see by the light of his eight-sided lantern the "holy face" of a mummy, wound in Yeats' "mummy cloths." Were this mummy that of Cleopatra or of Nefertiti herself, that boy would look twice before falling from the chapel's grace to necrophilia. The "false day" of his lantern would show her lipstick smudged or faded; for, however static and eternal she seems, time has changed her. She is "kissproof" now. The occasion may have been a visit to an old whore; but this supposed visit by a "boy of love" to the "private dark" is not unlike young Thomas' visits to the tomb. Plainly, he is dissatisfied. Maybe it is better not to pry into a dark past, even with "octagonal" lamp, which seems to have replaced forked language as instrument of discovery.

Told twice—by D. H. Lawrence maybe—to think and act with the blood, the poet, who has imagined that boy, defies time and stasis by motion. Everything is moving here; and we are out of doors, where field and roof, below and above, look the same to one so quick. Blood has replaced embalming fluid. But time, a long Egyptian gentleman, is still around, confusing past and present. His beard moves now in a static wind of the past. For Thomas, Egypt, meaning death and the past, was more tomb than womb, despite that pyramid. "Consider now," he says in "The Mouse and the Woman," "the old effigy of time, his long beard whitened by an Egyptian sun." (For Thomas on Egypt see 36, 44, 84-85, 88.)

They have told him things for many years, and there should be "some change," either in the telling or in its effect. The last couplet is a sudden change that works a change on the whole poem, transforming it. "No man more magical."

Here a real boy replaces the conditional boy, but even the real boy is not quite there; for he is in the past—a sunny past, however, of Cwmdonkin Park. (For this wonderful park see 19, 123, "Reminiscences of Childhood," and *Portrait of the Artist as a Young Dog*.)

Throwing the ball was action, but the ball, still up there in the light, is as static (unless in orbit) as the mummy—and as changed by time. Thrown in past time, it is out of time, in memory alone. This magical and enigmatic couplet, bringing radiance and change to a private dark, heralds the later poems and *Portrait of the Artist as a Young Dog*.

These two lines followed the present ending in the first printed version:

> Regard the moon, it hangs above the lawn;
> Regard the lawn, it lies beneath the moon.

Having persuaded Thomas to omit this ineffectual echo of Eliot and Laforgue, Vernon Watkins shares credit for making this a poem.

Watkins, 16-17. Fraser, 14. E. Glyn Lewis, in Tedlock, 181-82. Thomas recorded this poem, Caedmon, 1018.

I have longed to move away (1935; ms. 1933), *p.* 73

Fear kept the insulated man of "Ears in the turrets" from moving to the mainland. Here fear keeps him from leaving dead conventions. In short, like J. Alfred Prufrock and the boy of "A Prospect of the Sea," the poet was afraid of what he longed for. The problem in "I have longed to move away" is what he longed to move away from. Some have thought it the conventional morality and piety of the chapel. Some have thought it the conventions of society. Some have thought it his own poetic past. Triple talk or forked language allows these possibilities. But in a poem so muscular and neat, more than greets the eye is not what we expect.

The snaky "hissing of the spent lie" makes convention as religious as Eden, as social as the snakes around us, and as intimate as the worms of womb and tomb. Thomas seems equally critical of chapel, society, and self—all "terrible," but no more terrible than the prospect of removal. "The repetition of salutes" and the "calls and notes" make dead convention seem social. But "ghostly echoes on paper" of "ghosts in the air" can refer to his own early poems, as "spent" as everything else around him. Thomas was his severest critic.

He wants to move away from the obscurities of womb and tomb, to replace that lantern in a pyramid with the light of common day. But fear that some "unspent" force in old habit might explode to destroy his vision, deters him. This explosion, of course, could be social or religious, as well as poetic. "Night's ancient fear" of being alone in the dark haunts the black stairs and corridors of his present house and is likely to haunt the house he moves to. But neither night's fears nor "death's feather" (cf. 9, 15, 36), however light its touch, will make Invictus accept death or half-death.

"Pursed lips" at the telephone receiver are social terrors. "The parting of hat from hair" is both a gesture of politeness and a sign of terror. (Hairs standing on end lift hats.) That these lines are imitation Auden improves their social and literary bearing. But "Half convention and half lie" brings literature more plainly back to join society and religion. Poems or "fibs of vision" (48) are at once lies and fictions. Thomas' present poetry, as false and dead as society, is half and half. Its convention is both that of other poets whom he is imitating and his own tricks, grown stale from repetition.

In his quest of daylight and mainland Thomas tried many ways. A new poetic manner might help. Hence experiments such as this and "The hand that signed the paper" in the styles of those who, he thought, had found light and land. The tight, lean manners of early Auden and middle Yeats seem the models here. Such attempts at a clarity foreign to his nature may have helped his ultimate discovery of new matter: Fern Hill, Llareggub, the streets of Swansea, and Cwmdonkin Park, and a manner, **not** altogether lucid, but as much his own as that of the dark, early poems.

Fraser, 15-16. Stanford, 66-67. E. Glyn Lewis, in Tedlock, 182-83.

Find meat on bones (1936; ms. 1933), pp. 74-75

Not unlike "The boys of summer," this poem is a debate between age and youth, between father and son this time. Son wins, and the poet applauds victory of youth and life. Their debate, probably internal, between two sides of Thomas, is a kind of psychomachy, like Yeats' "Dialogue of Self and Soul." The structure is tight and dramatic. Father's advice occupies the first two stanzas; the son's reply occupies the second two; and the poet's recapitulation and comment, the last. The rhythm recalls that of the common ballad. But "sprung" lines, suddenly springing from regularity (at the end of each stanza and sometimes earlier) provide metric echo of, and proper vehicle for, the conflict of matter. Experiment in rhythm was as necessary as experiment in manner.

Father's advice to his son recalls Kipling and Housman. Make what you can of life, says this old cynic, for it is short, nasty, and brutish. The old dog tells the young dog (cf. 57, 65) to gather the lamb chops while he may: "Find meat on bones that soon have none"; for "the merriest marrow" and loveliest breasts are doomed to "winding-sheets." Let no prying lantern disturb those mummies (cf. 72). Just lay a flower upon the rags and go. This "ram rose," possibly a rambler rose shortened to combine male ram and female rose, as sentiment demands, seems closely related to the "ram rod" (194), unmistakably male. The last two lines of the first stanza, suitably sprung, are contrapuntal to the rest. Rhyme and dissonance suitably conspire. Breasts as "crags," accounted for in part by the cynical fancy, are also accounted for by "hags" and "rags."

Even more cynical in the next stanza, the old dog advises rebellion against nature and its laws, as tyrannical as the hand that signed the paper. Rebel not only against sun and moon, says this death-wisher, but against flesh, bone, and even the deathless "maggot" of life and death.

In stanza three, son, having taken the advice father gave in the first stanza, reports heartbreak, loss of weight, and ambiguous condition. "Took me for man," "My breasts," and the reappearing "ram rose" illustrate this ambiguity. His trouble and ultimate pleasure come of not having followed father's advice exactly. Instead of hanging the ram rose on her winding sheet, he put it "beside her" on the bed sheet, where it rose.

Bedding and "sweet waking" seem to have given son the courage, in stanza four, to deny father's denial of life in stanza two. In father's "dream," that of a Puritan moralist, Sin, now a dog, comes to heel, whistled out of Spenser's sensual "bower" of bliss and Circe's pigpen. ("That out of a bower of red swine"— if their redness is not too distracting—seems a line as nicely sprung as anything by Hopkins.) Ram risen in bed has affirmed Lawrence's life and love against cynical and moral objection. The feminine ending of the last line is appropriate and beautiful.

The poet's recapitulation in the last stanza reaffirms life as a happy companionship of light and dark, sun and moon. Even sea's kingly voice, alluding to stanza two, is a co-operation of mother and father. The matter in quotation marks (followed by an unexpressed "forsooth!") disposes of the negations that father must recant. "Before death takes you, O take back this," a magnificent line, is worthy of Yeats.

Stanford, 67-68.

Grief thief of time (1936; ms. 1933), *p.* 76

However obscure, this poem from the old congenial dark is not about self if, avoiding the perils of punctuation and taking the images as clues to sense, I have read them right. Time, old age, entrances and deaths seem the matter here.

Several difficulties slow us down. First, the punctuation. Commas where periods belong and no commas where they belong do their worst. Second, the puzzle of "Grief thief." Third, the form. The two stanzas, seeming ghosts of sonnets, tease us. Each has fourteen lines, to be sure, but octave and sestet, if there, are not apparent. The rhyming is not that of sonneteers. By replacing commas of the second stanza with suitable periods, you could arrive at something like three quatrains and a couplet. But more periods than that seem called for, and the form seems no more Shakespearean than Petrarchan. In Thomas' sonnets anything goes, but does it go this far?

1: Periods at the ends of lines four, five, eight, and ten may help. But just how does grief steal time? By deadening our sense of it, crowding all else out? The many combinations and possibilities of grief and thief haunted Thomas (e.g. 56, 63, 92, 182, 186). In "A grief ago" grief seems time. Does time itself steal time? Anyway, grief the thief or "knave of pain" crawls off and steals off the "moon-drawn grave" of the womb, making the old forget their "seafaring years" and the "sea-halved faith" of marriage that once made them indifferent to time—that blew that man down. The nautical metaphor, fully elaborated in "The Long-legged Bait," extends through the first stanza. Time and tide co-operate. The old "salt-eyed" salts have forgotten sea and the grief of life at sea, as statements in lines five and nine make plain. Sunken castaways could be forgotten children. The Ancient Mariner's albatross could be the guilt of all seafaring.

"Lean," "Call," "Cast," and "stumble" are imperatives. Let the old salt, however forgotten the life at sea, re-erect "the bone of youth" (instrument of life and death) and stumble back to bed, where she who, once at full tide "in a time of stories" (fabulous youth?), lies out of time and tide now, loving grief the thief who stole her life away. Loving this thief may mean grieving. The timeless victim of time is no more paradoxical than living. In brief, age, the effect of time, makes us forget time. Grieving makes us forget grief. Not this simple sense, however, but the richness of its presentation, which offers an experience wider than the sense, seems the value. We have been all at sea, and still are.

2: Now on land, the sea forgotten, Thomas elaborates the metaphor of thief, who becomes crook, slasher, and outlaw with sack of swag, caught in the act by policeman's "bull's-eye" or dark lantern, but not pursued by policemen's whistles. "Jack my fathers" seems, if punctuated, direct address. The poet is speaking to his forefathers, embodied in one Jack or knave. Fathers are all victims of thieving time, as the last line says. "The time-faced crook" is not only the clock but the "crooked worm" (10) or phallus, which steals the life it brings. Hypocritical and menacing, he carries a blade up his foreskinned "sleeve." This crook "steals down the stallion grave," like St. Mawr himself, with "swag of bubbles [cf. 108] in a seedy sack," surely the testicles. Time the thief is sex and sex, the thief of time, is grief; for womb is tomb.

Peeping at the intruder through a "eunuch crack" is an occupation for Susanna's impotent elders. Their bull's-eye is both dark lantern and eye of a bull. By such lights their peeping somehow frees grief from twin boxes, which are twin beds, twin coffins, or testicles—as you please. Freeing grief must mean encouraging it. The next hortatory lines are clearer with prefixed "let." Let no whistles chase the thief through time to death. Yet entrances are deaths, and the bubbles in his sack, "stolen" from forefathers, bite like phallic, deadly snakes and the "eye-teeth" of the "undead." (Thomas refers to Dracula in Quite Early One Morning and in the Watkins letters.) Let no occult "third eye," whether of Mme. Blavatsky or D. H. Lawrence, peep at the "rainbow," which, according to Lawrence, "bridged," like Hart Crane's bridge, "the human halves." But, whatever you do, "all shall remain" as it is "on the graveward gulf" of womb, tomb, and age, where all takes "shape," in sepulchral gestation, with great-grandpa and his thieves. A kind of merriness redeems the time and these dark regions.

The 1933 manuscript called for and received extensive revisions, made in 1935 and 1936. "Jack my fathers" is singular in the first version.

And death shall have no dominion (1933), p. 77

The first of his poems to be published (except for those at school), this lyric proves Thomas a lyricist from the start. Place in Twenty-five Poems proves nothing about time, nor does time always prove improvement. Resurrection, the theme, is plainly stated and restated with variation and example. Not theme, however, but rhythm is the triumph here—rhythm, symphonic vowels, grandeur of manner, and a kind of ecstasy. Like a preacher with "hwyl," Thomas is conducting a service for all the dead in certain hope of glorious resurrection. Nothing more ceremonious than this hymn of praise until "Ceremony After a Fire Raid."

Scansion reveals sprung rhythm in counterpoint with the running start and finish. Here, as in "the green fuse" and "Find meat on bones," Hopkins was the teacher. The fall of stresses, though fixed by the poet, awaits the reader's interpretation. At once flexible and formal, this "shape of sound" or "sound of shape" (58) challenges the reader's ear, voice, and sensitivity.

The thematic first and last line is from St. Paul, Romans 6:9: "Death hath no more dominion." Rising again from the sea in the first and second stanzas is based on Revelation 20: 13: "the sea gave up the dead" (cf. 7 and "The Enemies"). But these Christian references, proving only that Thomas had attended chapel, do not make this poem Christian. Here, as elsewhere in Thomas, Christian references are analogies for natural event or condition. Memories of the chapel, familiar enough for ready communication and useful for feeling and tone, were the very things for a ceremony of natural holiness—of holy dying and holy living or old Taylor transposed. The flowers of the last stanza, dying in the autumn and returning in spring, demand the parallel of Paul and Apocalypse. As Lawrence, another product of the chapel, used Christian parallel for life and rebirth in "The Man Who Died," so Thomas here.

In the first stanza, the dead, their bones picked clean, will reassemble parts on Judgment Day and become one again with wind and stars or nature. The third line, scrambling the elements that resurrection will unite, means the man in the moon (cf. "the manshaped moon" of gestation, 69) and the west wind, breath of autumn's being. "Stars at elbow and foot" sounds like Blake and Apocalyptic John. "Go mad" means die mad and go mad in the usual sense. Whatever their state at death and their state in sea or grave, men "shall rise again." "And" in the first and last lines is at once conclusive and inaugural, as the theme requires.

The second stanza is devoted to martyrdom and the pain of life, not that of hell itself, from which there is no resurrection unless Thomas, devoted to the devil's acre (46, 69), heretically thought so. (Compare the racking agonies of Hopkins' "Spelt from Sibyl's Leaves.") Tortured men may lose faith, but for all that, they will uncanonically rise; for salvation is not by faith but by nature. The play on "break," here and in the last stanza, recalls Hopkins' play on "buckle" in "The Windhover." The unicorn, according to Pliny's *Natural History*, is "the most fell and furious beast of all other." That those buried at sea "shall not die windily" seems almost too true unless "windily" means emptily or in vain.

Birds and waves of the last stanza recall Hopkins' poem of sea and skylark. Flowers also hammer through the ground in "I dreamed my genesis" and "intricate image." Hammering "characters" combine flowers, men, and letters, even dearer to poets than men and flowers.

Watkins says that Thomas, who preferred puzzles like "Now," included this grand, simple poem reluctantly. Excluded from *18 Poems*, it may have been allowed here as filler. Those who condemn this poem as rhetorical gesture forget that rhetoric is persuasive, gesture important, and oratory an art. That oratory can be more lyrical than Cicero knew is proved by this poem.

After the premature publication of this poem (1933) in a magazine, Thomas revised it substantially. The revised manuscript (dated February, 1936) differs little from the present version.

Watkins, 16. Fraser, 14. Stanford, 75-76. Ralph N. Maud, in *Modern Language Notes*, LXXIV (1959). Thomas E. Connolly, in *Explicator*, XIV (February 1956) Thomas recorded this poem, Caedmon, 1018

Then was my neophyte (1936; ms. 1932-33?), pp. 78-79

Each stanza falls into two parts, linked by rhyme which is sometimes exact and sometimes dissonant. Each second part is related to the first as the sestet in a sonnet to the octave. The general movement is from stasis to action. Embryo, birth, and childhood, the ostensible subject, prove to be a metaphor for Thomas' present immaturity. Thomas, says double-talking, self-critical Thomas, is embryonic and childish. Let embryo be his metaphor. Moving time is enemy again; but time's victim has not made much of time.

1: This "neophyte," literally something newly planted, is both embryo on its knees in the womb and a novice on his knees, praying. The "bell of rocks" is both a novice's grotto (cf. 147) and the womb. The "twelve, disciple seas," related to the "twelve winds" (e.g. 41, 63), combine time, amniotic fluid, and Jesus. "Ducked," the condition of the embryo, is also that of the newly baptized novice. To time and tide, who wind the "water-clocks," this ducking, which confuses day and night, is "green" or vital and youthful. The apparent oxymoron of "white blood" allows two readings, one of which requires a stop after "white." The novice is suitably dressed in white, and the embryo's blood is innocent after ducking. The meanings are as dense as the scenery and personae are strange. In grotto or on ocean ("where each kind doth straight its own resemblance find") we have enjoyed a green thought in a white shade.

"Hermaphrodite" is a good word for this dual creature, at once a slow, damp "snail" and a man undertaking life's voyage in a "ship of fires," love's fires, no doubt, and a pretty mixture of fire and water. (We shall soon encounter the other two elements.) "His," going back to the "twelve, disciple seas," reaffirms by a capital the presence of Jesus, who serves as analogy for novice and embryo. Like the pre-natal creature of "Before I knocked," the novice-hermaphrodite-embryo has foreknowledge. The second "His" makes Jesus equivalent to man, who sexually climbs "the water sex" or woman. Inserting "which" before "The climber" makes the syntax clear. "The green rock of light," opposite to the dark "bell of rocks" and the "green day and night" of the womb, is adult reality, vital as the rock of ages and our salvation. Does "bitten" (cf. "snapping," 147) include the work of a young sea dog?

2: The interrogative first half finds answer in an imperative second. The womb is now a watery labyrinth of scaly corridors with "tidethread" for clue. The "moon-blown shell" of the water-clocked seas is an image of birth. Botticelli's Venus rising from the sea (cf. 11, 63) separates Aphrodite from "sea hermaphrodite"; Hermes, god of analogies, may extend a hand to land her.

The amniotic voyage is over, the sails are "furled," and the voyagers have said good-by to "the fishes' house." But they have exchanged one "hell" for another. The "flat cities" seem Sodom and Gomorrah, flattened by the wrath of God. Myths of the labyrinth, Aphrodite, and the cities of the plain are succeeded by the "green" or vital and adult myth of Jesus. "Green," the key word (as in "Fern Hill"), changes color with each context.

Pictures, both photographs (cf. 16-17, 82, 103) and oil paintings, will show the newly born the nature of reality, a "landscape" now, which, though far from the original sea, is still salty—with "grief," thief of time. "Mirror," another picturing, whatever its syntactical place, calls for filling an ellipsis out. The "grail," goal of a quest, an artifact, and a container of precious blood, is time, pictured on canvas for the novice or child, still veiled but wanting to grow up. "Veil and fin and fire and coil" combines his recent amniotic trouble with future trouble (coil) from the fire of sex. "The green child," immature and vital, may owe something to Herbert Read's *The Green Child* (1935). Read liked Thomas as much as he liked Read; but we cannot be sure whether Thomas' green child entered the text before or after 1935.

3: The metaphor of picturing plainly proceeds, but who is the photographer? He who films Thomas' vanity, showing it up, may be time, Jesus, or child, or a triple composite. The "tilted arcs" (cf. 59) that provide light for the photographer's "shots" (cf. 17) are also the arks that, having come over the water, tilt on the shore to discharge children, their passengers. "Over the water" unites these Noahs with Christ, walking on water. The green child, having grown, is now playing in Cwmdonkin Park (cf. 19, 72, 123) with young Thomas, "headless" because "dumb" and talking only with his hands, "masked" because even young Thomas always had a mask on (cf. 147).

The photographer who winds the "clockwise scene" is now definitely time, who once wound "water-clocks" and a ball of "twine" for the labyrinth. The "ball of lakes" he winds (on fisherman's and photographer's reel) and projects on the screen is a memory of childhood that breaks the poet's "heartbone" (cf. 47). The picture of childhood on the screen of time and tide is "Love's image" or that of Christ and of Thomas' own childhood. "By a dramatic sea," a rich and admirable phrase, means beside the sea, not in it—and more. "Dramatic" may imply distance, impersonality, and action, but the heartbreak is personal, lyrical, and, since fixed in the past, static. Compare the ball thrown on the screen of memory in "Should lanterns shine."

4: Stanza four is a dramatic exchange between the poet and an indefinite figure who may be time, Jesus, and child again. Time with his sexual "scythe and water blade" lames the poet on his flinty, "year-hedged row" and kills his "history"—his memory and his life (cf. 199). Time is producer and killer of his production. The photographer of memories replies that snapshots cannot predict the future of anything so "shapeless" as a child. The "print" is that of the darkroom and of the foot treading to-morrow. Time tries in vain to console the frightened poet. The "green nought," which could imply mother, seems the empty green child here, his heart still unhacked by the scythe and still "unsucked" by experience. "O green and unborn and un-dead" splendidly summarizes the poem. Not only presenting the condition of embryo and child, this compendious line presents the poet's present condition, at once childish, embryonic, and frightened. (The "undead," neither here nor there, are suckers from *Dracula*.) Not taken in by time's consoling memories of childhood, the poet is mature enough to foresee his fate, but so was the embryo in the first stanza and the grail-questing child in the second. However necessary, coming up for air and light is a slow and terrible chore.

A manuscript about a neophyte in the 1930-32 notebook at Buffalo could have provided Thomas with little more than hints for what he was to make of the poem several years later. As one cannot judge his poems by the date of publication, so one cannot judge them by the date of the manuscript.

Altarwise by owl-light (1935, 1936), *pp.* 80-85

This sequence of ten sonnets (in which the sestets usually precede the octaves and rhymes are odd) has inspired more comment and caused more disagreement than anything else by Thomas. Some think it his greatest work and some, more moderate, think it the greatest poem of *Twenty-five Poems,* "nothing short of magnificent," as Dame Edith observed. Others think it a "splendid failure," a good bad poem, a bad good one, or a discouraging muddle. Some, led by Elder Olson, think it about Hercules in the zodiac. Others, thinking it the story of Jesus, hold that it announces new piety. Thomas, in Utah, had this to say: "Those sonnets are only the writings of a boily boy in love with shapes and shadows on his pillow. . . . They would be of interest to another boily boy. Or a boily girl. Boily-girly."

In general agreement with Thomas, I think that the theme is Thomas himself, the constant subject of his verse and prose. Although cheerfully allowing the presence of Jesus, Hercules, the stars, the zodiac, and a generally neglected voyage, I think them analogies, not to be confused with theme. Something like a thing is not the thing itself. Thomas, like Joyce before him, was always comparing himself with Jesus, God, and the devil. As microcosm, Thomas corresponded to the stellar macrocosm. Everything in heaven and on earth was his metaphor for Thomas, who, like Sir Philip Sidney's poet, was always "freely ranging within the zodiac of his own wit." Henry Fielding says: "an author will write the better for having some knowledge of the subject on which he writes." Thomas, who knew a little about the zodiac, knew himself entirely.

He was always complaining that words and analogies, his only way of getting at the object, got between him and it. Here the trouble seems to be that his words and analogies get between the critics and his object. Read in the context of his other poems and his prose, these sonnets seem another portrait of the artist as a young dog—of "a dog among the fairies." Beginning with his begetting, the story proceeds through childhood, and ends with the writing and publication of poems. This is the customary stuff of the novel of the artist's adolescence, here in miniature, however, and in verse, like Wallace Stevens' "Comedian as the Letter C."

These ten sonnets, once called "Poems for a Poem," are a fragment of what was to be "a very long poem indeed." In a note to *Twenty-five Poems* Thomas said: "The last poem in the book contains the first ten sections of a work in progress." As they stand, having progressed no more, these ten sections seem enough—

enough for me. As they stand, I find them rich and sea-changed. The moving whole has many fine parts. What more can a man this side of Joyce, Yeats, and Shakespeare do, and what more a man still this side of "Fern Hill," "The Long-legged Bait," and all the other autobiographies in verse and prose that were to make his later years illustrious?

Comments on the sequence: Olson, 14, 25, 54, 64-85, 88. Stanford, 69. Francis Scarfe, *Auden and After*, 106-10. W. Y. Tindall, *The Literary Symbol*, 183-85. Marjorie Adix, in *Casebook*, 285. Wm. Empson, in *Casebook*, 111. Fraser, 17.

I

The narrative—and Thomas said all poems should be narrative—opens with obscure magnificence. The first two lines and the last two of this sonnet are haunting, and in between are many wonders. Puzzling characters are around, doing strange things. A gentleman, a devil, an atlas-eater, a dog, a mandrake, an old cock, and another gentleman (or the same) crowd a landscape by Dali. Tropics and atlas make this unearthly scenery our earth, with stars on their rounds above. As we respond to these marvels, our minds, teased by hints, clamor for fact. Who are these people, we ask, and what are they doing? But we enjoyed the poem before asking this or we should not have asked.

"Altarwise," according to the dictionary, means as an altar is usually placed, and "owl-light" means dusk. "Wise" in "Altarwise" agrees with "owl" in "owl-light," as "light" with "Altar"—a pleasing confusion that may explain the choice of words. An altar is a place of sacrifice and worship. But whether the hero has been made wise by it or is skeptically wise to it is unclear. "The halfway house" is more complex. Thomas was interested in the zodiac, which begins with the Ram in March and, occupying its houses, gets half way round in autumn. (Thomas, under Libra, was an October man.) But "half-way house," in the context of Thomas' other poems, could mean womb or half way through life. (Compare the "half-way house" in Yeats' "Lapis Lazuli," 1938.) Since Thomas probably took the phrase from Hopkins' "The Half-way House," a poem on "the breaking of the bread," Thomas' house could also mean Eucharist or housel. In these holy, dark, vital circumstances and under stellar auspices, a gentleman lies "graveward," which, as any reader of Thomas knows, means womb and tomb. Thomas was fond of "furies." (See 20, "The Mouse and the Woman," "In the Direction of the Beginning." A poem of 1933, still in manuscript, concerns Orestes. Thomas must have looked into Aeschylus.) Sometimes Thomas makes the furies seven instead of three, sometimes, like Milton, he confuses them with the three fates, and sometimes, confronting them, he calls them by name. Under the zodiac, Megaera and her sisters seem fatal sisters now. I make this sense of multiple hints: the gentleman is either Thomas' father, daring his fate by begetting a son, or else the gentleman is Thomas himself in the womb, awaiting birth in fated October.

Father and son seem equally involved in the next four lines. Abaddon (from Revelation 9:11) is Apollyon, the destroyer, an angel of the bottomless pit. "Hangnail" seems cross or phallus, in both of which Adam and the devil are involved. "Incarnate devil" proves Satan a creator equal to God; and Thomas prays to Beelzebub in "Foster the light." "Fork" seems the gentleman's crotch, and the "dog among the fairies," Dylan himself among his contemporaries. Consuming the world or its image, he has, as a future reporter for a Swansea paper, "a jaw [nose] for news" and an ear for "to-morrow's [journalistic] scream." Dogs dig screaming mandrakes up. Thomas' mandrakes (e.g. 62, 69, "The Enemies," "The School for Witches"), probably from Donne, can mean children and genitals. The sense of all this excitement and horror seems this: Thomas, the young creative devil-dog-mandrake, is born. Since a son's birth is father's death, the young dog bites out father's mandrake and reports the news.

The emasculated "gentleman of wounds," like crucified Christ, is dead, with pennies on his eyes (cf. 151). Not only father, the gentleman as Christ, is son, a cock begotten by cock, conceived by egg, and hatched. The wonderful "Old cock from nowheres" (God, Jesus, father, son, and Lawrence's "Escaped Cock"), on one leg in the "half-way winds," is a weathercock and Christ on the cross. His unbuttoned bones are phallic (to allow cradle-scraping) and sepulchral. The "walking word" is Christ as Word and Thomas as poet (cf. "the walking circle," 70). As God is one with Jesus, so Thomas with father, whom he killed and replaced. The womb's "night of time" and "Christward shelter" are the "graveward" "half-way house" again for the phallic, long gentle-man. That the "long world's gentleman" (also long in respect of time maybe, but Mercator's projection in an atlas makes lati-tude long) is both father and son is suggested by an implied pun on sun, which moves in the last line between the tropics. Sun is God or father and sun is Son or Jesus. Since Father and Son are consubstantial above, so below are father and son. Both Father and Son create by the Word, and down here a poet is born—a long fellow to "the fellow father" (35). An "atlas-eater," he has consumed the world he embodies as microcosm and rules like a magus by wizardry.

Edith Sitwell, in Treece, 146-47. Thomas' reply and explication, in Treece, 149-50. Ralph N. Maud, in *Explicator*, XIV (December 1955). Bernard Knieger, in *Explicator*, XV (December 1956). Erhardt H. Essig, in *Explicator*, XVI (June 1958).

I I

Child growing up to die is the theme. As man, the microcosm, is a metaphor for all things (15), so one term of every metaphor involving man implies his death and all stories of man take death's shape. The "planet-ducted pelican of circles" recalls Capricorn, Cancer, and since, according to the bestiary, the young bird kills the old bird by feeding on its arteries, son killing father by biting his mandrake out. This bird with a poet's large mouth is as mi-crocosmic as an atlas-eater. The "gender's strip" corresponds to the tropical zone of the macrocosm. Compare "the short spark," which fertilizes the egg in the "shapeless," shaping womb, with the "red-eyed spark" of genesis (27) and the "short sparks" of "Prologue to an Adventure" (147). Compare the phallic "long stick" with the failing stick (22) and the leg that scraped the cradle in I. In short, here are the long and short of creation. Uniting with "shooting up," the "long stick" produces the meta-phor of the ladder made by Abaddon and Adam, the ladder of death, life, and aspiration. "Jacob to the stars" or climbing from midnight to light (cf. 32, 34, 40) recalls "star-set at Jacob's angle" (43). But climbing this ladder holds for a child the terror of climbing the black, back stairs to bed. Climbing to light or grow-ing up means death, but death, in nature, means resurrection, ac-cording to the "hollow agent" (womb, tomb, skull, phallus).

Hairs, roots, and feathers—whether of pelican or cock from no-wheres—thrust up through skin or ground like daisies (cf. 33, 77). According to Matthew 10:30, "hairs of your head," like falling sparrows, are numbered. "Nettles" could imply the crown of thorns and "feathers" the Holy Ghost, both bringing hope of renewal, like the "hemlock," which, though in one form a poisonous plant (33), in another is an evergreen in a "wood of weathers" or reality. The imagery throughout is that of the preceding poems, "Foster the light" in particular.

This sonnet of Dylan, the suckling, growing up lacks the density and magnificence of the first. Nothing here like those great final lines of Capricorn and Cancer. But "You by the cavern over the black stairs," which concentrates the horrors of childhood, is a good line.

Bernard Knieger, in *Explicator*, XVIII (November 1959). Elder Olson makes astrological comments on all the sonnets. For Thomas' astrologer and his disastrous baby on the merry-go-round see "After the Fair."

III

The metaphor of sheep, unfolding from lamb to ram, through wether, mutton, flock, and fold (cf. 194), includes Thomas' present and future conditions, the seasons, and the globe. As a child of one or two, Thomas is like the lamb of God or Jesus. His "knocking knees," which combine knock-knees with terror and knocking to get out (cf. 8, 22), remind him of his "three dead seasons" (nine months) in the "climbing grave" of the womb. (Compare "running grave," 21. "Climbing," which recalls the ladder of II, is only one of the intricate connections that link these sonnets.) But back to our muttons: "Adam's wether," who "horned" Thomas down in genetic "garden time" must be father. A wether, the ram who leads the flock, is generally, but not always, castrated. If emasculate now, like the old gentleman who lost his mandrake, father must have lost his parts by giving them to a son. The "flock of horns" is the flock he leads: horned sheep or devils perhaps, but hardly cuckolds. "Butt," combining verb and noun, the butting ram and his object, also combines and divides head and tail. This combination of opposites leads to antipodal skull and foot or death and sex. (Compare "the poles of skull and toe," 29.) If skull suggests Golgotha, the garden could also be Gethsemane; for Christ and Adam are both around. Their "thunderous pavements," through which hemlocks thrust, are laid by the "short spark" (II).

Adam and Christ, falling and rising, lead to Rip Van Winkle, sleeping and waking, like Finnegan. Like this earlier Rip, young Thomas wakes from sleep in the "timeless cradle" of the womb, where he has dipped in the "descended bone" of death and sex. There or here, as "Rip of the vaults," he is lord of tomb and womb. In short, as we already know, he is alive and something of a rip. "I took my marrow-ladle/Out of the wrinkled undertaker's van" is one of Thomas' most wonderful pictures, surrealist in all but rational control. That the van is ripped and wrinkled adds to the fun. Translated, the "undertaker's van" is only the womb, and the "marrow-ladle" is only what serves life and dishes it. But the picture, greater than the translation, is diminished by it. Better to enjoy manifest wonders without laying them on the couch.

Rip brings ram back to mind by sound. Starting as white lamb, Thomas will grow to be the black "ram rod" of "Lament," the only one who is not cold mutton in a flock of muttonheads, a ram among the ninnies, and "the black spit of the chapel fold" (194). But ram unites this butting future with an innocent present. Spring lamb becomes ram of spring. As a sign of the zodiac, the Ram ushers in the poet's spring as old winter shuffles off. (The sense is clearer than the syntax here.) As unemasculated wether, Thomas the ram, young or old, is a bellwether, leading the flock and boss of the fold. The ladder of the wether's weathers rings because it has rungs. The antipodes, which bring us back to the globe of the first sonnet and the poles of skull and foot, ring spring out twice, like a clock—an ambiguous clock; for ringing twice could mean either that the child is now two years old or one. The sun, moving between Capricorn and Cancer, brings the world two springs a year. If young Thomas is the whole world, he is one year old. If only a hemisphere, like someone in Plato, Thomas is two.

This merry sonnet, all but metaphysical in tightness and wit, shows the hand and rod of a fairly old ram and a young rip.

The opening line of this sonnet was taken by economical Thomas from a poem in his notebook for February, 1933.

Bernard Knieger, in *Explicator*, XVIII (January 1960).

I V

A little older, young Thomas troubles mother with embarrassing questions about sex and obstetrics. (Compare the child's questions in "Why east wind chills," the undertaker's questions in "The Horse's Ha," and the unanswerable questions of "My world is pyramid.") Questions here of "genesis" and the "short spark" are as plain as the questions of shade, shape, and Pharaoh are ghostly. If Pharaoh, as king, is father, Thomas in his pyramid is the "echo." His "shape of age" must be four or five by now. The "wounded whisper" seems mother, wounded by bearing Thomas and by his questions, which are "hunchbacks to the poker marrow." Their shape, that is, is that of the question mark. The poker marrow (spine or penis, bone of life and death) carries the burden of an embryonic hump, which may grow as large as H. C. Earwicker's.

With his question of the "burning gentry" the bad boy gets more embarrassing. These gentry (the "proper gentleman and lady," 55) are his parents making love. One sixth of the twelve winds (e.g. 41, 69) is two winds, those that blew parental fires out. The "bamboo man," a poker without marrow, is father in mother's "acres." Did mother corset with bones the "boneyards" of her belly for a boy as "crooked" as the "crooked worm" (10) and the "time-faced crook" (76)?

Peculiar among these sonnets, this one is not inverted. A sestet of a sort follows a sort of octave.

No buttons can conceal the "hump of splinters" (from bone, bamboo, and question marks) in your womb, says this boy, back there by imagination's help; for "My camel's eyes will needle through the shroud," a combination of sewing, hiding, undertaking, and Matthew 19:24.

Optics and photography, suggested by those needling eyes, bring the story of this inquisitor to a close. (For photography see 16-17, 78-79, 103.) Pictures taken in the darkness of the "breadsided field," the acres of mother's womb, reveal "Love's reflection" in the face of the embryo (cf. "looking-glass shell," 102). Conceived in love, he is love's reflection. The "mushroom features," growing in the dark, are those of Dylan Thomas, who must have studied his reflection in the mirror and reflected on it. His picture is an unfortunate "close-up" on the wall of ancestral pictures. The photographer's arc lamp (cf. 59, 79) turns in the amniotic sea to the ark of Noah's flood. Even as a little boy, Thomas was obsessed with wombs, he says. Maybe he is also saying, as he has said before, that his poems of womb and tomb are childish.

V

In the sestet, the boy, a little older now, is playing. With the octave he begins a voyage. This Odyssey or Aeneid, which reappears here and there through the rest of the sequence, is an analogy for the voyage of life, as Mr. Bloom's voyage through Dublin is an analogy for a day's journey.

The first line is memorable. "Two-gunned Gabriel" from the Wild West means that young Dylan, playing in the park or at the farm, has become Marshal Dylan of Dodge City. (For Thomas playing cowboy and Indian see "Reminiscences of Childhood" and "The Peaches." Note "two-gunned, Cody-bold" in "Quite Early One Morning." When I said that I had once seen Cody or Buffalo Bill, Thomas was consumed with envy and admiration.) But the sheriff Gabriel is also a seraph, angel of the Annunciation and the Last Trump, in charge, therefore of birth, death, and rebirth. (Compare Hart Crane's "religious gunman" in "The Marriage of Faustus and Helen.") Though the wild winds of "the windy West" seem Shelley's "breath of autumn's being," Thomas is enjoying his spring. By a pun, Gabriel's Apocalyptic trump introduces a game of cards, another metaphor for playing. But cards also mean trickery, here the trickery of the chapel. Young Thomas, who had a Sunday-school certificate on his bedroom wall ("The Fight"), is "tipsy from salvation's bottle." Yet, neither altogether drunk nor altogether tricked, he remains as "black-tongued" as the "black spit of the chapel fold" (194). The deceiving Sunday school "trumped" cards up from "Jesu's sleeve": king, queen, and jacks, the royal family, in fact, and that of Cwmdonkin Drive. "The king of spots" implies death, father, and, if father and son are one, acne perhaps; and Thomas, a jack (or every man Jack), is also the knavish king. The old gentleman as son has become a "fake gentleman in suit of spades," useful for digging in the park and for bringing death to mind. What this faker says occupies either the first three lines or the sixth. His "Byzantine Adam," rising in the night, seems precocious erection. Adam implies genesis; and Byzantium, between Asia and Europe, is neither here nor there. The emphatic placing of "Rose" may bring a further suggestion of Yeats, here, maybe, to hail the emergence of a younger creator.

Since sailing from Byzantium finds parallel in *Moby Dick*, the legend of Jonah, and the Aeneid, two layers of analogy separate us from the facts of Swansea. Ishmael Thomas in a city of the "plain" owes as much to the Bible as to Melville. This outcast was cast out at bloody birth. The "climbing sea" from Asia that threatens to overwhelm the outcast Byzantine, is mother (the "climbing grave" of III), threatening the independence of her child. But Jonah's Moby or father saves the drowning lad; for although father and son are one in one sense, in another, father is still father and son, son. A Freudian contest between parents for their son (cf. "I fellowed sleep") continues through the arctic and marine imagery of the conclusion.

"Cross-stroked" combines swimming and rowing with weeping Jesus, stricken on the cross of Adam's sin, as salty as tears, sea, and Lot's wife. "Pin-legged" on a hill, recalling "on one leg" (I), is the crucifixion. These images of the boy's paternal saviour are fixed in the Arctic, by "waste seas" on "pole-hills." The "frozen angel" is both announcing Gabriel, frozen by the crucifixion, and the frozen town of Archangel in Russia, land of the "white bear." This white masculine bear is opposite to the female "black medusa," a petrifying marine creature, swimming in the warm Black Sea. (The cold Kara Sea of Russia and the warm Sea of Azov, part of the Black Sea, figure in "The Orchards.") As a dreadful creature of the sea, the black medusa is parallel to the singing "sirens" here and to the "furies" of the first sonnet. (Thomas' women, whether mothers or girls, are generally terrifying: the girl in "A Prospect of the Sea," for example, and the "serpent-haired" and "stone-turning" siren of "In the Direction of the Beginning," who sings while a white bear listens and sailors drown among whales and furies.) "Our lady's seastraw" makes Mary in the manger another menacing mother on the "deadweed" (VI), where sirens sing or play the oaten straw. (Compare the "straws" of the "rooking girl," 13.) But sirens are the poet's Muses. Women, whether marine vertebrates or invertebrates, are dangerous and necessary.

But why does the white bear, black siren's opposite, quote Vergil? To tell young Aeneas of the voyage before him? To warn him of sirens along the way or of the Virgin? (Vergil is commonly spelt Virgil because thought to allude to the Virgin in the Messianic Eclogue.) Or is the Arctic bear hinting the delights of fishing the warm Mediterranean with long-legged bait? A Russian barbarian, is the bear commending the classical and the civilized to a young poet? What songs the white bear sang, though not beyond all conjecture, are a puzzling question.

Those "milky mushrooms," no longer Thomas' features (IV), are mother's poisonous breasts, which "slew" the child's hunger and may slay the child. This sonnet celebrates the weaning of those "mushroom features."

M. E. Grenander, in *Notes and Queries*, V (June 1958).

V I

"Cartoon," going back to "mushroom features" (IV), means Thomas' caricature of a face, slashed because the reflection of wounded parents (I, IV). Still contending over him, father and mother equally encourage their wounded boy, who, in this sonnet begins to write his poems under their auspices. Both shape his early poems. Parental contention and co-operation are presented in images of fire and water, which unite in "the tide-traced crater."

"Tallow-eyed," the young poet with vision impaired by his light writes in "a book of water." Father provides the candle and lamp, and mother provides the page. So provided for, their son burns "sea silence on a wick of words," composing the "oyster vowels" of "medusa's scripture" by "lava's light." "Pluck . . . my sea eye," says mother to her cocky son (cf. "suncock," 64). "Lop . . . my fork tongue," says father, the Satanic patron of forked language (cf. 27). The symphonic vowels of their encouragement and advice serve as poetic example. That mother is medusa and that Satanic father is as "pin-hilled" as Jesus we know from sonnet V. His "nettle," however, seems to combine the crown of thorns (cf. "tree of nettles," 41) with the sea nettle, medusa's cousin.

As "love" or "Love's reflection" (IV) and as "old cock from

nowheres" (I) now, the young poet acts on this advice. Whether to use or destroy it, he plucks out "the stinging siren's eye." He lops or moderates the youthful exuberance of his "minstrel tongue." The "fats of midnight" are the midnight oil he burns on his wick while blowing tallow from the "tower" of father's creative candle. Singing salt unites siren's song with tears and "salt Adam" (V).

Back at his game of cards (V), the boy is a "joker" now. But "Adam, time's joker" is the father-principle in his writing as the paper he writes on is "a witch of cardboard," the queen or mother principle. Adam begets poems on his witch, another dangerous lady. These early poems of the womb, "an evil index," spell out "the seven seas" of his perilous voyaging. His Muses, the terrible sirens he encounters, are "bagpipe-breasted ladies in the deadweed," close relatives of "seaweedy" (55). The instruments of these surrealist ladies blow gauze bandages through his slashes, enlarging them. "Manwax" is from father's candle. The wound connects the boy with wounded parents and Christ, the best analogy for sufferers who create by words. As Jesus unites Son and Father, so, by analogy, he unites father and son. We know from "Foster the light" that God, Satan, and mother, equal creators, conspire to pluck "mandrake music" and blow music of the sea.

VII

The young poet's words are a "Bible-leaved . . . book of trees." We know from "Especially when the October wind" that Thomas associated words with trees; and we know that he associated these "written woods" with the tree of knowledge and the cross, "the scarecrow word" with "Genesis in the root." But the language of one poetic light makes one great-rooted blossomer of these two trees.

The poems of Thomas, the Word, are his "Lord's Prayer"; but stamping it on minute grains of rice shows becoming modesty. (Since rice is seed, however, it seems more fertile than the heads of pins on which the Lord's Prayer is commonly inscribed.) Thomas' poems are his cross (e.g. "tree of stories," 48, and "tree of words," "The Visitor"). Doom to those who deny the "windturned statement" of his branches or the "rocking alphabet" on his treetop.

In the octave, the poet returns to his Muses, those surrealistic and wonderful sirens (VI) with "the teats of music," who now stuff his wound with the sponge of the Passion. Singing sirens, they have scales in three senses: music, fish, and balances (cf. the "scaled" siren in "In the Direction of the Beginning"). As "sea-sawers," they move up and down with the waves and the "rocking alphabet," fiddling as their bagpipes blow. Balancing, these fishy girls sing to the unbalanced. Their sponge (another marine animal) sucks life out of paternal Adam, whose bell-voice connects him with the bellwether and the chimes of III. The bell, uniting with the book and candle of the preceding sonnet (cf. 92), may imply the excommunication of "deniers" or else of Ishmael, the poet (V), cast out by society. And it is true that Thomas' poems are sometimes less communications than excommunications.

The "Time, milk, and magic" of siren-song or poetry are as old as genesis, "the world beginning," and, serving as the Word, its beginner. But siren-song, in time and of time, brings "heartbreak." Whether from the "bald pavilions" of knightly old father or from Bethlehem, mother's "house of bread" (cf. "bread-sided field," IV), whether from maternal "rose" or from the "icicle" of the paternal white bear (V), song breaks hearts—like Yeats' images; for time, song's essence, its burden, and its enemy, "tracks the sound of shape." (For tracking time see 21-23; for time in the sound track of a phonograph see 39, 42-43, 139; for poetry as the sound of shape see 58 and "Prologue to an Adventure.") The "ringing handprint" of the "bell-voiced" creature and creator stamps the prayer. Hands, once used for pulling the chain (11) and for signing deadly treaties (71), are put to better purpose now; and the hands of parents in his poems are slowly yielding to his own as time's tune replaces womb's time.

VIII

This portrait of the developing artist continues with the poet's crucifixion; for Thomas, like Stephen Dedalus, was always mistaking himself for our Lord. Here, suffering, creative Jesus-Thomas hangs on his "tree of words," one or all of "three crosses" on the "mountain" of Golgotha. Mary weeps beside him now and, later, at the "gallow grave," his tomb. A concentrate of the queen, medusa, and siren, in the preceding sonnets, "our lady" (V) is the feminine principle directing the poet, his Great Mother and his Muse. That much is fairly plain. The problem is the speaker, who sometimes seems Mary, sometimes Jesus, and sometimes both together. Jesus "wept," but Mary seems to say His words. The sonnets leading up to this one suggest a possibility: as Thomas has joined and replaced his father, so here he joins and replaces his mother. As he becomes the long world's "gentleman of wounds" (I), so he becomes "the long wound's woman" here. A union of masculine and feminine principles is necessary for creation. Such union would account for the speaker, who seems son and mother at once. Autobiographically, it would mean Thomas' acceptance of the parents who shaped and advised him (VI). Woman may be terrible, but if you cannot beat her, join her.

"Time's nerve" is at once Jesus and the poet, who sings "Time's tune" (VII) with all its heartbreak. The "vinegar" offered to Jesus is on Adam's "sponge" (VII). The "bright thorns" wept by Jesus-Mary are the "pin-hilled nettle" (VI). "Bird-papped" Mary recalls the "planet-ducted pelican" (II) and suggests the Pigeon. Her tears are "pins" because she weeps that "pin-hilled nettle" and the nails.

"Jack Christ" (from Hopkins' "That Nature is a Heraclitean Fire") means Hopkins' "Jackself" (from "My own heart"). But the syntax, like the speaker, is unclear. Is "Jack Christ" directly addressed by either or both the speakers or is He in apposition with "sky"? "Each minstrel angle," going with "sky" and "heaven," could mean ministering angel, as some have thought; but, if referring to poetry, it could mean the minstrel's angles or poetic tricks and devices, of which Thomas had plenty. That some of the nails of the cross were "heaven-driven" leads in one way to predestination and in another to the poet's inspiration.

The nipples that issue a "three-coloured rainbow" seem those of papped and bagpipe-breasted Mary, of Jesus, making a new covenant, and of the poet, joining heaven and earth in the manner of D. H. Lawrence. Although in the middle ages the rainbow was sometimes thought to have three instead of seven colors, it is not certain that Thomas knew this. Here, three could be the poet's triple revelation, triple talk uniting earth and sky, or his triple nature, a compound of father, mother, and self.

The poles remind us of the globe (I) and the antipodes

(III). That this world, which is both the poet as atlas-eating microcosm and the macrocosm to which he corresponds, is "snail-waked" means that he has been slow to develop and the public slow to respond.

"All glory's sawbones" is plainly the poet of life, death, and glory in the character of Jesus, the divine healer "by the tree of thieves." (Grief is thief, thief is time, and Thomas is crook or fake, as we know from other poems.) "This mountain minute," combining great and small, space and time, refers to Golgotha again. But how does the sawbones "unsex the skeleton," which seems sufficiently unsexed? Maybe this skeleton is the result of removing the sexual flesh. Maybe bone, as in many other poems, is phallic and needs unsexing. Maybe the poet, possessed by death like Eliot's Webster and Donne, sees the skull beneath the skin. In Thomas' development, this vision would be that of his early poems, those of womb and tomb. The "sun" probably unites light, father, and son again, but what is sun's "blowclock witness"? Clock tells time, and blowing, as of Gabriel's trump or the poet's mouth, is poetry or "Time's tune" (VII). "Blowclock" is the very word for poetry. But the word blow has seventeen meanings or more, and who can tell from this context on which of them Thomas is also playing? "Blowclock" could mean the weathers' wind or a time bomb with green fuse.

Jesus suffered little children of earth to come unto him. "Heaven's children" could be their equivalent and another union of above and below. But Heaven's children could be Jesus and poet, and Mary could be speaking her Son's words. Muse, after all, speaks through poet.

This poem, a fine-sounding and teasing concentrate, shows what Thomas meant by "I, in my intricate image." "Greek in the Irish sea," this romantic poet is something too much.

Marshall W. Stearns, in Tedlock, 120-23. Francis Scarfe, *Auden and After*, 106-10.

IX

With the boys of "Should lanterns shine" and "my world is pyramid," we visit Egypt to inspect mummies, which serve the poet now as images of printing. When set in books, the poems he has written with all the pains of crucifixion are mummies of themselves (cf. 88-89). They are embalmed; yet publishing them is a kind of resurrection. As VIII is "the crucifixion on the mountain," so IX is "the resurrection in the desert," that of Egypt's pyramids and of the modern wasteland. Pyramid or tomb is womb again.

In the sestet, "oracular archives" on "parchment" are poems, set in "the caps and serpents" and the "oil and letter" of inky typography, and printed by "the glove of prints" or "the ringing handprint" of VII. Glove has covered hand. The printed playing cards of V introduce king and queen or father and mother, the poet's creative principles and a subject of his poems. Mummies of prophetical king and queen, buckled like Hopkins' windhover, are inspected by "the lamped calligrapher," Jack Thomas himself, who, having set them down, embalmed them in lint, cloth, henna, and natron (or nitre, a word of Egyptian origin). The "halo" of printed poems is their glory.

The octave notices the scholars or critics who rant about these "oracular archives." Unable to see life in mummy cloth ("bandage" and "linen") or in the gold mask on the mummy's face, they see death alone. If, as uncertain syntax allows, the gold masks are on the features ("such features") of critics, these masks are pretentious deceivers. But "the linen spirit"—the spirit of rag paper or of poems on Yeats' mummy cloth—unites "my long gentleman" (Thomas, one with father and love's long tool) with "dust and furies" (cf. I). The poet sees life in the dust of death and in the terrible women—furies, sirens, and the medusa—he has joined. A "gentle wound" connects the poet as priest and king in pyramid with Jesus in the tomb, ripe for resurrection.

"World in the sand" means not only that his world is pyramid but that his enduring poetry is built on the shifting foundation of time (cf. 55). "The triangle landscape" includes pyramid, delta, and, according to Freud, the female principle. On sand maybe, the poet's world or poetic pyramid is built of "stones of odyssey," gathered on his voyage through life, which, Vergilian once (V), is now Homeric. "Ash" is a tree of life and a creative wand, as well as dust; and "garland" is what a poet wears. "Ash" and "odyssey," suggesting Joycean auspices for triumph, make the poet one with Stephen and Bloom, and the stones of odyssey, wandering rocks, maybe. "Rivers of the dead" around the poet's neck, which may be the Nile and the Styx, suggest The Book of the Dead, watery poetry of the womb, the weight of poetic tradition, and the albatross of the Ancient Mariner.

Imperative mood in the last four lines means hopeful prayer for triumph rather than its announcement. More than pyramidal resting place, a "bed" is that part of a printing press on which the printer's form, filled with type, is laid (cf. 40). As reporter for a Swansea paper, Thomas must have known about "putting the paper to bed."

X

Hortatory "let" proves nothing happening here and now. So conditioned, this "tale's sailor" may drop anchor off a harbour, not in it, and enjoy a distant prospect of garden and nest on shore. His "Christian" odyssey (IX), strangely combining the Christian and the pagan, suggests Joyce's *Ulysses* again. Christ and voyage, Thomas' analogues for himself and his career, are no more Christian than Mr. Bloom and his day—and no less.

"Atlaswise" recalls "Altarwise," the "atlas-eater," and the globe of the first sonnet. Like Atlas, and wise to deceptive Hercules maybe, the poet balances his "globe": the macrocosm, the microcosm, and, since he has inscribed "Time's ship-racked gospel" of a Christian yet secular voyage on it, his poetry. Reluctant to enter the "dummy" or fake harbour (cf. "the symboled harbour," 41) that the deceivers promised him in Sunday school (V), he will hold off, "half-way off" in a "half-way house" of another sort. His voyage, unlike that of the fisherman in "The Long-legged Bait," is not over.

Such harbours, seen through birds' eyes, are "winged," but "rockbirds" are as much at home on shore as the Pigeon on Peter's rock. These harpies of the shore may "spot" (see or defile) the seafaring poet's word, "blown" by poetic winds on Gabriel's trump. Blown images that confuse "December's thorn" with "a brow of holly" (cf. 3) are those of Thomas' poetry, which mixes the holly of Christmas with the thorn of Good Friday in a pretty but unorthodox arrangement, distasteful to holy birds on shore.

"The first Peter" differs from his "rockbirds." Let him ask "the tall fish . . . from the bible east" (fish is an icon of Jesus) about the garden. The "rainbow's quayrail," on which Peter leans, is that of heaven, the quays of the harbour, and the "three-coloured rainbow" of Thomas' poetic arc or ark. "Quay," the key, unites them all. Let Peter ask about father, peeling like a stick of rhubarb in mother's "foam-blue channel" to sow the flesh of child Thomas and the Holy Child around a ghost. (Blue is Mary's color.) Their union makes a "flying garden," either ascending Jesus or the Eden of childhood (cf. 179) and poetic desire. (Compare the "flying heartbone," 47, the "flying heaven," 101, and the "flying grail," 44.) Every microcosmic poet his own Eden. The "sea-ghost" is Thomas still at sea (like a Flying Dutchman) and on a sea coast—little better than a "rockbird." Joycean puns have taken over to lighten proximate triumph.

Let this hoped-for garden be as "Green as beginning" in Eden, with its two trees ("two bark towers"). Let this garden happily fall with Adam (cf. 174) and rise on "that Day" which unites Apocalypse with Genesis, first suitably confused at last with last. On that day the poet may find his wormy "nest of mercies." His building worm is Eve's destructive serpent, "the rude, red" phallus, equally creative and destructive, and the poet's writing finger (cf. 10); for in Thomas all worms are united. Golden "straws" of his venomous nest are those of the "rooking girl" (13) and our lady (V). But what of an ambiguous nest (smaller but safer than harbour, though no less disagreeable) in a "rude, red tree"? Nest for cock or pelican (I, II) perhaps? Tree, always associated with word, suffering, and knowledge, must be this poet's poetry and his cross. "Rude," a possible pun on rood, may also suggest the present nature of his poetry or that of its readers (for red may be a pun on read); and "red," as we know from "Our eunuch dreams," may bear political meaning. But this poem, no more political than religious, is about poetry, the word of Thomas, and himself.

"Altarwise" and "tree," the first and last words of the sonnets, say all—ambiguously. Devoted to his ceremony, the poet is wise to it. His star-crossed self, nailed to this great, composite tree, finds hope of mercy there and hope of blossoming. The ending, like the beginning, of this sequence is obscurely magnificent in sound and shape.

William Empson, in *Casebook*, 113-14.

The Map of
Love, 1939

Of these sixteen poems, which reappear in *The Collected Poems*
in their original order, some were written between 1937 and 1939
and some between 1930 and 1933; for, to fill the volume up,
Thomas raided his notebooks again. The early manuscripts at
Buffalo of seven poems are almost altogether unlike their final
versions in *The Map of Love*. Thomas used these manuscripts as
foundations for later constructions. The date of the construction
seems more significant than the date of the foundation; for a
poem is not its origin.

Since in this volume Thomas sometimes replaces generalized
womb and tomb by actual places, people, and occasions, it is
tempting to draw conclusions about his emergence into the light
of reality. But actuality, as Ann Jones proves, was there from the
start. "Once it was the colour of saying" bids good-by to his old
manner and announces the new. But this is an early poem and
the old manner survives the announcement of its death.

The threat of war and his marriage, which provided a new
theme, may have moved Thomas to seek old poems of actuality

out for refurbishing. This preference could indicate a change. Change is apparent in the loosening of rhythm.

Because the pleasure-bird whistles (1939), *p. 86*

The occasion of this poem, originally called "January 1939" (in memory of Yeats, maybe), was a visit to London in December, 1938: "I've just come back from three dark days in London, city of the restless dead. . . . Out pops a lamp-post covered with hair." That this nightmare was moral is plain; for the living dead of London, says Thomas, see "no difference between good & bad" (Watkins, 49).

A Puritan's vision of Vanity Fair, the wicked city of destruction, this poem takes its place beside "The Countryman's Return" (for the text of which see Watkins, 85-86), a poem excluded from *The Collected Poems*, "Prologue to an Adventure," and *Adventures in the Skin Trade*. The shades of John Bunyan and Lot direct these visions of chapel-eyed Thomas, as he "walked through the wilderness of this world."

Free verse, relieved by irregular and fugitive rhyme, carries an intricate structure of images, of which the chief are supper, snow, and Sodom. The bird and beast of the opening and the fable of Lot's wife are as "convenient" for the moralist's purpose as the fabulous insect of "To-day, this insect." The poem of the pleasure-bird, a sermon as good as any of the sixty sermons of Bunyan, proves that Thomas also preached in parable and exemplum. Opening with a riddling question is not beyond such preachers.

The "pleasure-bird" has been blinded by wicked men (cf. "The Visitor") to make him sing; but the "horse" (Pegasus, the winged horse of poets?) has been no more than partly blinded by those pleasure seekers in their pleasure domes. His song will be the bitterer for their attempt. Exemplary bird and beast, cooked in the poet's pie, are supper for his mood and his readers.

"Snow," not only that of wintry wind plucking a metaphorical goose (cf. 135), is dope, a "drug-white shower" for the sinners of London. January, licking snow, is "the tongue of the year." The licking tongues of dopes, uniting with the "wild tongue" of the poet, put one in mind of pleasure-domed Coleridge, another "enamoured man" in the "deadly wood" of hairy lampposts.

The poet's fiery eyes, inimical to the snow around him, have not been blinded by "hot wires"; for his eyes are forked "twigs" of the "tree of words," and his tongue is rooted. Breaking from its tombs (in mouth, city, and womb), the tongue escapes as if cut from its "red, wagged root." Red may combine anatomy with Puritan politics, as tongue combines food, dope, sex, and poetry. The flying tongue does not look back, but the horrified poet, like Lot's wife, turns for a final look at the city of the plain, undiscouraged by the "fable" of this "salt person."

This fabulous wife, frozen like an icicle into a statue of salt, is "one story out of the bum city." Standing one story high above the flattened ruins of story, she is cold, white, and static amid a hot and rocking muddle of toppled towers (cf. the icy woman, "salt and white," of "In the Direction of the Beginning"). "Bum city" and "the mauled pictures of boys" make London Sodom and sodomy its sin (cf. xv and "Sodom To-morrow and London," 175). Thomas has escaped from sods and dopes, who "fixed" him in horror. Since Lot's wife and the dopes are equally, though differently, "fixed," double talk becomes triple.

At once supper and grace after meat, this poem offers a geographical conceit as dessert. The morally and geographically "upright man" of the "antipodes" (cf. 81) is tumbled, his stomach turned by the stomachs of London's dead, who have not come to Thomas' supper. (*Don Giovanni* may have crossed his mind.) The "table," which joins "fable" by punning rhyme, is both that of this supper and, "altarwise," the table of communion. Thomas the Puritan is cook, server, and celebrant.

Puns seem at odds with the dominant tone and feeling, but Gwilym's sermon in "The Peaches" also horses around. Here is the sermon of a seeing horse among the fairies. Llareggub, where Thomas was to seek refuge, is Sodom's opposite, at once more backward and less.

Not really about an experience in the bum city, this poem is about the experience of making a poem about an experience in the bum city.

Olson, 55, 59. Treece, xi, 137-40. Watkins, 49, 54, 55-56, 85-86.

I make this in a warring absence (1938), *pp.* 87-89

Dylan and Caitlin were lovers. Hence this quarrel. Its history, originally called "Poem to Caitlin," then "Poem (for Caitlin)," was written in 1937, a few months after their marriage. ("Not from this anger" has a similar theme.) That Thomas thought "warring absence" a great poem is no guarantee of value, nor are the pains and time he lavished on it. He thought it worthy of the *Criterion*, a journal with "snob-appeal," he said, but it did not appear there.

The form of this dense and driven poem is curious. Stanzas of eight and seven lines alternate. Terminal words agree in a single consonant: "n" in the first two stanzas, "s" in the third and fourth, "n" in the fifth, "d" in the sixth and seventh, "n" and "m" in the eighth, "s" and "r" in the last. Approaches to sprung rhythm relieve metrical regularity.

1: The "harbour" he had hoped for at the end of "Altarwise" proves poor anchorage for tongue and "proud sailing tree," rude and red no more. Tongue and tree are both phallic and poetic. Shaped by the creator's hand, Caitlin's "handshaped ocean" shapes the creator's hand (cf. "manshaped," 69). The "quaystone" (cf. "quayrail," 85) of her harbour is the keystone of an architectural enterprise that, implying the rainbow (cf. 85), proceeds through vault, groyne, house, and column. "Groyne" includes anatomy, breakwater, church, and overarching trees. Thomas' aspiring tree will drive branches up through vault, groyne, and house to the "marrow-columned heaven" of Lawrence's delight. But the "house" still seems a "half-way house."

Caitlin's "warring absence" is either coldness or actual departure. The "ancient, stone-necked minute" combines old and new, long and short, harbour and stubbornness. (Parenthetical "praise is blessed" shows his need of her praise.) "Pride," the important and difficult word, can mean female sexual desire. She has stopped praising and desiring his phallic "mast and fountain" and the proud tree of his poetry.

This dazzling abundance of images says too many things at once for ready agreement or synthesis. The effect is scattered.

But maybe the poet's confusion is the point of this confusion.

2: Her pride in and for him and his pride in accomplishment, both amatory and poetic, are cast off like old rags, weeds, and scrawls of breath. "Opium head" (cf. "poppied," 5, "snow," 86, and "hophead," 43) makes the neglected poet a dope. Nautical imagery of rope, knot, and reefed sail brings us back to the harbour. Sailing or anchoring there is plainly sexual. Her pride, driving her to a "bread and milk mansion in a toothless town," is both infantile and senile. I cannot believe that she has gone home to mother.

3: That "her proud absence" makes him confuse prickly "nettle" (cf. 83) with soft pigeon and innocence with guilt is further evidence of his confusion. A metaphor of grotto and oyster shell brings Virgin, siren, and Venus to mind. "Shameful oak," may be the once-proud "sailing tree" of this druid. From syntactical obscurity and imagistic disagreement a little comes: however enclosed she is in cave, shell, and renewed maidenhood, pearls and other signs omen "whalebed and bulldance" (cf. 167-69). A pride of "lions" is also in the sexual offing; but present pride is as unrewarding and sterile as "sucked stone." "Huge as sandgrains," returning to "ancient minute," is the large and small of time, measured by sterile sand. As the senses of pride multiply, like these grains of sand, we must follow Thomas to the dictionary.

4: Her contraries seem Thomas as beast and priest and herself as fire and ice. His "grave foot" implies sex and death while his "hand of five assassins" recalls old habits, to which he may have resorted in this emergency, and the hand that signed the paper. As his architecture aspires, so does he—in vain. Following the "cold flintsteps" of his hot phoenix up the "cinder-nesting columns" of his heavenly temple, he becomes icy and "limptreed," shut out by ring and lock, new images of enclosure, from the noon and summer of his climbing desire. (Compare climbing a sexual mountain in "Adventure from a Work in Progress.") This beast's "herd" seems starved of firebird's fire. (Compare the firebird of "A Winter's Tale.") The last line is the climax of a darkly splendid shape of sounds, rhythms, and hints.

5: Like angry Samson, the poet makes the jawbone of an ass his instrument. Better than making now, destruction may open things up. His "warring sands" are those of beach, Caitlin, and time. His destruction of east and west leaves few directions. Hanging "beheaded veins" on the "wringing shell" of her absent heart illustrates his surrealistic extremity. Yet even destruction is creative when the bird-picked jawbone of this poetical ass brays a little. Forgetting Samson but not those "warring sands," the poet becomes a wave, sprawling to ruin, on her beach. Since Dylan means wave, the "tide-tongued" poet has found a suitable place for ruin. A kind of gaiety redeems his fury.

6: Skeleton, wave, and ruin suggest submarine entombment, one "rood" or seven or eight yards down. As sunken tree, the rood, far below "marrow-columned heaven," lies in a "water-pillared shade" no Samson could pull down. The aqueous world of Thomas is pyramid again and he, having regressed, is mummy (cf. 36, 44, 72, 84), wound in "emerald linen" to suggest the Emerald Tablet of Egyptian Hermes, perhaps. ("As above, so below," said Hermes Trismegistus.) There "love's anatomist" lies until his own "sun-gloved hand," wielding a diamond, saves him. However sunken (cf. the sunken cathedral, 167), a pyramid aspires to light, and tomb becomes womb. As a shape of light, a diamond is a poem, and so the submarine "sharp wind."

7: Meanwhile he lies "linened" in his pyramidal anchor-ground, hearing voices, his own apparently. The "inchtaped lips," paradoxically crying, are those of a mummy that pleasingly combines female lips with two worms: inch and tape. "Topless" recalls fallen Troy. "Taut masks," drumming, are those of African mummies, swathed in "hank and hood." Mummy or embryo in womb is the image of the poet's regression; and mummy voices speak his guilt. His is the "tongue that lapped up mud," and he the "lizard" whose forked tongue forked him back through the "lockjaw bed" of Samson's jawbone and mother's "mouth of seed." "Tongue" and "lizard" unite the poet with father, and "mouth" with mother. (For "venom" see 85; for "fork" see 26, 27, 37.) As "lockjaw" is the poet's disease (cf. 14), so a "breath-white, curtained mouth of seed" is the death of poetry. But the "dead ascend," these internal debaters allow, from the tangles of "groin's endless coil" (trouble, umbilicus, and spiral). Ascent and manhood offer hope, beauty, and a jaw forever. Yeats may preside over spiral, mask, and mummy cloth.

8: Reborn, he hails the "terrible world" as brother; for pardon has fallen from Caitlin's "cloud of pride." The "once-blind eyes" of the embryo have "breathed" the "wind" of poetic vision. Breathing eyes are no more apocalyptic than the fleshing of a "once-rindless" poet's hand or the fuming of a poetic, phallic tree. The womb's cauldron, root of this tree, has produced a "burning bird" or phoenix, fit companion for the firebird of stanza four (cf. "burning bride," 134). What matter that the phoenix is singular? The packs of terrors that have dogged the poet flee his resurrected "ghost in bloom."

9: Seas of life have delivered Caitlin from cloudy pride. No lightnings flash; the winds are calm that once raised trees, like Dylan's hair, in terror and turned "soft snow's blood" (red-white, warm-cold) to ice. Sunny Caitlin offers a prospect of "quiet countries." Though infant "prides," sucking her "pale, nippled air," threaten other clouds and warring absences, the poet makes this poem now in "a forgiving presence." In a letter to Watkins (30-32) Thomas tells what he meant the last lines to mean. If his intentions differ from our guesses a little, we need not fret; for we have nothing but the text to go by.

Close connections between this well-intentioned, muddy poem and "Altarwise" help prove that autobiographical and this its sequel. Anticipations of "A Winter's Tale" are no less instructive.

When all my five and country senses see (1938; ms. 1932-33), *p.* 90

This "many sounding minded" sonnet is as strangely shaped as the other sonnets. A decade, if we can call it that, is followed by a quatrain. Synesthetic correspondences bring Baudelaire's "Correspondances" to mind. Probably ignorant of this, Thomas seems to be saying that poetic vision comes not from mind but from heart and senses. Hand, eye, tongue, and ear conspire in a poem and, as each sense includes the others, so the heart includes the lot. Seeing or vision, a great composite, is at once sensual and beyond the senses. What these spies and witnesses see is the death of love. Not this idea but an arrangement of noble lines, in which idea is working, creates this radiance.

"See," "mark," and "eye" acquire importance from place. "Country" implies the fresh, the green, and the innocent. The five seeing senses correspond to the five touching fingers of the poet's hand, which is both creative and destructive (cf. 11, 71, and "hand of five assassins," 88). "Green thumbs," promising fertility, are country thumbs. The "vegetable eye" of the nail's "halfmoon" connects "country" with "zodiac," above with below. (For zodiac see 27, 80, 130. Cf. "the half-moon" of the writer's "thumb-nail," "The Orchards." "The lashes of her fingers lifted. He saw the ball under the nail," "The Burning Baby.") Since this "handfull zodiac" or macrocosm in a microcosmic hand is connected with a vision of love's death, the hand's activity may be more or other than poetical. "Young stars" could be sperm that a "pared" nail pares and freezes. "Wintered by," recalling Hopkins' "worded by," demands a semicolon instead of a comma. Meanings distract us from a pattern of wonderful sounds and rhythms.

"Whispering ears" also see love's death, this time that of Venus on shell and beach (cf. 11). "Whispering," "breeze," and "syllables" remind us that ear and tongue join fingers in creating a poem. (Tongue may hint taste, otherwise absent from the conspiracy of senses.) Since "lynx" means light and sharp sight, a "lynx tongue" sees as it cries—like a poet. "Fond wounds . . . mended bitterly" happily approaches chiasmus. Nostrils seeing love's "breath burn like a bush" equates goddess with God and this bush with the merrily burning bush of "The Burning Baby"; but love's breath burning and smelling is a good definition of Thomas' poetry—of some of it anyway.

The conceit of one and five would have pleased Hopkins and Browne. Though singular, the heart is as "sensual" as the five senses. Five witnesses or seers are no better than one. Indeed, they seem less, for they may fall asleep. "Love's countries," the field of the "country senses," are various, as those fingers see when they "grope awake." "Break," the final, ambiguous word, proves senses fall apart or open up like hearts. The death of love is a breaking thing.

Query: Since "when" and "will" imply that the senses are not seeing yet, can the speaker be another foreknowing embryo, whose senses will "grope awake" at birth? Or is the speaker a young man complaining about present capacity while welcoming the death and heartbreak his sensual future holds?

Watkins, 62. Olson, 96. James Zigerell, in *Explicator*, XIX (November 1960).

We lying by seasand (1937; ms. 1933), p. 91

Something sinister hides behind the grace of this grave, gay lyric, which Dame Edith called an "unsurpassable technical achievement." Stresses of the sprung lines, falling from four to three at times, rise to five at the end. This movement, complicated by periods of various length, is accompanied by sounds. Dissonance, assonance, alliteration, and rhyme, both terminal and internal, weave a pattern—here, for example: "That's grave and gay as grave and sea." This great interwoven line, inspired by Hopkins and, through him, by the Welsh, concentrates the feeling and the theme of the poem. Working with the parts that serve it, the theme emerges uncertainly. But what this thing of words certainly communicates is itself, proving Wallace Stevens right. "Poetry," he said, "is the subject of the poem."

Among the elements that agree and disagree to compose the poem and hint the theme are yellow and red, sea and sand, sand and rock, stasis and movement, present and future, calm and uneasiness, sterility and love, heaven and earth. Yellow, uniting sand with moon and heaven, becomes "golden" and "sovereign." The "sovereign strip" we lie on (cf. "the gender's strip," 80) seems calm, curative, ruling, and stable as the pound. Apparently eternal, yellow sands, nevertheless, are temporal and sterile. As winds blow the grains, the redness of "red rivers" and "red rock" impends.

"We lying by seasand, watching yellow" enjoy a temporary "one-coloured calm" that "should cure our ills," all the fears and troubles that come from "the grave sea" of womb and tomb. But who are "we"? Thomas and a girl or Thomas and his "intricate image"? And how "lying"? Simply on or near a beach or making love? Maybe the latter; for we mock those who, favoring sterility and redness, follow hollow pursuits in a desert which is not that of the yellow sands. The sands of time are fertile as well as sterile. ("Each golden grain spat life into its fellow," 24.) We mock dry men who mock life.

Chief among these mockers seems T. S. Eliot, whose poems yield Thomas' images of sterility: "red rock," desert, hollow, rib, canal, and cicada. What matter if Eliot detests the desert that Thomas associates him with? Dry bones enough to keep the metaphysics warm. And Eliot readily joins the sterile moon as "dry tide-master"; for he rules the tides of contemporary verse. Not altogether villain here, Eliot seems convenient example. After all, to have created an "alcove of words" of dry materials in a wasteland is an accomplishment beyond mockery. I have heard Thomas mock Eliot, and I have found echoes of Eliot in Thomas' poetry. Eliot's rock is red and Thomas, who also hated dryness (see 12, 38, 60), preferred "green rock" (78). But both the sands where Thomas lies and Eliot's red desert are "grave" in several senses. Thomas' "red rivers," unlike the "red river" of Eliot's "Virginia," could be political or arterial.

A little tired of monotonous yellow, one calls for another color, maybe green, but "calls with the wind"—in vain? However calm and sovereign, "The lunar silences, the silent tide" (another interweaving of great beauty) are no cure for what ails the poet. "Heavenly music" (of wind and poetry?), hurrying over the temporal sands, ends calm by movement, while uniting above and below. The "golden mountains and mansions" it hides maybe dunes (cf. "A Prospect of the Sea") children's sand castles, as Dame Edith thinks, or Bunyan's heaven. "Bound" here by our yellow ship, we wish in vain that wind would blow red rock away.

"But wishes breed not," a stale inversion, seems a flaw. But it could be a calculated descent to make the brightness of the ending brighter. Hopkins used such tricks.

No wishes can prevent "rock arrival" or political threat to yellow calm. Has Eliot's red rock yielded to its political opposite? What of Thomas' commitment to the left? Certainly not communist here, the impending red rock must be Hitler's war, for which, Thomas may have thought, Eliot, commending fascists in his *Criterion*, had done his bit. Maybe that is why this rock assumes the shade of his rock, which Thomas, of another red on his yellow sand, may hold accountable for a threat to peace.

This golden weather cannot last. It will break like a ribbed heart and disintegrate like a weathered hill in the contention or union of two political reds. These two are outer reds, and blood, a third red, is inner. "Heart's blood," recalling "red rivers," may be their opposite. But this symphony in yellow major makes all reds irrelevant save the broken heart's.

It is tempting to find a source for Thomas' red rivers in the "red river" of Eliot's "Virginia," but Thomas' rivers flow in the 1933 manuscript and Eliot's river appeared in 1934. When Thomas rewrote his poem in 1937, he retained the occasional beauties of the primitive text. His schoolboy verse, still in manuscript, is plainly under Eliot's spell—together with that of Noyes and Flecker.

Edith Sitwell, in Tedlock, 149-50. Henry Gibson, in Tedlock, 152-54. E. Glyn Lewis, in Tedlock, 180. Fraser, 20. Treece, 103.

It is the sinner's dust-tongued bell (1937), p. 92

A regression to an earlier manner, this poem falls victim to a syndrome. Lost in the rich confusion, one critic thinks the theme a black mass, celebrated by Satan. Another thinks it an announcement of the poet's religious conversion. Unable to agree, I cannot blame; for these quarreling images invite hypothesis without affording proof. Here, before us, are images of ritual, fire and water, sex, destruction, creation, magic, and child. Time and grief (cf. "Grief thief of time") are everywhere. Maybe it is best, taking what is there as it is, to avoid hypothesis altogether. But it seems likely that Thomas, up to his old tricks, is revisiting time, process, death, and creation—creation of poem, world, and child. Taking metaphor of church and child literally is our danger. We can be sure that, after abandoning his chapel, Thomas was never called to church by any bell, whether "dust-tongued" or "black-tongued" (2), both deathly. And we can be sure that the unmarried poet who wrote this poem had no child, unless some bastard.

1: Time, personified as "sulphur priest" or devil with hourglass and torch, is conducting a service to which a "dust-tongued bell," at once temporal, sexual, and poetic, calls a black ram rod, lamenting sins. Time sets fire to a black aisle of the church and a "firewind" blows out the candle. Altarwise grief, who accompanies time, lover, and poet, tears out the "altar ghost." Grief's destructive and creative action, like all the actions of this stanza, implies sex and poetry. Their holiness demands a church that is neither Presbyterian nor Catholic.

2: The church choir sings a minute, but time sings an hour— since life is short, art long, and both in time? They sing of time and grief, like all poets. Time's slow-growing, creative "coral" and grief's drowned "sepulchre" introduce a metaphor of sea and sunken cathedral (cf. 167). The "whirlpool," a possible allusion to *The Waste Land*, may mean "Death by Water," and the "prayer-wheel" (cf. 182) makes the service Buddhist. "Moonfall" combines setting moon with submarine landfall. The "sailing emperor" is the sun, God or Son, who, walking on moon-drawn water, leaves tide-prints (cf. 141). From the "dashed-down spire" of the sunken and sexual cathedral, a bell strikes the "sea hour," like a ship's clock, through the metal of a diving bell (cf. 42). This familiar imagery of womb and tomb suggests embryo and poem. Moon, emperor, and son, a holy family, are engaged in life's deadly, creative process or ritual.

3: In the "calm" of the sunken cathedral the candle of sex and poetry is out for a time and the flame "dumb," above the "loud and dark" of nature and under her snows and thunders. Grief's ritualistic bell, book, and candle (anticipated in the first stanza), though commonly used for exorcism of altar ghosts or for excommunication (cf. 83), are used now, suitably "drenched" by sinking, for the baptism of "cherub time," the embryo who will be the child of the last two stanzas. The "weathercock" of the sunken steeple (hardly a Catholic decoration) prays for the child on time's coral, symbol of sea change and growth. The weathercock (cf. 80, 145) is paternal and the silent bell in his steeple, maternal. An "emerald" bell suggests creation's green, the sea, and the Emerald Tablet (cf. 88) of Hermes Trismegistus, who reappears as the sorcerer of stanza four and the astrologer of stanza five. Hermes, the god of transformation and correspondences, is the god of writers, as Stephen Dedalus affirms. Hermes and Shakespeare's coral add poem to embryo.

4: Born white, the child, climbing the blue wall of day, acquires color. From the womb's blank winter comes a boy of "dark-skinned" or tanned summer. That this child's caul and shroud are "crabbed" (cf. 19) proves marine origin. The "stone tocsin" of the sunken church paradoxically and splendidly rings "Ding dong from the mute turrets." A "sorcerer" or Hermetic magus is a transformer, and an "insect," as we know (from 41, 47), is an articulated product of metamorphosis. The poet's poetry wakes us up.

5: Coming right out, the poet makes a statement: time is the child, cast out and shaped for death's "curfew." The "holy room in a wave" (cf. 154-55) is sunken church and womb. Though called to this church by their curfew bell, love's sinners worship their child, a "hyleg image." Hyleg, a term from Hermetic astrology, refers to casting a horoscope (cf. "cast" in the first line). "Hyleg" figures with stars in the 1933 manuscript of "When once the twilight locks." Of no use there, the good word found use here. The prediction of the stars, embodied in the "urchin" (sea urchin and child), is grief, born at "nightbreak," not daybreak. No ceremonial spice or incense can sweeten parents' plague. A "hyleg image," which may imply *heilig* in this context, is also a poem. Poetry predicts grief and, as we know from "Altarwise," crucifixion.

Olson, 58. Stanford, 83. E. Glyn Lewis, in Tedlock, 176.

O make me a mask (1938; *ms. 1933*), *p. 94*

This defiance of a hostile world is not unlike "To Others Than You" and "I have longed to move away." More than a defiance of the sods, dopes, spies, and critics around him, however, this slight, repetitive poem is a prayer for a protective mask. But Thomas was always masked. What if not a mask is his "intricate image," what his calculated obscurity, and what, for that matter, his barefaced face? But no face or "armour" could keep him from giving himself away—not even the mask on his mummy (89).

"O make me a mask," the opening exhortation, recalls Blake and middle Yeats. Transferred adjectives make the "enamelled eyes and the spectacled claws" of crabbing enemies more terrible. Even if the "nurseries" of an innocent face, already a kind of mask, partly conceal the "rape and rebellion" within, Thomas must assume a less revealing concealment—some good persona for a bad actor.

Silence might be proper mask. Let the "tide-tongued" poet be tongue-tied and dumb. However paradoxical, a silent persona, gagged by "a dumbstruck tree," might discountenance "bare enemies." (This tree, of course, is the rude, red tree of words.) A dumb persona would certainly silence the sharp tongue that fails to defend his "prayerpiece" now. This pious persona is a "sweetly blown trumpet of lies," and lies are fictions or "fibs of vision" (48). Let his future persona blow poems bitterly or blow no more.

Let his unprotected "countenance of a dunce," with its "mushroom features" (82), be covered by "armour and oak" (cf. 40, 87). Yet, let this prayerpiece seem to weep; for the mask of sentiment would veil "dry eyes" and the "belladonna" or poison behind them. Let others betray themselves, as he has done, by a "nude mouth" or by a boyish "laugh up the sleeve" (cf. 96). Compare "The bare boy's voice through a stone mouth" and the masks of the moon in "The Orchards." A laugh up the sleeve was tried and rejected in the manuscript of "My hero bares his nerves."

Despite intricate rhyme and experiment in flexible rhythm, Thomas found this prayer for maturity and adjustment "unsatisfactory." And we may guess why; for this confusion of masks unmasks him. The long 1933 version, nothing like this, was revised in 1937.

Watkins, 39-40. E. Glyn Lewis, in Tedlock, 184.

The spire cranes (1938; *ms.* 1931), *p.* 95

An intricate image, this tightly elaborated conceit proves debt to the metaphysical poets. Here is a poem as ingenious as something by Donne himself. Thomas thought it a "curious thought." Herbert Read found it an "abstract arabesque." Any good poem must be that, but, like any good poem, this is more than that. The image of a spire with birds and bells plainly serves as analogy for poet and poem. "The spire cranes" is another poem about poetry. Sprung rhythm and verbal echoes show debt to Hopkins, who also aped the metaphysicals. Couplets, an unusual form for Thomas, improve the feeling of tightness while dissonance and failure to close the couplets with a stop maintain the air of freedom.

This "spire," aspiring and creative, is holy phallus and the poet's holy tower of words (19, 41, "The Orchards"). Either a noun or a verb, but more nearly the latter, "cranes" introduces bird (cf. the bird "on one leg," 80) and the action of bending like a derrick (cf. 58). The "statue," a stone nest for birds, is either the spire itself or a statue on it. Aspiring birds dive from their spire to bite the dust and the salt froth, like the images of "my intricate image' (41-42). "Carved," "feathery," and "throats" make these birds poems as well as sperm. "Spilt sky" marks the union of above with below. "Weed," "heel," "pelter" (a form of pelt), and "plume" may come from Hopkins' poems on birds and spring: "The Windhover," "The Sea and the Skylark," "The Caged Skylark," "Henry Purcell," and "Spring."

Chimes, imprisoned in the spire like birds in their stone nest, also escape. Bells (commonly associated with poetry) are "music for silver lock / And mouth." Silver lock could be the poet's control of his silver tongue. But as uncontrolled outlaws, these sounds in time fall to Keats' "priestlike" waters. Control and freedom are aspects of poetry. Bird and chime ("Both note and plume") plunge from the "hook" of the craning spire—but they are hooked and must return or effect an arduous escape.

These "craning birds" are a parable of choice for the poet. If his poems "jump back to the built voice" of their creator, they are solipsistic—made for the poet alone. If they fly out like the bells to the winter of reality, they are communications. "With winter to the bells" seems a reversal of with the bells to winter.) "Prodigals," both wasters and returners, are private poems, and their wind is "dumb." Should the poet choose habitual privacy or publicly come forth? The last, magnificent line, a compromise, is saved from privacy by Biblical reference.

The present version of this poem is different from and better

than the early version in the 1930-32 notebook. The changes
and elaborations show Thomas' craft and the process of creation.

Watkins, 31. Herbert Read, in *Seven* (Autumn 1939).

After the funeral (In memory of Ann Jones) (*1938; ms. 1933*),
pp. 96-97

Thomas loved tombs and tombstones. Plainly of the graveyard
school, this elegy differs from its predecessors in *The Collected
Poems* in being for an actual woman, his "peasant aunt," who had
helped make holidays at Fern Hill green and golden. (Ann Jones
is the heroine of "The Peaches.") That this emergence from darkness into light involves a tomb seems curious, though he is not in
it and old habit dies hard. Thomas was a complicated man and
this elegy is more than elegiac. Writing about Ann Jones, he is
also writing about himself writing about her. She and her bard are
his heroine and hero. But other contrasts provide drama, movement, and excitement. A conflict between conventional mourners
at her grave and mourning Thomas occupies the first part, and a
conflict between his image of Ann and Ann herself, the second.
Here, as image and reality coincide, the poet, transfigured, becomes one with one of his images—not, however, with the monstrous one. An agreement of imagination and fact assures elegiac
consolation, the poet's triumph, and the triumph of life.

This tightly elaborated structure, in which all parts work toward a climax that contains and transforms these working parts,
draws upon the resources of rhythm and sound. Springing rhythm,
looser than Hopkins' sprung verse, gains values from assonance,
dissonance, and, above these, alliteration, until final rhyme concludes a shape of sounds.

The mourners at grave and wake, sterile mules feasting on
"tear-stuffed time and thistles," are happy that the undertaker's
tapping on Ann's coffin is not on theirs. "Mule" is an adjective
and "praises" a noun. Such "snivelling" praises are less for Ann
herself than for Ann as "one peg" in a general grave. The "lids"

are of her coffin and their eyes as they hypocritically cry up their sleeves. (Thomas once laughed up his sleeve, 94.)

Ann's real mourner, a "desolate boy," shaken by tapping and smack of spade, "sheds dry leaves," the pages of her elegy (cf. xvi), which, though sincere, is inadequate; for this private apocalypse breaks only one of her bones to light. His "dry leaves" are not unlike the "stuffed fox" and the "stale fern" that decorate Ann's parlor, where her elegist stands alone. Fox and fern are facts, as we know from "The Peaches," and "humped Ann" was a fact. But, abandoning facts, this ingenious elegist, as false in his way as the mourners in theirs, succumbs to hyperbole, the temptation of druids and bards. What have poor, humped Ann and her stuffed fox to do with a fountain flooding parched Wales? (Compare the Welsh flood in "Author's Prologue.")

None more self-critical, however, than this elegist, even with his mask of druid on. His image is a "monstrous" conceit, "magnified out of praise." Ann needs no hyperbolical druid. Her broken body lies "dumb and deep" and her death, no flood, was "a still drop" (cf. Yeats' "green drop" in "Fergus and the Druid" and "water bead," 112).

But conflict among ingenuity, self-awareness, and grief cannot keep a good "bard" down. Ann's undismayed bard calls all seas and woods to her service now—all "the ferned and foxy woods," which, though living, correspond to her stuffed fox and stale fern as the "brown chapel" she attended corresponds, if only by contrast, to the chapel of holy nature. Her love attended both. As its sign let four birds from the four directions form a cross (cf. "the birds . . . flew crisscross," "The Horse's Ha").

A tombstone cutter now, her bard raises a "skyward statue" on her grave. It may be that "her flesh was meek as milk," but somehow the monument is appropriate—even in the rain of "a crooked year." However appropriate, this image "carved from her" is inappropriate, too. The self-critical bard plays his still monstrous image against real Ann. From this some of the poem's glory.

"I know her scrubbed and sour humble hands" is one of Thomas' best lines, which, though owing much to alliteration, rhythm, and a scale of dark vowels, owes more to naked reality. Things rather than ideas of things have begun to detain the poet. Religious "cramp" and "wits drilled hollow" recall the "brown

chapel" of Sunday, not that of nature. Ann's son, Gwilym, main-
tained an even browner chapel in "The Peaches," and his *hwyl*
was louder than her "damp word." "Her fist of a face died
clenched on a round pain" is another great apprehension of the
actual.

Now actual Ann and sculptured Ann unite. The monument
"of [and to] the hewn voice" becomes one with Ann's "seventy
years of stone" to "gesture" and "psalm" her poet forever. (Gesture and psalm are verbs.) "Storm me forever over her grave" may
be a weak line, as Thomas conceded. But, he said, he wanted it
weak—in order, perhaps, to improve the strong last lines by
dramatic contrast.

Ann's death becomes her poet's life. No longer stuffed with dry
and hyperbolical leaves in her parlor, the poet's foxy lung cries,
"Love." (Crying love, 107, is what a poet does, and the love of
Man, as Thomas says in his prefatory "Note," is what a poet must
have. For Thomas as fox with a "foxy tongue" see xviii and 21.
For strutting and swanking Thomas see 100, 147.) No longer a
stale fern, the poet struts and lays seeds to restore a black sill.
Fox and fern, becoming images of life, have become one with
poet and reality. Ann herself and writing her elegy have made her
poet a poet.

The original text of this poem (in a 1933 notebook) lacks all
the merits of the present version: druid, monument, chapel, fox,
fern, and Ann's sour hands. Embalmed in "natron" and "mummy
paint," Ann is less important than her hypocritical mourners and
the gossips of Glamorgan.

Watkins, 39-40, 57-58. C. Day Lewis, *The Poetic Image*, 123-25. Francis
Scarfe, *Auden and After*, 115. Fraser, 19, 21. Herbert Read, in *Seven* (Autumn
1939). John Malcolm Brinnin, *Dylan Thomas*, 236-41. Marshall W. Stearns,
in *Explicator*, III (May 1945). Stanford, 86-87. David Daiches, *Poems in
English*, 744-45. Thomas recorded this poem, Caedmon, 1043.

Once it was the colour of saying (1939; *ms.* 1932-33?), *p. 98*

Our expectations, aroused by two quatrains, are disappointed.
Instead of a third we find five queer lines. Instead of the sonnet

our eye may have fancied we find thirteen lines with the couplet in lines nine and ten. Such violations seem jokes. As the form evolves the unexpected, so the matter. What begins plainly enough ends darkly in a puzzling image of light.

Thomas is saying good-by again to his early manner—his old, colorful verse, which, as "soaked," "capsized," "seaslides," and "drowned" imply, is all wet. Compare "the colour of saying" with "colour in a shape" (70). With this colorful manner he associates his brightly colored past, at school, at the seaside, and in the park. Although Cwmdonkin Park figures in "October wind" and "Should lanterns shine," Thomas has not learned all its possibilities. Here, childhood memories, part of a rejected past, do not clearly announce the use he was to find for them. But, knowing this use in "The hunchback in the park" and "Reminiscences of Childhood," we may read welcome into this farewell.

He has come over a hill, and the damp weather has turned around (cf. 114, 165). On the hill's ugly slope is "a capsized field," a brilliant concentration that delights British critics, whether from public schools of the first class or of the second. More than overturned by time and wet, "capsized" means the size, they say, of a school cap, that of Swansea Grammar School. (Hell's Kitchen High, which calls me old boy, has no cap; yet there too the little victims played, regardless of their doom.) "The gentle seaslides of saying" that the poet "must undo" are damp poetic habits and playing at the seaside on slides or on slides in the park. "Charmingly drowned" in his early verse, such memories must rise, crow in a new dawn, and kill. (Killing and undoing are the nature of reality. Cf. "I saw time murder me," 79.) His images must roar, in other words, on heaven's hill (44).

Back in the "reservoir park" by night, he and the other naughty boys annoyed "cuckoo" (mad in spring?) lovers under the trees after the hunchback, sufficiently plagued, had gone home. "The shade of their trees was a word of many shades." This line includes lovers and poet. For them shade was off-colour protection. For him trees were words, and shades of words were the colours of saying. Summer lightning, unwelcome lamp to lovers, was creative spark to him. "The poor in the dark" are both lovers and this poor poet of womb and tomb.

"Now," he says, his "saying" will be his "undoing" (cf. "I

must undo"). This ambiguity means many things: undoing his past, both personal and poetic, by new poetry, for example, and his future by truth and devotion to a killing art. This is fairly clear, but the last line is baffling. How does one wind a stone "off like a reel"? Opposite to water, stones could be the heavy reality he will encounter or the heavy past, now hard and dry. The reel could be that of a fisherman in the reservoir or at the seaslide, fishing for memories, or that of a photographer (cf. 16, 79, 103), snapping memories by "a lamp of lightning." Movies, implying light and projection, preserve the past. If reel is real, is the poet promising a union of memory and reality in new light? Anyway, "cockcrow," "stone," light, and undoing promise a change from charming drowning.

Watkins, 21, 52, 53-54. John Wain, *Preliminary Essays*, 184. Fraser, 19-20. Treece, 102.

Not from this anger (1938; ms. 1933), p. 99

Of another amatory crisis, this little history is as dark as the formidable history of Caitlin's "warring absence." Fourteen lines, some shorter than the rest, and a scheme of odd rhymes tease our expectations of a sonnet. "Unsatisfactory," said Dylan Thomas.

The girl's "refusal" is climax and Dylan's "anger" is "anticlimax" or consequence. His "lame flower" bends like a "beast" (cf. 88) to lap "singular floods" in a hungry land. Lawrence's beast and flower are here, but not his bird. "Singular floods" may be autoerotic as well as lonely and strange.

Anger and singularity cannot create "a bellyfull of weeds" (cf. "lovebeds of the weeds," 12, and "seaweedy," 55), children with "tendril" hands across the seas. Amniotic seas are "agonized," to be sure, but why "two seas"? Two pregnancies? Or is the boy, all at sea, another sea?

The "square of sky" seems a window over the bed. In the window's frame the "golden ball" of the sun, uniting above with below, contrasting fertility with sterility, reminds him of the "circular smile" of perfect love. This circle is squared. And, according to the pathetic fallacy, the sky pathetically sags.

Her refusal, like the sunken bell (cf. 92, 167), cannot create poems. As anger breeds no children in her womb, so it breeds no poems in his mouth. Far from receptive, the "burning mirror" of his eyes (cf. "enamelled eyes," 94) is objective and reflective. What is worse, this mask offers fire for her water, and, hiding him, shows her up. Art may be a mirror held up to nature, but not his art to her nature. That this anger bred even this poem is a paradox.

The manuscript of this poem (in a 1933 notebook) was recast in 1938, apparently with Caitlin in mind. The first two lines remain much the same.

Watkins, 39-40.

How shall my animal (1938; ms. 1930), pp. 100-01

Rhythms indebted to Hopkins prepare for Welsh sounds, also indebted to Hopkins: "Sigh long, clay cold, lie shorn," for example, and "Lie dry, rest robbed, my beast." Examination of these masterly lines shows an interweaving of alliteration, rhyme, and vowels in subtler agreement and disagreement. Elsewhere, internal rhyme ("sigh . . . high . . . dry" and "drops . . . lops") improves the symphony. And there are more great lines. "To trot with a loud mate the haybeds of a mile" recalls Hopkins as "And clap its great blood down" recalls Yeats. A process of terminal sounds also improves the symphony. Agreements (in "s" and "l" in the first stanza, in "s," "t," and "l" in the second) become increasingly complex in the last two. Interrogatives in the first two stanzas yield in the third and fourth to declaratives and imperatives. The craft of Thomas, demonstrated here, needs no further evidence.

What seems at first encounter another vision of embryo and birth seems something more at second and third. More than embryo or Thomas as "beast" (cf. 88, 99), the "animal" (which, a snail at first, becomes octopus, horse, turtle, fish, crab, and bird) suggests the poet's *Anima* or creative imagination and the poem it makes. This, then, is another poem on making a poem and on the nature of Thomas' poetry—still embryonic or newly born, maybe. The bestiary is metaphor for these.

1: The poet's "cavernous skull" is the womb and tomb of his animal *Anima*. Skull as "vessel of abscesses and exultation's shell" brings Baudelaire's "horror and ecstasy of life" to mind. The gestating poem, an invoking thing evoked by druid or magus, has a "wizard shape" and "weird eyes." Question: how can this thing endure "burial" in "shrouding veil" or caul "under the spelling wall" of druid's spell, poet's words, and skull? But cap, veil, and spelling wall do equally well for print. How can a poem endure the confinement of printing? (For printing as entombment see 84-85.) The poem should be free, drunk, flailing, quarreling with the "weathers" of reality. How, without this, can it draw the macrocosmic circle of the skies down to its microcosmic vision? Thomas seems resolved once more to leave his low-vaulted past for loftier and lighter chambers.

2: Magnetizing towards the stallion seems to make Lawrence's St. Mawr or Yeats' winged horse a mare, but trotting with a "loud mate" leaves sex indeterminate. (For Pegasus see 86 and stanza 4.) Anyway, *Anima* or imagination is feminine—"queen of the faculties," as Baudelaire puts it—and creation demands coupling in a "midnight blaze." Lion and horse, head, heel, and shoe, pleasantly confused, imply union of opposites. "Brute land," "country days," and "Love and labour and kill" imply external reality, for whose "quick, sweet, cruel light" the horsing *Anima* longs. Sprouting, the bursting of black seas, and red corpuscles imply birth from water and soil. No longer a wet crab, the beast, "parched" now and raging in the light, must rejoice. Fine lines ensplendor this joyous stanza, along with nicely sprung co-operations of vowels: "locked ground sprout out." We are attending the birth of a poem and the rebirth of a poet.

3: "Fishermen," fishing for fabulous creatures with inadequate "bent pin" and Eucharistic "bridebait" (cf. "The Long-legged Bait") seem other poets, Eliot among them. (Eliot published this poem in his *Criterion*.) They fish the tides, but Thomas fishes in his "curl-locked . . . temple-bound" head, the animal cavepool of the first stanza. Here by the aid of "spells" he examines his octopus, caught and crucified in the cranial "bowl of wounds and weed." He masters his catch as a poet must. This clasped "fury" recalls the long gentleman's "furies" (80) and the furies called by name in "In the Direction of the Beginning." "Atlas" and "horn," also recalling "Altarwise" (80, 82, 85), imply the poet's functions: holding up the daylight world and balancing it by sound (cf. "the globe I balance," 85). "Never" in the penultimate line may mean that the beast must be transformed to become a poem; for a poem is not its origin. But why "few seas" (cf. 2) instead of all? This may imply the selection and limitation of art, as balancing the day on a horn adds point to sound.

4: High and dry on stone (cf. 98), the beast lies caught and shorn. The "scissors" that cut his hair (and probably his umbilicus) are those of life and death, of midwife, of the third fatal sister, and, maybe, of the tailor as creative critic or of the poet as barber. (Thomas was obsessed by scissors, e.g. 12, 21, 24, 147.) More than this, these scissors are those of Delilah cutting Samson's "thicket of strength." However shorn, Samson (cf. 88) will pull the pillars down. (Love's "hewn" temple must be the poem and the poet's "curl-locked" temples. "Carved bird" and the rest seem decorated capitals of the poem's pillars.) The "wrackspiked maiden mouth" (cf. 54) of the *Anima* also unites creation with destruction. Clipping, though apparently destructive, must subdue the bestial poem's "rant." The burning bush (cf. 90), plumed like the Phoenix with Lawrentian and Mosaic flames, seems another moderator of the ranting "gesture of breath." Now a plumed bird, the beast must fall to earth with "red feathers" and die. (Compare "flying heaven" with "flying garden," 85.) Whether from sea or air, the beast, clipped and controlled, must "lie dry" in the light of common day, down to earth in the "whinnying light" of horseplay. But day brings night and life, death. The "grave" of the poem is the dying poet's heart. From the head of the poem's origin we have reached the heart. From womb of a sort we have come to a sort of tomb.

The images that make this point get in each other's way. Whatever the beauties of sound and shape, this "gesture of breath" wants clipping.

Although the manuscript in the 1930 notebook is quite different from the present version, that manuscript establishes the theme as poetry and poetic inspiration.

Watkins, 39-40. Treece, 83. Stanford, 84-85.

The tombstone told when she died (*1938; ms. 1933*), *pp. 102-03*

A letter to Watkins shows that Thomas liked this "Hardy-like" poem more than it deserves. As the previous poem needs a little clipping, so this has had a little too much. For him, however, the clarity that denudes it was an experiment in light. Having emerged from the dark, damp womb, he stands in a graveyard in the rain, contemplating a tomb, and, like Masters of Spoon River, making a fitting story up. Necrophilic fancy lends pathos to this married virgin's tombstone, but the tombstone of Ann Jones, erected by the poet, claimed his heart. This virgin's stone, however, becomes one of the first milestones on the way to Llareggub, Milk Wood, The White Giant, and all the countries of humanity and love. The humor and gusto that relieve the pathos there are suitably lacking here. Sentimental Thomas was to be saved by humor.

The sense is all but immediately clear. Two surnames on the stone, married name and maiden name, direct the poet's fancy. A "virgin married" must lie here after a life of frustration that drove her mad. She died long before Thomas was born. "More the thick stone cannot tell," a fine line, tells almost all. Later, gossips told him more, and he fancies the erotic and obstetrical fancies of a madwoman who died before "bedtime." She corroborates these gossips through the "clipped beak" of the bird on her monument

Tomb in Thomas' early, or even middling, world is never far from womb, which figures twice in this poem. The girl had died before Thomas entered "the looking-glass shell" in his "mother's side" (cf. 82) and long before the "rainy tongue" of his devilish, innocent youth celebrated womb and self, "a secret child." Centered in her womb, this "mad heroine" of a film hears the womb "bellowing." "Blazing," a word deliberately picked, seemed suitably "violent" to Thomas, and "dear," however "dangerous" and "daring," suitably pathetic and "very moving." (Hopkins and Yeats had dared such dangers.) "Bellowing," "devilish," and "innocent" also seemed *mots justes* to their chooser. The "hurried film" (cf. 16, 79, 82, 98), he said, represents "the winding cinematic works of the womb."

The rhythm is sprung. The structure is tight: as the hand of the virgin's husband, for example, plunges ineffectually through her hair, so her hand through the hair of her imagined son. "Plunged" in the twelfth line accounts for "floods" in the last. But movement is the formal triumph. Three end-stopped lines dramatically introduce, after the manner of Beethoven, a free run of six lines. A single end-stopped line interrupts the flow, which resumes with a run of ten lines. And then the flooding conclusion.

The virgin's husband, conspicuous in the early manuscript (considerably revised in 1938), is a farmer, and the virgin dies in her wedding dress.

Watkins, 43-45. Ihab H. Hassan, in *Explicator*, XV (November 1956).

On no work of words (*1939; ms. 1933?*), *p. 104*

Four self-contained yet logically related triplets suggest terza rima as Thomas' sonnets suggest sonnets. Scanning the first line proves the rhythm sprung. But this freedom, within tight structure, does not extend to the movement, which monotonously pauses at triplet's end—except for the initial pause in the last. The triplets of Wallace Stevens are more flexible.

Poets—Hopkins and Yeats, for example—like to write poems about being unable to write poems. Handy, moving, and less paradoxical than it seems, this subject primes the pump.

On the occasion of "no work of words now for three lean months" Thomas lets "rich year," "big purse," and "poverty" dictate an elaborate metaphor of money (pounds, marks, currencies, treasure, expensive, rake, pay, and count), which leads to giving, taking, and two givens: manna and dew. The colon at the end of the first triplet introduces three parallel infinitives of taking, lifting, and surrendering. These infinitives may serve as thesis, antithesis, and synthesis. The poet's structural "craft," is more in evidence, until the final lines, than "the lovely gift of the gab."

Poetry, says Thomas, is a gift, like manna or dew, from

heaven. "Hungrily," apparently misplaced, applies more properly to taker than to giver. The poet, a manna puffer, takes his heavenly gift to give it back to heaven. But now the lovely gift, like a lift in its shaft or a horse (cf. "blind horse," 96) in his shaft "bangs back," frustrated by dead end. The forked concentration of "blind shaft" denies the shaft's blindness.

"Lift" means raise or steal. To take, not from heaven, but from the works of previous poets ("the treasures of man") is deathly, however pleasing. ("Mature poets steal," says T. S. Eliot in his essay on Massinger.) To steal "currencies of the marked breath" or other poets' poems is to forsake creative mystery and to replace good dark by bad. To surrender one's gift by stealing or submitting to silence is to die twice, poetically once and once actually.

By the ancient, druidical woods of his Welsh blood, Thomas swears never to take either to, only to, or in order to destroy or imitate this world, which is either the place of our daily work or which, according to Kant, each man must create. Of whichever kind, this world is not manna-dropping heaven. But what is "the nut of the seas" that Welsh woods must dash down to? Trees are the spelling words of the "syllabic blood," as we know from "Especially when the October wind." Trees bear nuts, but here is a nut of the seas, and woods dash down like waves. Aside from the possibility of reversal: are the trees of land exhorted to drown themselves or to rescue a drowned nut—nutty, "tide-tongued" Dylan, perhaps? Is this nut the nucleus of the alien sea or the fruit of the womb that must be brought to light and land for use by wizards? Whatever this nut (and it is there in the earliest manuscript) or the purpose and manner of dashing down, the last lines, endlessly suggestive, have a fine sound. What more should we ask of a "many sounding minded" druid?

A saint about to fall (1939), *pp. 105-07*

The way to light from womb and tomb was encumbered with tombs and wombs—or else, walking toward light, like Orpheus, Thomas looked back; for womb and tomb were hard as hell to abandon. But there is a difference sometimes in the point of view. No longer his private places, seen from within, tomb and womb are sometimes those of others—tombs of Ann Jones and a married virgin, and here the womb of his wife. This poem, once called "Poem in the Ninth Month," is addressed to his unborn child. "In September," an earlier title that accounts for the frightening imagery, refers to one of Hitler's crises. Fear of war in the fall of 1938 becomes fear for the saintly child, about to enter a terrible world. This poem tells the child what to expect. Syntactical obscurity vies with clotted imagery to conceal this revelation from all but the shrewdest child. Yet something emerges somehow for all but the dullest adult. Free rhythm responds to each requirement.

The typographical divisions in the American edition are misleading. This poem, as reference to *The Map of Love* assures us, has three stanzas of seventeen lines each. Within these stanzas are four quatrains and one line for good measure.

1: An enormous sentence—if it can be called this—discloses heaven or the womb on the eve of violent birth. Thomas was always confusing womb with heaven; but, as earth below knows explosion, fire, flood, and agony, so heaven above or heaven within. The embryonic saint, falling on earth like Adam or, like Lucifer, falling from heaven to hell, is suffering and rising Jesus— or, to give analogy its due, like Him. Hymns praising Him are ceremonies after fire raid and flood. "Flames and shells," becoming devotional objects, fittingly combine fire, water, and destruction from the air.

In the celestial air raid, "flats" (plains, apartments) are "razed" and raised by an explosion which also raises the saint like a kite above the "last street." Kissing the hem of his shawl is a sign of devotion during this ascent. What fire has left is flooded out, and the saint, once blown up, goes down to the bottom of the sea. The flooding wave praises destruction of father's house (at Laugharne and mother's womb), artfully "woven" on the sands of time. "Song by rock," joining "hymned," appropriately suggests "Rock of Ages" and Toplady, its composer. The unwinding of song and the winding down of the clock introduce the sunken bell of a ship. ("Chucked," a wonderful word, means patted lovingly or thrown away.) "Ship-work," which is "musical" because of song and bell, refers, like all other images to the works and days of the womb, "the blood-counting clock" of nine months. "Behind a face of hands," which combines clock with grief thief of time, is surrealistic if taken at face value. (For shipwork and flood see xvii, 141; for streets of the holy city see 109; for fire and flood see 143-46.)

Flood becomes fire again. The volcanic eruption (cf. 83) of birth disturbs the "wind-heeled" angels of the "whirring feather-lands." Watery womb becomes "fireball." Does "etna" suggest falling Empedocles? Saint seems the subject of "hymned" and "sang," the main verbs, maybe, of what cannot be called a sentence. As his flock of attendant angels is "shrivelling" in the fire, the saint becomes Christ, "the quick / Cut Christbread spitting vinegar" on the cross. Christbread or Eucharist, quick cut and cut to the quick, includes the spilled "wine" and the burning "rick" of grain. "Vinegar and all" combines a squinting grammatical construction with a pun: and gall, in one sense, "and all / The mazes" in another.

What does this confusion add up to? The violence of birth is a foretaste of violence on earth. Birth and life are agony on the cross. Eucharistic everyman must be consumed. Certainly this confusion imitates the confusion of birth and world. We know that art is imitation, whatever that may mean; but should art be as lavishly mimetic as this?

2: "Glory cracked like a flea," a "grotesque contrast," said Thomas, must come here as a necessary shock. After that first stanza, a short, complete sentence is shocking, to be sure, and any great line shocks us awake. This great line unites shocking opposites: the great and the small, the abstract and the concrete, creation and destruction, earth and heaven, the infra dig and the dig. This insect, bringing us down to earth, is today and the world we breathe. The fleas of Laugharne crack at doom.

"Candlewoods," resinous pinetrees literally, are holy candles of the Son, holy woods in the sun, poems maybe, and, when burnt, the cross. "Black buds" are uncertain and certain promise. "Fishgilled boats" of blood combine Christ as fish, the embryo recapitulating phylogeny, and mother's feeding corpuscles. The "scuttled sea"—maybe crab-crowded but surely a dazzling reversal and union of sea and ship—is the womb at the moment of birth. Both "leeches and straws" in the hold of the scuttled womb promise sucking (cf. "milk in your mouth"); and straws are for a manger. This fall from falling amniotic heaven leaves one "crocked bell." Meaning impaired, killed, soiled, or drunken, "crocked," a great word, joins birth and religion with poetry and child with father. "Wake in me" assures this identification.

Becoming hortatory, the rest of the stanza is father's advice to son and self. The main verbs (wake, puzzle, stare, see) are imperatives. Let the child see, as father sees, what threatens both: "a war of burning brains and hair." The length and movement of this ponderous line suit the horror.

This house in the mud of the squawking shore is the poet's house at Laugharne, to which he has fled, as if "flicked," from London, "the carbolic city" (cf. 86). (Dissatisfied with "carbolic," Thomas was unable to find a better word. For deadly acid see "The Lemon.") Mud and cloud, sour and sweet work in a structure of opposites. "Bed of sores," uniting mother and child, lightens puerperal bedsores.

3: Hortatory verbs (strike, raise, throw, wail, wake, and cry) continue to direct the action. "The time-bomb town" is heaven, womb, and Laugharne. Raising the eardrum combines embryonic development with the hearing of horrors. Throwing Cerberus a stone or bone fits our hell. Though still in the "dark asylum" of the womb, this child of nine months is "lapped" (probably in several senses) by "herods," only one of whom threatened Christ. "Wail . . . That the eyes," as well as the ears and heart, are destroyed by horrors. If "agony has another mouth to feed" refers not only to Jesus, everyman, and this world, but also to father's budget, cheerfulness breaks through. If "dishrag hands" and "sponge" refer not only to Jesus on the cross but also to mother in the kitchen, cheerfulness breaks through again.

In "the old mud hatch," mud may be adjective or noun and hatch may be noun or verb. The "bolt" seems primarily an image of fear, and the "stranger" seems to combine emerging child (cf. "iron head," 108) with menacing Herod.

Be this menace what it may, "Cry joy." These are the important words (cf. Isaiah 40:5-6; 66:10); for however bad, life is good, and this "noble fall," like Adam's, is happy. The "witchlike midwife second" of birth flicks (cf. "flicked") on sunlight by a switch and bullies the child from his "girl-circled island" into rough seas. "Bullies," "bullring," and "island" (cf. "mazes") bring the Minotaur of Crete to mind. (Compare the black sail of Theseus, 10. In the 1930's Picasso also found the bull a fitting image of our world.) The rhythm of the last lines, intentionally "ragged," accords with violence. The last line, in contrast with "you so gentle," said Thomas, "must roar."

Watkins, 45, 47, 49.

'If my head hurt a hair's foot' (1939), pp. 108-09

The pregnancy that detained Thomas in "A saint about to fall" detains him again. But, in spite of many echoes, there are differences here in theme and treatment. The first poem is a celebration of child and womb. The second, a celebration of child and mother, is a step forward—from impersonal organ to person. This poem has attracted more critical attention than the first; for not only more humane, this is simpler.

Thomas, his own critic, called it "a series of conflicting images" which is "deeply felt," he felt. Other feelings differ. Elizabeth Drew and John Sweeney found the poem "luminous." Treece found it "turgid." Denouncing Thomas as fake—as great a fake as Yeats or Hopkins—Robert Graves called it "nonsensical" and "disgusting."

Nothing by Thomas could be plainer than this debate between embryo and mother. In the first three stanzas, the unborn child gallantly offers to stay where he is should his birth give mother pain. In the remaining three stanzas, mother replies that, once started, the process of life must continue to the end. There is no going back. But there is looking back: Thomas wrote this poem about two months after the birth of his polite and gallant son.

Occasion, theme, and feeling are of less interest than method. We are familiar with the process of conflicting images and with quarrels among words from incompatible areas. But here, directed by Hopkins, are advances in rhythm and sound. Excellently sprung, but freer than those of Hopkins, the lines unsystematically display all the devices of Welsh sound: alliteration, as-

sonance, dissonance, internal rhyme, and chiming vowels. Consider "Pack back the downed bone" or "Bump on a spout let
the bubbles jump out." Nothing more symphonic since Hopkins,
and no better shape of sounds. Thomas was learning, moreover,
that sentences need not begin with the beginning of a line or end
with its ending. Beginning within the line has rhythmic importance. Now, no longer obtrusive and alone, fine lines serve the
whole. The critic Stanford, dismissing this symphony, found
Thomas "deaf to sound."

1: Hair and foot, anatomical extremes, find reconciliation in
"hair's foot" at the pubic middle. Promising no harm to this,
the embryo, still "unpricked" in several senses, also promises no
interference with father's "spout." This imagery is at once familiar and extravagant—but so, after all, a speaking embryo. Compare the "bubbles" of unpricked breath with the "swag of
bubbles in a seedy sack" (76). "The worm of the ropes" seems
umbilical, phallic, and deathly. Better polite death than playing
the bully to parental loving, however "ill" or ill-timed. "Clouted,"
which echoes "out," involves amatory striking and, by anticipation, swaddling. Note the vowels of the fourth line.

2: He is "game" and his game words fit this parental cockpit.
Let him remain like a poacher with dark lantern in the "snared
woods" of the womb or, a bird himself, let him "duck time."
Blamelessly dancing in the dark on father's spouting fountains is
better than becoming a nuisance in the light and air of loud and
bloody birth (cf. 155). The "ghost with a hammer," in apposition
with "air," is as menacing as light. Reluctance vies with politeness to prevent rushing this ghost of air in the crouch of "bunched,
monkey coming."

3: If his birth gives the feet of mother's hairs pain, let her
"rage" him back to the "making house" or womb. "A cross place,"
childbed (cf. "a bed of sores," 106) is mother's bother and crucifixion. Compare the "riderless shape" of the returning steeplechaser with "the riderless dead" (42). The "nine thinning
months" of reversed direction are opposite to the nine fattening
months of gestation.

4: Mother says, "No," but, like Mrs. Bloom's first word, this no
becomes yes at last. Thrust your "iron head" (cf. 107) out at
whatever cost, she says. No dream of the "dazzling" heaven of

Christ or the "nacreous" peace of Venus, no fear of pain can make her change what, after all, is inevitable. You must thrust to escape what there is no escape from: "none, none, none." The poetry may be in the pity, as Wilfred Owen said. But more than moving, the last two lines are a triumph of movement.

5: Empty and dark as a cave and "husked of gestures," she is awake to anguish, death, and necessity. The child, bumped on a spout and "forever unfree," must be "bounced" from the womb as from a pub. (The pub in "The Peaches" is called "The Hare's Foot.") Slang, apparently at odds with high compassion, intensifies it here. "This way" is toward light and death. "The rim of the grave" (cf. "breast of the grave," 143) is womb and tomb, both of which are crying houses.

6: There is no choice. There is no return for "dust-appointed" seed. "Fat streets" and "thin ways" are of womb and tomb, as shut to coming or return as metaphorical and literal stone. But the last line of suffering cries joy; for life is "endless beginning" and miracle. Joyous, ultimate "open" counteracts desperate "shut" in the penultimate line as endless beginning contradicts inevitable end. A less admirable version of the last line, given in a letter to Watkins—"And the endless, tremendous beginning suffers open" —is another proof that poetry consists of right words in the right places, put there by poets, but who knows how? So put, the words of the last line share glory now with those that end "Ceremony After a Fire Raid."

Watkins, 58-60. Thomas, "On Reading One's Own Poems," *Quite Early*, 169. Graves, in *Casebook*, 165. Drew and Sweeney, *Directions in Modern Poetry*, 111-12. John L. Sweeney, Introduction to *Selected Writings*, xviii. Stanford, 85-86. Olson, 44. Treece, 103.

Twenty-four years (1938), *p.* 110

As womb put Thomas in mind of tomb, so his birthday put him in mind of the day of his death. This lean celebration of the fatal, vital years belongs with "Poem in October," "Poem on His Birthday," and "Especially when the October wind," first of the series but not altogether typical of it. By lucky accident his springing forth coincided with the year's autumnal decline. Congenial by timing to a poet of tombs, his birthday, like anyone's, justified concern with self. Whenever else is one more fittingly one's hero? Thomas was "terribly pleased" with his "Twenty-four years."

The agreement in sound and sense of "years," "tears," and "fear" pleased him, no doubt, but the last line, bold yet linked by a sort of rhyme with the quiet first line, pleased him more. This final line, written years earlier and retrieved from a notebook, now finds, he said, its "inevitable place." A very good line, it concentrates many feelings and ideas. "Advance" and "forever" seem courageous, enterprising, and hopeful. But "as long as forever," reconsidered, abandons eternity for time or mixes them. To a pious man, forever means life after death. An impious man's long forever is his short life. Here, pious and impious together, Thomas is serious and ironic, hopeful and discouraged. Playing with what concerned him most was his joy forever, as long as he lived.

He worried unnecessarily about the parenthetical second line, which, it is true, means nothing certain. But a good line, exceeding sense, may invite satisfying guesses by sound, rhythm, and hints of sense. "Labour" could mean Adam's curse and Eve's or any trouble of the day. If obstetrical, labouring makes this "grave" the womb. Burial of the dead, leaving The Book of Common Prayer, could mean begetting a child. "Fear" belongs to life and death; fear of the walking dead could be fear of, or for, the living or of living. "Walk," anticipating "advance," must be distinguished from "strut." Rich in possibilities and more emphatic than what it seems to interrupt, this fine-sounding parenthesis, plainly of life and death, is suitably elusive. We should be foolish to ask more of it than it offers.

The history of Thomas begins in the third line. As embryo-tailor (cf. "Once below a time"), he sews the "shroud" for his life and death. His journey, a "walk to the grave," is under "the meat-eating sun" of time. "Shroud" is both flesh and winding sheet, and the grave he advances toward is sexual experience as well as tomb. "Dressed to die" in his shroud of flesh, he is dressed to kill, dressed for death, and, by a familiar pun, dressed to make love. Compare the "sensual strut" of jaunty young Thomas with his strut as a "strutting fern" (97) and his swanking in astonish ing disguises (147). His veins "full of money" (corpuscles literally) pay for his jaunt. As he struts, his blood is spent—and his meat eaten.

The "final direction" is his end in two senses: death and chosen course. Since "elementary" means basic, ultimate, rudimentary, and pertaining to first principles, "the elementary town" could be womb or tomb. As the poet lives to die, so he dies to live and to renew life.

Watkins, 47-48, 49. Fraser, 20. Stanford, 83, 88-89. Geoffrey Moore, in Tedlock, 257. Andrews Wanning, in *The Southern Review*, VI (Spring 1941). Karl Shapiro, in *Casebook*, 178. John L. Sweeney, Introduction, *Selected Writings*, xix.

Deaths and Entrances, 1946

The *Collected Poems* is faithful to the text of *Deaths and Entrances*, with these exceptions: for "Paper and Sticks" Thomas substituted "Do not go gentle," a poem from *In Country Sleep*; he added "Once below a time" from *New Poems, 1943*. Most of the poems of *Deaths and Entrances* are vintage Thomas of the years 1939-45. "The hunchback in the park" and "On the Marriage of a Virgin" are no less sound; for Thomas remade the early texts in a good year.

The Conversation of Prayer (*1945*), *p. 111*

The two climbing the stairs to bed with arising prayers in mind may be Thomas and son or Thomas as man and boy. Literally, they may be talking about the prayers they are about to say. But the words "conversation" and "turns," the clues to sense, have many senses. Talking together is but the most familiar sense of "conversation," which carries from its Latin roots the idea of turning around, transposing, returning, answering, interchanging, exchanging. To converse may be to converge, approach, convert, or reverse. "Turns," a limiting word, makes turning about or interchanging emerge from these possibilities (cf. "turned around," 114). "Prayers" in the first line is "Prayer" in the title, where two have turned to one. Whereas the plural allows talking about particular prayers, the singular, making prayer general, puts emphasis on turning around. These words in mind, we should have no trouble with the sense of the poem. The prayers meditated on the stairs will be reversed in time: the boy's prayer will be the man's as the man's approximates the boy's. Interchange brings man and boy, confronting life, together—more or less.

A structure of interchanging rhymes, fitting this idea, brings it out. "Prayers" and "said" in the first line rhyme with "bed" and "stairs" in the second. "Love" and "room" in the third line rhyme, crisscross, with "whom" and "move" in the fourth. This interweaving, with the effect of chiasmus, embodies in sound and pattern the idea of exchange, which terminal rhymes also support. The rhyming of the last word of the first line with the last word of the fifth and the last word of the poem makes extremes converge. This poem of a conversation is a conversation of sounds.

Such oral trickery, distantly Welsh, seems almost too clever. But the poem is saved from the virtuosity of the craftsman by his humanity, tone, and feeling—by heavy sounds, brooding movement, and ritualistic or incantatory repetition. As the elements of sense, sound, rhythm, and feeling admirably conspire, the effect of their singular interaction is single. Nothing like this co-operation of craft and feeling in recent works of words.

In the first line "about," which, doing double duty, belongs with both "prayers" and "to be said," may anticipate the turnabout on which the poem hinges. The identity of the "dying love" upstairs is unimportant. Whoever the woman and whether she is ill or well, she must die one day. The point is the man's awareness of death and the boy's indifference. Anapaests and conjunctions of two unstressed syllables with two stressed syllables ("in her high room," for example) dominate the rhythm, which becomes troubled in the last line.

In the second stanza "Turns" gains importance from place.

The pattern of internal rhymes is that of the first stanza until "sound" in the fourth line adds a further agreement. Grammatical structure, no longer coincident with stanzaic structure, provides interweaving of another kind. Movement becomes an interchange between two structures.

The third line of the third stanza, a return to the opening line of the poem, and the repetition of "Turns" in the fifth line mark the turning point of the structure. Two questions, preparing the way for turning, provide suspense. "The same grief flying" anticipates the conversion without weakening it. Turning on "the quick and the dead" (from Acts 10:42 and The Book of Common Prayer), their prayers become common. As the man's prayer turns about on finding his love quick, so the boy's prayer will turn on finding the quick soon dead. ("Climbs," the *mot juste*, is transitive. Compare "climbs" in the first stanza and "arise" in the second.) Someday, like Hopkins' grieving Margaret and the girl of "In Country Sleep," the boy will know the grief of time and life. Even now, before he has changed place with the man, a dark dream may drag the boy to the man's bitter knowledge. Though the man's prayer is granted for the night, the boy's, still about to be said, may climb unheard in the coming night.

Internal dissonance of "fire" and "care" in the last stanza and assonance of "grief as deep" and "made grave" improve the dark symphony. The "made grave," prepared and awaiting the sleeper, is the made bed upstairs.

Mary Ellen Rickey, in *Explicator*, XVI (December 1957). Robert C. Jones, in *Explicator*, XVII (April 1959). Geoffrey Moore, in Tedlock, 255-57. Fraser, 26-28. John Wain, *Preliminary Essays*, 184. Stanford, 92-93. Watkins, 126.

A Refusal to Mourn the Death, by Fire, of a Child in London (1945), p. 112

The war "of burning brains and hair" (106), feared no more, provided elegiac Thomas with welcome replacements for Ann Jones and the married virgin. Here, the girl to be mourned has ruined house or street for tombstone to tell where she died. In **burning babies and water to put them out** Thomas found an agreeable subject. Fire and water are destructive and vital. Brightness falling from air to earth rounds the cycle of elements out. A burning baby, moreover, has religious importance, as Robert Southwell's poem proves. The "majesty and burning" of the child in "A Refusal to Mourn" dim the fires of "The Burning Baby," a short story, but not those of "Ceremony After a Fire Raid," the ultimate celebration.

Ritual turns on paradox. Here, the ceremonious elegist paradoxically refuses to mourn what he mourns—or, as William Empson says, the poet says he will not say what he says. But holy paradox and holy airs, less than orthodox here, serve romantic piety alone. Nature is "holy," as Thomas tells the sleeping child of "In Country Sleep." We come from nature and return to it for secular renewal with the bees and flowers. From this the comfort that elegy demands and for this the holy images are metaphor.

1: The words from "mankind" to "humbling" compose a grand, Germanic, unhyphenated adjective, which modifies "darkness," our origin and our end—or, as the imagery of making, light, and sea implies, our Genesis and Apocalypse, our first light and our last. Lawrentian darkness fathers Lawrence's "Bird beast and flower" to establish the idea of nature and romantic holiness and to make mankind one with other living and dying creatures. "Making" and "fathering," the words for creation, are displaced from their proper objects to show the unity of man, beast, and flower. Properly speaking, creation, which fathers man, makes the flowers. "Tumbling in harness," the sea of Genesis and Apocalypse seems a horse—Poseidon's maybe—driven by the moon and to be ridden by the river. The rhythm is freely sprung. Rhymes and near-rhymes maintain an appropriate balance.

2: On the day of doom Thomas, as mankind's representative, must return to the seed and water from which he came and to which this child, also mankind's representative, has preceded him. "Zion," "synagogue," and "sackcloth" bring holiness from the Old Testament to natural water and seed. The "water bead" (cf. Ann Jones' "still drop" and the "water drop" of "A Prospect of the Sea," 133, 135) recalls Andrew Marvell's microcosmic "Drop of Dew" and Donne's tear as world in "A Valediction: of Weeping." "Bead," while maintaining the air of ritual, violates that of the Old Testament. They tell no beads in a Zion, whether

Jewish temple or Protestant chapel. "The ear of corn" (wheat), a natural congregation of grains, becomes a synagogue or supernatural congregation. Zion and synagogue establish the holiness of nature, for which no Jewish wailing in sackcloth and ashes will do. "Sow my salt seed" is complex. Since seeds and drops of water are fertile and salt is sometimes sterile, "salt seed" is a kind of paradox, implying maybe that as you sow, so shall you weep. Sterile, fertile weeping joins praying the "shadow of a sound" among the poet's refusals. Both may imply the elegy he is writing while refusing to do so.

3: Any punning elegy or "grave truth" would diminish the "majesty" of this child's death, which becomes that of all "mankind." Christianity, replacing Judaism, provides the stations of the cross, which romantically become "the stations of the breath": life, poetry, and all human, rather than divine, suffering. Jesus is the embodiment of mankind, and mankind is one with bird, beast and flower, poet and child. The force through the green fuse moves them all through life to death.

4: Meanwhile "London's daughter" lies deep in London's hell with the "first dead," those killed in the first raid and Adam and Eve themselves. All have returned to their dark origins, the water bead, the ear of corn, and the earth. "Grains beyond age" are seeds and sands of time, "long friends" in respect of time and by congregation in a long ear of wheat. (Compare "long sea," 42, "long world," 80, and "grains," 143.) The daughter's mother seems both London and the earth, darkly veined with rivers or, as Empson thinks, with ore. Earth's water, like the water bead and the elegist, is "unmourning" because it is the water of life and renewal. Here is water to put fire out and bring seed to light. (Compare the watery ending of "Ceremony After a Fire Raid.") The "riding Thames" is a river of life, flowing out to the harnessed sea, maybe in order to ride it. Individual river puts out to general sea. "Rode" is sexual (125), but a rider is Thomas' image of time (58) and the girl of "In Country Sleep" rides to sleep (181). (Compare Hopkins' "it rides time like riding a river" and his "riding" windhover.) Thomas' "riding Thames" can include any or all of these possibilities—or others.

The last line, rising to majesty, provides elegiac consolation for the simple reader and for the alert, a pleasing doubt. "The first death," recalling "the first dead," could be that of Adam, Eve, Jesus, this child, or anybody. (Compare Donne's "an *issue* from the *first death*," "Death's Duell.") That "there is no other" death after the first means, as the context demands, that death is followed by perpetual life: Christian heaven or natural rebirth in bird or flower. In either case "death shall have no dominion." But, whatever the demands of context and the elegiac tradition, this line is ambiguous. "After the first death, there is no other" can mean that death is death. There is no other because, once dead, you are dead for good. A poet as aware as Thomas of what he was about must have intended this ambiguity, which seems there to combine with admirable exactness and condensation his two beliefs: that life is eternal and death, final. The believing unbeliever, at once holy and secular, hopeful and desperate, believed what he knew to be untrue. This great and fitting conclusion to a structure of paradoxes precisely joins what a double talker wants with what he knows.

Flocking to this poem, critics disagree. For some, especially followers of F. R. Leavis, "A Refusal to Mourn" is vague, pretentious, and, compared with *Daniel Deronda*, repulsive. For others it is the most remarkable poem of the war and one of the great poems of our time. Dame Edith admired "its dark and magnificent, proud movement." Honest Mr. Empson has what should be the last word: "a good deal which I feel I haven't got to the bottom of."

William Empson, in *The Strand*, March 1947. Edith Sitwell, in *Casebook*, 126-27. Henry Gibson, in *Tedlock*, 151-52. John Wain, *Preliminary Essays*, 182. Fraser, 29. Robin Mayhead, in *Scrutiny*, XIX (Winter 1952-53). John Davenport, in *Twentieth Century*, February 1953. Stanford, 96-98. John A. Clair, in *Explicator*, XVII (December 1958). Thomas recorded this poem, Caedmon, 1018.

Poem in October (1945), *pp. 113-15*

Differing in light and movement from its predecessors in the great sequence of birthday odes ("Twenty-four years" and "Especially when the October wind," which was once called "Poem in October"), this poem of October, written in August, 1944, begins the celebration of childhood that was to culminate in "Fern Hill" and the reminiscences of *Quite Early One Morning.* In "A Prospect of the Sea," a story, Thomas had revisited the farm, also the place of "After the funeral." In other poems he had revisited Cwmdonkin Park (e.g. 19, 72) with its "star-gestured" children, himself among them. But here he emerges from the limits of that park as from those of the womb before it. Here, discovering all the green and golden light of childhood, he discovers a measure as young and easy as his theme. This coming to light, toward which he had struggled so long through darkness, may be a retreat—what psychologists might call regression; but let them worry about that while we, enlightened by glory, freely range an actual yet visionary place. Thomas, too, was lost in admiration of this "Laugharne poem," which, he said in a letter to Watkins, must be read aloud for its "lovely slow lyrical movement."

Verlaine, whom Thomas knew little or nothing about, has the exact words for this sort of thing:

> De la musique avant toute chose,
> Et pour cela préfère l'Impair
> Plus vague et plus soluble dans l'air,
> Sans rien en lui qui pèse ou qui pose.
>
> Il faut aussi que tu n'ailles point
> Choisir tes mots sans quelque méprise:
> Rien de plus cher que la chanson grise
> Où l'Indécis au Précis se joint.

Thomas' movement of light and sound in time and place depends for its precision and imprecision in part upon a loosening of rhythm, in part upon dream syntax, and in part upon the stanza's shape and concerts of vowels within it. Terminal assonance has replaced habitual dissonance or rhyme. (In the second stanza, for example, "name" agrees with "days" and "gates"; "horses" agrees with "rose," "road," "border," and "awoke.") Internal vowels are no less symphonic: "Of the town closed as the town awoke." These sounds of words and words of sounds are as simple as the public image they compose.

Not here that old contention of weird images in a private dark.

Not here a speaking embryo or some burning babe or a nameless boy on the stairs. The child is Dylan himself, discovered by new lighting and improved by time.

If we must look beyond memory, brought back by Laugharne, for a literary inspiration, we must look to Henry Vaughan, whom Thomas praises in his essay on Welsh poets (*Quite Early One Morning*) as "a magician of intervals." Quoting "The Night," Thomas admires Vaughan's "sacred landscape" with visionary figures. Not this poem, however, but "Regeneration" and "The Retreate" seem more immediately relevant. In "Regeneration" Vaughan walks abroad in the morning to encounter two places and two weathers, as Thomas was to do in this poem. In "The Retreate," as everybody knows, Vaughan anticipates the glory of Wordsworth's "Intimations of Immortality," which Thomas must have known. He was to see, in another part of Wales, Vaughan's "Bright *shootes* of everlastingnesse," to share his desire, and to approximate his condition:

> Happy those early dayes! when I
> Shin'd in my Angell-infancy.
> . . . .
> O how I long to travell back
> And tread again that ancient track!
> . . . .
> But (ah!) my soul with too much stay
> Is drunk, and staggers in the way.

1: "To heaven" may mean toward or offered to. Since heaven is womb in the earlier poems (101, 105), it is also tomb. Here, while retaining these intimations, it means, primarily, ascent toward light up "heaven's hill" (44), where images rise and roar. Not roaring now, the images are descriptive. As the poet leaves Laugharne in the morning (cf. "Quite Early One Morning"), he finds nature holy. The water prays and the herons, like those of "Over Sir John's hill" and "Author's Prologue," are priests. The "knock" of boats is at once unlike and like (since this is a birthday) the knock of birth (8). In the earlier poems the boat, now part of the scenery, would have been a metaphor (e.g. 87).

Scanning these flowing lines seems less useful than sensitive abandonment to them. Our voices will know how to read them, but their best interpreter was Dylan's voice.

2: Even here "the winged trees" that fly his name, though literal, are trees as poems (cf. 19), too. (These winged trees were "bare" until Thomas, remembering that October is leafy, changed the word.) The name flown by poetic birds and trees may be "High tide," the English equivalent for Dylan and his description. High or not, the poet walks through a lovely confusion of farm and shore, of actuality and memory, "over the border" of times and weathers. "Gates," closing as the town awakes, imply rebirth (from a public womb) on this birthday. Dylan climbs heaven's hill toward sunlight in the autumn rain, a birthday "shower" of all his days, as the heron, returning to water, dives. This side of the border, birds and things, however holy, are wet.

3: Over the border and onto the hill, above the clouds below, he suddenly comes into October sun, which, confusing seasons and climates, is both springlike and summery. Confusion of seasons portends timelessness. Two weathers and two times attend the autumn that makes him a larkful of springs. His poetic development has found its fitting image.

4: Down there, "pale rain" and "snail," assonant and wet, join the autumnal castle, "brown as owls," and "the dwindling harbour" (cf. 167). "Beyond the border" are gardens of spring and summer, clouded by larks alone. The "tall tales" link the "hobnail tales" of childhood (181) with "fibs of vision" (48). The last three lines, repeated in the seventh stanza, are pivotal. Two weathers in one day seem marvel enough, but here are two times as well. "The weather turned around," embodying more than weather and its ponderous yet sudden movement, unites weathers and times. For the rest of the poem there are two actual weathers and two times, one present and one past, both simultaneous. Present weather turning to evoke a past allows what Ford Madox Ford called a "time shift" and Proust, a "privileged moment." In the twelfth book of "The Prelude" Wordsworth calls such moments "spots of time," which bring back "renovating" glimpses of "youth's golden gleam."

5: This turning from October sun brings back the forgotten summer of childhood at Swansea and Fern Hill, abounding in fruit; for two times involve two or more places. "The green chapels" (cf. the "brown chapel" of Ann Jones, 96) and "the parables / Of sun light" prove nature holy again and childhood holy. "Parables" and "legends," "the tall tales" of the previous stanza, are the fictions and wonders of childhood. "And," which dominates the syntax from here on, as it dominates the syntax of "Fern Hill," serves logic less than dream. According to Freud, "and" is dream's chosen connective. Sunlight and green trees are the glory of Fern Hill, recaptured—all that "I saw in the turning." Like "The Conversation of Prayer," this poem turns on the idea of "turning," which replaces "border" as principal word. If "sun," significantly separated from "light," is another pun on son or the boy himself, this stanza is his parable of "sun light," and he, one of the boys of summer.

6: "The twice told fields" of the recaptured past are its twice-told tales, the wonder book of childhood's green parables and golden legends. "That his tears burned my cheeks" makes boy and poet, past and present, Laugharne and Swansea, one. The "summertime of the dead" is the boy's past (cf. "Return Journey"). As his ghost whispers "the truth of his joy," so "the mystery" still sings alive in nature.

Mystery singing alive and truth of joy are good descriptions of this poetic co-operation of boy and poet—the conscious poet, whose vision, as usual, is double. Seeing the object, as in "After the funeral" and "A Refusal to Mourn," he sees himself writing about it. No poet has written more telling descriptions of what he has written.

7: Repeating elements of the first, fourth, and sixth stanzas, this is a recapitulation. However moving, the vision is static. "The weather turned around" is not a new turning but a return to the first. "The long dead child" is from "the summertime of the dead." No baby but a child's "true joy" (cf. "the truth of his joy") sings burning in this poem. Like Blake's child, this child says, "Joy is my name." Though the poet still stands in the "summer noon" of childhood, he is aware of the town below, "leaved with October blood"—of trees and of his October heart, which sings this truth. May he write poems as good as this on this heavenly hill "in a year's turning." "Turning," the great word of transformation and time, is, as it should be, last. Time's magic has evoked the timeless-ness of art.

Stephen Spender, *Poetry Since 1939*, 45. John L. Sweeney, Introduction, *Selected Writings*, xviii. "Pleasure Dome," a Columbia record (ML-4259), includes Thomas' reading of this poem.

This side of the truth (for Llewelyn) (1945), *pp. 116-17*

Perplexed by plain words, condensation, and his six years, Llewelyn, who, as saint about to fall, had been advised before, may have found himself unable to profit by father's disenchanting advice on the present occasion. For discouragement as profound as A. E. Housman's, father approximates Housman's neatness. Tidy triplets of two or three sprung stresses to the line and rhymes, pretty good on the whole, reveal the moral untidiness of things. Plain words allow ambiguity, however, and with ambiguity a little hope.

Subjects separated from their verbs and qualifiers from what they qualify should cause no trouble. The sense of the first stanza easily emerges: from your position, my son, you may not see that all is predestined, meaningless, and doomed. "This side" of a truth that has two sides seems father's view that "all is undone." In spite of his blue eyes, Llewelyn, on that side, is blinded by youth to father's vision of futility. The skies, "unminding . . . of innocence and guilt" are amoral and indifferent. All is fixed before you start. Whatever your human gestures and desires, you must come to dust, the "winding dark" of winding sheet, clock, and labyrinthine process. Lack of expected rhyme makes "make" and "dark" stand out.

Once a Puritan (in "Because the pleasure-bird whistles," for example), Thomas has abandoned, for the moment, his old moral certainties. Puritan predestination has become Hardy's mechanical determinism. A pretty thing to tell a six-year-old about. This boy would be better off in Sunday school and father, back in chapel.

Nature's indifference to "innocence and guilt" proves that "good and bad . . . blow away like breath" across "the grinding sea" of life and "go crying" into a dark as alien to morality and human gesture as the skies. "Moving about your death" is the process of unholy living and unholy dying. Death, the last "element" (cf. "elementary," 110), is as fundamental and final as the last line of "Refusal to Mourn" has led some readers to suspect. There, natural process offers some hope and the green fuse is still green. Here, souls fly to a chaos where death has dominion.

Three paradoxical similes describe their flight and the nature of things. "Stars' blood" and "sun's tears" unite above and below, inorganic and organic, light and dark, fire and water, joy and sorrow. "Moon's seed" unites light sterility above with dark fertility below. Do not think these unions hopeful, however. They are the "rubbish" of a cosmic dump and the "rant" or empty rhetoric of the sky.

"The wicked wish," established at, and going "down" from, the beginning of Lawrence's bird, beast, and flower (cf. 112) and from the beginning of the four elements, seems not only the original sin of Genesis but the sin of predestination, nature's wicked wish that is "cast before you move." Worse than amoral, nature seems immoral now.

But the last three lines soften this indictment by ambiguity. Whatever you do or say, die you must as your words and deeds must die. Since we are what we do and say, Llewelyn, equivalent to his deeds, truths, and lies, is dying with them. If father, conventionally punning again on "die," means making unjudging love (die today in another's bed, my son, for tomorrow you die alone in your own), the advice is unsuitable—for the time being. A lad of six finds sex of this sort beyond him. Maybe "die" means die. "Unjudging love," however, is plainly ambiguous. Far from unjudging, God's love is judging. Nature's is unjudging; for nature is morally indifferent. But how can indifferent nature love at all? "Unjudging love" can mean father's uncritical love of his son; but since father is likely to die before his son, how can son die in father's love unless it survives somehow amid the rubbish of indifferent nature? Maybe the "unjudging love" is Llewelyn's —what he must live to die by. In a loveless universe, he must love without judging. Unless indifferent by nature, Llewelyn may be puzzling still. What side of what truth is father on?

E. Glyn Lewis, in Tedlock, 172-73. Treece, 120. Watkins, 126.

To Others Than You (1939), *p. 118*

As plain and bitter as some poems of embittered Yeats, "To Others Than You" invites comparison with "I have longed to move away" and "O make me a mask." In sense, this poem is not unlike "Because the pleasure-bird whistles," where Thomas condemns the sods and dopes around him. Now, like Joyce, he finds himself surrounded by hypocrites, deceivers, and betrayers. The virtues of "To Others Than You," a challenge to such enemies, are feeling, tone, and satiric vigor. Instead of Pope's classical couplets, romantic Thomas found free verse compatible. The nasty dissonance of "good" and "cloud" at the end, agreeing with previous disagreeable agreements, fits the feeling all help to carry.

The first line, suitably separate, is challenging. Calling out is challenging to a duel. "Friend by enemy" makes each hypocritical friend an enemy. One by one and together he calls them out as he cries out upon them. Not waspish Pope himself could crowd a line with more.

An elaborate metaphor of money occupies the next five lines and, maybe, the sixth and seventh. Counterfeiting and deception bring one sense of Joyce's forging to mind. The "bad coin," a counterfeit, is at once a probing eye in its socket and, by a pun, a coin jingling in a pocket. Since coins are put on (though not in) the eyes of the dead (cf. "penny-eyed," 80, "coins on my eyelids," 151), this image helps make his enemies deadly. Palming a lie unites monetary and thaumaturgic deception with moral (cf. "winning" and "enticed"). "Brassily" makes the coin in the eye a penny, but "twinkling bits" make it a piratical piece of eight, of which two bits are a quarter. One bites a bit to test it, but the "sweet tooth" of Thomas' love seems too innocent for that. "Sweet tooth" and "sucked" (the "necessary" words, said Thomas) make him a child among these deceivers and thieves— not child enough, however, not to pay them out as they pay out false coins.

"You" includes all enemies, one by one or together. The title, which adds to the sense, defines "You" ironically as all but the enemy reading this. (Hitherto, titles have commonly, though not always, repeated opening words.)

"Conjure," a play on words, introduces a parallel metaphor of conjuring on the stage. The enemy's "smiling act" tricks his audience with mirrors and "quickness of hand." (Young Thomas, less innocent than he now appears, had knuckle-dusters in his glove, 21. Compare his "laugh up the sleeve," 94.) Fooled by this act, Thomas lays his heart under the "hammer" of deceiving auctioneer or destroyer; for metaphor shifts under the pressure of a feeling too strong for tropical consistency. This innocent, betrayed by hypocritical gaiety and frankness, has thought the composite deceiver "a desireless familiar," the phrase (taken from "The Orchards" and given a whole line for emphasis) out of which this poem grew. But the best line, in Thomas' opinion, is "While you displaced a truth in the air." The break after this line (not there in the earlier versions) is emphatic.

Love, truth, and stature cannot cope with such liars—stilted boys, towering above this innocent shorty with "their heads in a cunning cloud," displacing truth up there and down here, too.

Watkins, 68. Fraser, 34. Stanford, 124.

Love in the Asylum (1941), p. 119

Triplets contending with sense, which cuts across them, compose a fitting structure. The six triplets fall into two divisions of three, the first rhymed a b c, the second, d e f. In each division the first triplet has two short lines and the other two triplets, reversing the pattern and the rhythm, have two long lines. Whether long or short, each line is sprung. The first sentence, escaping the confines of the triplet, occupies four lines. The second sentence occupies five lines, and the third, six. This progression works dramatically up to the climax of a self-contained triplet, which also brings a process of sense, in happy co-operation with pattern, to climax.

The title of this celebration of marriage states the theme better than the first line, serving as title, would have. More than a madhouse, an "asylum" is also a refuge; but this house of refuge, occupied by a madman, admits "a girl mad as birds." (For poet as madman and for madwoman with birds see "The Mouse and the Woman." Shakespeare, as Thomas knew, associates poets, madmen, and lovers.) More than mad as birds, this committed girl, like her successors in Thomas' "A Winter's Tale" and "Unluckily for a death," is a bird. "Bolting the night of the door" with her "plume," she bolts the door against the night outside this refuge.

Mazed in the strait bed, she adds delusion to a room already "nightmarish." (Reversals of expected order—e.g. "Strait in the mazed bed"—suit this madhouse.) Meaning narrow (cf. "narrow" below), "strait" implies strait jacket here. Like the girls of "A warring absence" and "I fellowed sleep," this bird-girl is associated with clouds, which she brings down to the room for all its heaven-proofing. Committed to his dark room, Thomas has resisted heaven of cloud or star. This cloud-girl, "at large as the dead" in her confinement," seems a restless ghost as she walks the floor or "rides" in dreams of the "male wards." (For the poet's jealous suspicions of Caitlin's dreams see "Into her lying down head.") These imagined wards are oceans, perhaps, because projected by a dreaming cloud.

As bird and cloud, she is "possessed," in two senses, by the skies, whether colliding with "the bouncing wall" of her padded cell or sleeping in the strait "trough"—of Circe's victim? The "madhouse boards," worn by her walking, are worn by Thomas' "walking tears," as Christlike as the "walking word" (80) and as Godlike as the "walking circle" (70). As sufferer of the word, Thomas is Christ, and as creator by the word, God—and so "All, men my madmen" (23). Sometimes madmen think themselves Napoleon or Theodore Roosevelt; sometimes, Christ or God.

Bringing clouds from above to the heaven-proof madhouse, this girl brings light to its occupant. Although "taken by light in her arms" can mean taken in her arms by the light of dawn, it probably means that in her arms he is taken by the light toward which he has darkly aspired through all his heaven-proofing. The union of trough below with cloud and star above is tardy. "I may without fail" paradoxically qualifies certainty with possibility, but certainty wins as "may" becomes can. With the madwoman's help he will "Suffer the first vision that set fire to the stars." "Suffer" makes the poet the "walking tear" again, as the working vision of Genesis again makes the poet God. By opening the roof and bringing vision, the girl has enabled the madman to see the fires of stars above her watery clouds. Created by her, but proceeding beyond her, the suffering seer creates a world—indeed, a universe crowded with stars (cf. 121-22), which, a product of the creative word, compose a word. That word is this poem.

Compare this successful madman with the madman who fails at the end of "The Mouse and the Woman":

> The woman had shown him that it was wonderful to live . . . how pleasant the blood in the trees, and how deep the well of the clouds. . . . He opened his eyes, and looked up at the stars. There were a million stars spelling the same word. And the word of the stars was written clearly upon the sky.

Stanford, 121-22.

Unluckily for a death (1939), *pp. 120-22*

Originally called "Poem (to Caitlin)," this poem belongs with "A warring absence," "Not from this anger," and "Into her lying down head," a sequence on the troubles of marriage. These coagulated poems, which Thomas prized above their merits, gave him as much trouble as they give readers now. He worked them over and over in the vain attempt to shape something he was too deeply involved in for easy shaping. A shaper requires distance from his object and clear sight. Obscurity of image and syntax, increasing as he reworked the text, may also be protective. How better can a poet, compelled to reveal, conceal things so revealing? But more than revealing concealments or concealing revelations, these poems may be attempts to work his problems out. Himself his audience, the poet needs no other.

An earlier, almost completely different version of the poem (available in the Watkins letters and in *New Poems*) is instructive. Reconstruction made this labyrinth darker and more labyrinthine. Maybe a labyrinth leading to, yet hiding, mixed bull was the proper shape for such mixed purposes. Less shape for us than puzzle.

Irregular assonance and approximate rhyme do little to lighten the free verse of these four stanzas, which, although of fourteen lines, are not four sonnets. The first sentence, a syntactical maze of twenty-four lines, is as monstrous as the monologue of Lucky in *Waiting for Godot*. But that yields a little sense at last and so does this. Fortitude is what the reader needs—and time.

1: Unluckily for the death that awaits him, the lucky, holy poet seems trying to say, resurrection is possible, although the woman, its agent, is a problem: hot, cold, constant, inconstant, and unawakened. That Lawrence's phoenix waits with death under the unlit pyre of death and renewal is sinister. This singular bird must sit on top of it and burn. "For the woman" may mean unluckily for, waiting for, or pyre for. "In the shades," she is still in the dark, "under the cloud" of the second stanza, or ghostly "among the scudding dead." "Saint carved," an adjective lacking its hyphen, belongs with "dedicate," another adjective. Though the stony, sacred image of a saint about to rise, she is "sensual" and unsaintly. No hot kiss on her "clay cold" mouth can assure the constancy of this sensual statue, however dedicated. The "winds" of external reality, poetry, and love have not freed this carved saint from the "wintry nunnery of the order of lust," which denies love. Hot and cold, clay and flesh, cloister and hearth, love and lust, and all the other incompatibles reveal the poet's problem.

"Beneath my life" may qualify "order of lust" or mark a return to the "phoenix under." "That sighs" may refer to "my life" or "nunnery"; for both may sigh for the "seducer's coming," the one like Bloom and the other like Mrs. Bloom (cf. 125). If "that" refers to "nunnery," the seducer may be Thomas, some Boylan, or, paradoxically, love to open lust's cloister. The "sun strokes," significantly separated in the manner of Joyce to allow several meanings, are triumphantly sexual and deadly; for the stroker is stricken by heat and light. Season of fulfillment, "summer" suits the "seedy shifting" of its boys.

2: The metaphor of religion that detains us in the first stanza (saint, choir, cloister, order, nunnery) continues through the second (hosts, wound, ceremony, celebrated, communion, breviary); for love, as Lawrence affirms, is holy, and for an icon-hunting product of the iconoclastic chapel Catholicism is ultimate and icon-crowded. The sentence, uncertainly proceeding from the first stanza, leaves us in doubt about "loving." Who is loving and where and what? Is she loving his "holy lucky body," is it loving her, or are "sun strokes" loving? "Sea banged guilt" may be specifically amniotic, generally vital, or hairy in the surrealist manner. As she "in shades," so he "under the cloud." Is this cloud "against love" or is his body caught and held against love to be kissed "in the mill of the midst," which, certainly not that on the Floss, seems sexual? But "midst / Of the descending day" seems deathly. Our evening is upon us. Being "cut" to the quick or wounded "in the order of the quick" (not "the order of lust") marks the triumph of love, imaged by a single evening "star" and by "communion" between sun-stroked "suns." Lawrence, the poet of the phoenix, seems behind both evening star and these two stars in holy balance.

Whatever the syntax, the idea seems to be that love—even love as complex as this—is a "ceremony of souls." His fleshly "wound," like Christ's, assures divinity. Her "inch and glance" (repeated in the penultimate line of the poem) unite flesh and spirit. He will "chant" no more "a saint in shades" while her "prayed" and inching flesh turns the pages of their "breviary." Yet the death-biding and pyre-awaiting two are lonely together. The end of this stanza returns to the beginning of the first. Is Caitlin the phoenix, uncooked and tolerantly unshooed, under his pyre? (She is a firebird in "A Winter's Tale" and "I make this in a warring absence.") Is phoenix phallic? Is resurrection erection? Or, as the colon implies, is this singular bird as double in communion as that evening star? Finding the answers out seems hardly worth the bother.

3: Answer and, for a change, plain statement appease us here while metaphysical gaiety brings light to gloom. Thomas' exemplary zoo, a pleasing conceit, proceeds from the singular, double phoenix and the death-biding two of the previous stanza. Each of his beasts is as double and each as monstrous as marriage. But recurrent "I see," which controls the structure, implies vision or revelation. Look! We have come through.

The first beast of marriage is a "tigron," a mixed and dubious animal, half tiger and half lion—like the "tiglon" in the Bronx zoo. The "androgynous dark" where this tigron weeps is as dual as he-she. But, like Blake's tyger and the phoenix, this noon-maned beast, "striding to holocaust" by night, will burn bright in love's regenerating fire. Mules, equally dual, are mixtures of horse and ass. (Compare "mule's womb," "In the Direction of the Beginning.") Though sterile and stubborn, these mules will bear "minotaurs" for Thomas' labyrinth (cf. "mazes" and "bullring," 105, 107; "bulldance," 87). Minotaurs, as mixed as such mothers, must have mixed-up sires. The duckbilled platypus (*ornithorhynchus anatinus*), a mammal that seems mixed with bird, must yield, when broody, "a milk of birds." This zoological vision, as ingenious as the conceits of saint, nunnery, and phoenix, is merrier.

The second vision makes the carved saint in black habit of "shades" a "symbol" of a desire beyond his capacity in spite of his Rabelaisian "great crotch." The "giant continence" of a thwarted Gargantua and modern "guilts" seem impediments.

The third vision answers our questions about the "unfired phoenix." ("Herald" echoes Shakespeare's "The Phoenix and the Turtle.") If the phoenix is an "arrow" aspiring to the "heaven" of the womb, this bird is as phallic as any of Freud's. An arrow of "the renouncing of islands" seems sadly mixed; but everything around here is a little mixed, and islands renounced mean an end to insulation. No lover is an island.

With answer comes plain statement of the Lawrentian theme: all but flowering togetherness (a word Lawrence used twice in *Lady Chatterley*) is "monstrous or immortal." Immortal or spiritual love, as bad as islands, is renounced in favor of mortal love. (Compare Stephen Dedalus' renunciation of immortal for mortal beauty.) But, after the monsters of the marital zoo, what can "monstrous" mean? Is the poet dismissing such conceits as below love's dignity—and Lawrence's, or has the poet forgotten them in his heat? Anyway, the result of monstrous or immortal love is death, and its daughters (not sunny sons) are the grave. But if grave is womb and women are the better half of love's double-backed beast, why are grave and daughters worse than earth and sons of the last stanza?

4: The phoenix seeking heaven is plainly the phallus, and the "carved nunnery" is plainly the womb in which the phoenix sexually dies. That desire persists after such death makes it eternal if not immortal. No success unless he bows to his saint's blessing and walks like genetic God in the cool of the evening in her "mortal garden." He is God and she is Eden. That it takes a saint to make God creative is theologically dubious enough to try a saint's patience. And why, since Thomas has renounced immortal love, has this god got "immortality" for companion in his "mortal garden"? Immortality, "like Christ the sky," may be the spiritual half of a marriage of above and below, of sky and garden. If this is the point, the denunciation of "immortal," like that of "monstrous," seems an inconsistency that revision should have got rid of—unless the confusion is meant as paradox, which love, like religion, is never without. "Christ the sky," God's walking companion, is as Welsh as Evans the Produce in "Old Garbo" or Dai Bread and Organ Morgan in *Under Milk Wood.*

Caitlin's "translating" glance has lost him in this theological and amatory maze. The "mortal garden" and the "young stars" of Genesis signify the poet's genesis. Joining garden with manger and poet as God with poet as Christ, this double walker is born "like Christ the child," who, like "Christ the sky," is every inch and glance a mortal immortal.

"Lucklessly" marks a return to the beginning of the poem. Without the lucky, holy poet she can have no more luck than he without her. His "vaulting bird" is a jumper and a seeker of vaulted womb, tomb, and nunnery (cf. "Rip of the vaults," 81). Her "inch and glance" (repeated from the second stanza) do not spin off "the globe of genesis," but, making him a maker, enable him to do so. In this sense, the "living earth" of his creation is her "sons," as the grave of improper love, her daughters. "O my true love, hold me" is the climactic, plainest, and most moving sentence of this turbid poem.

Watkins, 63-67. Stanford, 122-23. Caitlin Thomas, *Leftover Life to Kill, passim.*

The hunchback in the park (1941; ms. 1932), *pp. 123-24*

As the thought of marriage commonly brought involution and obscurity to Thomas' poems, so the thought of childhood brought clarity and, with it, compassion and agreeable pathos. Here, Cwmdonkin Park in Swansea is memory's center. "I wish we were there now," Thomas told Watkins in 1946. This magical park, which figures briefly in other poems (19, 72, 98), comes to poetic fulfillment here. But it shines on in the prose: "Reminiscences of Childhood," "Return Journey," and "Patricia, Edith and Arnold," a story of the young dog.

In the last of these, the park holds two alien worlds, that of the pathetic adults and that of the naughty boy. He has no understanding of their affairs, they, none of his. In this nostalgic poem of the hunchback, the park holds the same two worlds, that of the "solitary mister" and that of his tormentors. Each world locks the other out and each is the other's opposite, yet each is like the other; for both are dreams and both innocent. As the innocent boys, playing in the groves, make up tigers and sailors, so the innocent old man, daydreaming, makes up a woman for the night. Both dreams are "made" (an important, repeated word) in the "unmade" park, the reality that dreams employ and their occasion. In story and poem, however, there is a third world, that of the poet, remembering and understanding what is beyond his dreamers' innocence. "The hunchback in the park," a vision of three worlds and two times, is a richer poem than it seems on first looking into.

That the hunchback, an "old dog sleeper," lives in a "kennel" is significant; for young dogs tease him and these dogs, old and young, one and many, are seen by an artist no longer a young dog.

Although the sense is easy, certain elements call for notice, the "garden lock" of the first stanza, for example (cf. "twilight locks," 4). This lock, not only that of the gate, is a water lock that lets "water enter" and a garden lock that lets in "trees." Trees and water, depending on their observers, enter with them and leave with them at night. Locking each other out, these dreamers make and remake their unlocked garden "Until the Sunday sombre bell at dark"—a beautiful, sad line, as great in its way as this concentrate of glory and regret: "And the groves were blue with sailors." The "loud zoo of the willow groves" in the fourth stanza, more than a childish mixture of beast and tree, prepares for tigers in the fifth—tigers on the grass, alas. And alas for boys "innocent as strawberries." These strawberry boys will surely follow, as they follow now, the old dog to a "kennel in the dark." "Dark," the last word of the last line, solemnly echoes "park," the last of the first; and these words, the keys to the poem, figure again in the last line of the first, and the first line of the last, stanza. The pity is that life will have burdened these straight backs and crooked them before closing bell and kennel time. Although the poet knows that every dog has his day and night, his groves, recaptured, are still "blue with sailors." *still day dreaming—as a thing—*

What also redeems his sadness is the gaiety of art. Stanza and rhythm are a mechanic's delight. (Long ago, behind the woodshed, I used to smoke a tobacco called Mechanic's Delight.) Sprung in the ripest manner of Hopkins, the rhythm allows variety within the stanza's frame. A line may begin with a stress or with one, two, or three unstressed outriders. Within the line, three or four stresses fall at odds with expectation. An appearance of careless crudity, shared with old ballads, hides sophisticated craft. Lack of finish is the finished craftsman's play and, for matters like this, the fitting form. Matisse made pictures that a child could make, perhaps. Thomas, also playing with sound, plays rhyme against dissonance and assonance.

The broadcast version of this poem (see Notes to the English edition of *Quite Early One Morning*) has a period at the end of the first stanza, and the version in *New Poems* has a comma. Early versions have a period or a comma at the end of the fifth stanza. Thomas was fussy about such determiners of rhythm and sense. From the 1932 manuscript Thomas saved the opening lines, a phrase here and there, and the general idea. Rewriting the poem in 1941, he made it what it is, with its tigers and sailors. I did not include this poem in my prefatory list of his best poems, but now I think I ought to have.

Thomas, *Quite Early One Morning*, 6-8. Watkins, 109, 134. Fraser, 29-30 Treece, 114-15. Stanford, 113-15. S. F. Johnson, in *Explicator*, X (February 1952). Thomas recorded this poem, Caedmon, 1043.

Into her lying down head (1940), *pp.* 125-27

Another in the marriage sequence, this poem is less turgid and more amusing than its predecessors, "A warring absence" and "Unluckily for a death." Thomas, who thought these poems "important," worked them carefully up and worked them over with care. "I never worked harder on anything," he said of this. Plainly, his road to poems of marriage was paved with good intentions. Or—to shift metaphor—the more he stirred, the more he stirred things up.

This poem is partly saved from sediment by humor and, with humor, the achievement of a distance remarkable in something so close to home. In their asylum, Thomas had fancied Caitlin's dreams of the "male wards" (119) and he or Caitlin had ambiguously sighed "for the seducer's coming" (120). Such suspicions and sighs get full play in this poem of "betrayal," which he tentatively named "One Married Pair" and "Modern Love." But as Joyce, obsessed by betrayal, made his obsessions art by humor and detachment in *Ulysses*, so Thomas, in his degree, here. In this nightmare of jealousy, Mr. and Mrs. Bloom preside over the house of Thomas. The intruder who threatens it is as "furnace-nostrilled" as any of Mrs. Bloom's twenty-five suitors, as Bloom sees them—and as comic. Like Bloom, Thomas attributes incredible potency to his "column-membered" rivals. That these are as ghostly as Bloom's were real adds to the saving fun. It is not for nothing that Thomas called Swansea "little Dublin."

Like Mrs. Bloom, Thomas' darling meets—or, rather, is suspected of meeting—"once seen strangers . . . on a stair." (Mrs. Bloom met a stranger on a stair of the Gaiety Theatre and another in the pit.) The last lines of the first part confirm the presence of worrying Bloom. The "enamoring island," acorns for pigs, and "luminous charms" suggest Circe, whose presence is established by direct reference in an early version of the poem in the Watkins letters and *New Poems*. Here the hypothetical seducer from "shining Hollywood" carries the "runaway beloved" to "Circe's swinish, coiling island." (Compare the "wiving sty," the sly, rooting "swineherd," 197-98, and the piggish "trough," 119.)

In Joyce's Circe episode Bloom dreams horribly of rivals. Here Thomas dreams that Caitlin is dreaming of his "enemies" entering bed. However serious such imaginings, they are absurd. No wife is ruined by her dream alone, still less by a husband's dream of her dreaming. But the real subject of this poem is doubtful Thomas or how it feels to be a husband.

I

Beginning with plain statement of his fears, Thomas proceeds, by way of enormous metaphors, to Biblical, literary, and historical analogies. As Caitlin dreams of infidelity, perhaps, Noah's "now unkind dove," like a "rekindled" firebird (cf. 120-21), brings male intruders, not an olive branch, to Thomas' ark (cf. xviii), afloat on "a raping wave" among "unreined" whales. (For whales as rivals see "The Long-legged Bait," 168-69; cf. "whale-bed," 87.) Their "green grave" is sea and womb. Their "fountains of origin" are spouting genesis (cf. 87). Though they are not altogether parallel to Don Juan, King Lear and Queen Catherine (of Russia?) seem examples of potent youth and mad age. Samson, still unshorn, is "drowned" in the "raping wave" of his hair. (For Samson see 88, 101, 130.) All, capable of "colossal intimacies," seem threats to Thomas, though Catherine's threat remains as uncertain as Lear's. Both mad, maybe both threaten the asylum from within.

Blades and scythes are phallic and deadly. The "haycock couch," made by scythe, is that of the ladies of "The White Giant's Thigh." The cock, sexually riding and climbing, is the bird of the "rushing grave," which, in "The Long-legged Bait," "Rose and crowed and fell" (168).

"Sleep-walking" the isle of Man, Caitlin is as innocent as a swaddled, newborn babe, yet the "swaddling loin-leaf" connects her with fallen Eve. "Laid" (cf. 169-74) is slang; and "acorned sand" seems both falling time and seed. "Sleep in a newborn sleep" recalls Yeats' erotic "Lullaby."

II

Part II, developing from these suspicions, concerns Caitlin's welcome to these male-moaning Boylans and Thomas' response to this. The "numberless tongue" of more than twenty-five suitors may also mean that, lacking numbers, they are unpoetical. Boylan, says Molly Bloom, "doesnt know poetry from a cabbage."

Such "super-or-near" men, who undo the jealous poet's faith and hang his walls with "baskets of snakes," are either more than human or less. But she thinks them as glamorous as the deflowering "thief of adolescence" (cf. the Thief, 185-86, and his various predecessors, 76, 118). This lover, as "oceanic" (vast and womb-projected) as those in the "oceans of the male wards" (119), makes his "bad bed in her good" or, by squinting syntax, in her "good / Night." As he enjoys the "white gowned" (innocent and nightgowned) wife, she cries from the "middle moonlit stages" (cf. "ivory stages," 142) of imaginative action by night to the "tiered and hearing tide" or the falling levels of attentive Dylan, who seems also in the theater's gallery. A "nightpriest" with "wingbeat" foul as a harpy's, celebrates her "holy unholy" marriage "with the always anonymous beast." Beauty, beast, and celebrant are figments of dream. The blow to "pride" seems to be that Thomas has no "lovely part" in the dreams he dreams she dreams. The never anonymous husband, as imaginary cuckolds know, never has a chance.

III

It's only nature, as Bloom and Molly separately conclude. But here attempts at similar consolation yield to despair. Four analogies from nature—of sand, bird, grass, and stone—prove no help as they gradually descend a scale of length and richness.

The first analogy, suitably Homeric, of "two sand grains together in bed" (cf. "The Map of Love": "two-loves-in-a-grain of the million sands"), lying singly together, serves as image of marriage, life, and death, the "covering sea" and anonymous "nightfall." These "heaven-circling" grains recall Blake's "eternity in a grain of sand" and Mr. and Mrs. Bloom in bed. The voice of the shells on the beach confirms Thomas' fears of "betrayal" by echoing Kipling's view of the deadly female. Not only that of the shell, "one voice in chains" (cf. 180) may be that of the poet, enchained by life and art. If "golden" goes with "betrayal," it may mean sand or sperm; but if it goes with voice, it means art. (Compare "water veil" with "green, laid veil," 174.)

The second analogy, that of the "she bird," anticipates "A

Winter's Tale" and recalls "Love in the Asylum." For all that her treeforked husband, master of the tree of words and forked language (19, 27-28, 128), enfolds tomorrow's poetic flight, she sings to the intruding hawk. By "Carrion, paradise, chirrup my bright yolk" she may mean flesh, love's pleasure, and egg.

The brief third and fourth analogies of grass and stone, one with meadow and hill, fail to console. From these analogies on, the last lines of the poem, differing almost entirely from those of the early version in Watkins and *New Poems*, are disconsolate. Humor is dead and Homer, too. Lying together, the two are "alone." "A man torn up ["a loveless man" in the early version] mourns in the sole night"—of his soul, maybe. The "two wars" between which she lies "alone and still innocent" may be the first and second wars or those of warring absence. Her "incestuous secret brother" seems the intruder of her dream, the twin she has created. Such "second comers . . . bury their dead" (beget children) and "perpetuate the stars" in "her faithless sleep."

This poet's end is his beginning. "No other men," as young Thomas maintains in vain in "One Warm Saturday," "must lie and love in her head."

"I made such a difficult shape," he says of this elaborate invention. The stanzas, parallel to each other in structure, begin briskly enough but end, ponderously sprung, in long lines and troubled rhythms. Terminal and internal sounds, a mixture of rhyme, alliteration, assonance, and dissonance, increase discomfort. (Note these strange agreements: bed-eyelid, times-climbed, hair-ear, chains-declaims.) "Sleep to a newborn sleep in a swaddling loin-leaf stroked and sang" combines balanced alliteration and assonance in the ancient Welsh manner with the rhythm of Hopkins.

Watkins, 92-95. Treece, 111. Stanford, 119.

Do not go gentle into that good night (1951), *p.* 128

A villanelle consists of five or more tercets and a quatrain, all on two rhymes. The first line ends the second and fourth tercets. The third line ends the third and fifth tercets. The quatrain ends with the first and third lines. New context makes each repeated line a little different in sense or feeling. This tricky shape, which pleased young Stephen Dedalus and the poetic artificers of the 1880's, pleased Thomas, who, amorous of prosodic mazes, was a formalist at heart. Choosing a shape so artificial for a matter so close to heart is as much a conceit as springing the rhythm, even moderately, within so traditional a shape. Forms and their violations were his delights. (Compare Empson's "Villanelle.") "Do not go gentle" would not be half so moving without the ritualistic repetition with variation that the form demands. Thomas had found the inevitable form for his purposes.

Growing up and slowly moderating his concern with womb, he liked his father more and more, and, like Freud's good boys, forgave the old man in "I fellowed sleep" before the last good-by. Father taught English. That Thomas, rejecting engineering or law, accepted English as his profession proves his father easier to forgive than most or Dylan more forgiving. This poem on "an old kind man brave in his burning pride" is one of the most moving tributes of son to father in all literature. Written on the occasion of his father's illness, perhaps that of 1945, when, as Thomas told Watkins, "the world that was once the colour of tar is now a darker place," this poem remained unpublished until after the old man's death. Then Thomas supplemented this loving exhortation with an elegy.

The fathers of fiction are figures of fun. Joyce, who loved his father, made Stephen despise Simon Dedalus, a caricature of Joyce's father. Thomas, who loved his father, made young Sam Bennet of *Adventures in the Skin Trade* despise his school-teaching father and, what is worse, deface the papers awaiting grades on his desk. Escaping this convention, "Do not go gentle" is no fiction in the sense of lie.

The simple theme is embodied in two rhymed words, "night" and "light," which, like "dark" and "park" in "The hunchback," stand for death and life. Do not accept death quietly. Thomas prays, but, raging, affirm life while dying. "Rage against the dying of the light" is an evident echo of Yeats' "raging in the dark" ("The Choice") as "be gay" in the fifth tercet is an evident echo of Yeats' "Lapis Lazuli," a poem Thomas liked to read aloud.

"Light" is what he strove for. "That good night" is more complex. "That," Yeats' favorite demonstrative, implies distance here and rejection; yet that night is "good" somehow, as end perhaps to a natural and inevitable process which, accepting as we must, we must rage against. "Good night" is also good-by, an implicit prayer.

The four tercets that follow the first give examples of four kinds of men, who, knowing all at last, meet death variously and alike. "Wise men," the first kind, seem philosophers of a sort. Knowing all at death, they "know dark is right." As ambiguous as "good," "right" may mean natural, inevitable, or suitable for them after lives such as theirs—suitable because, however "forked" or ambiguous their words, they were not forked lightning. (For forking see 26, 28.) Because of this frustration and thought's dark inadequacy, they cannot call night good. "Good men" seem moralists, Puritans perhaps, who, having avoided dancing waters in life's "green bay," cannot accept death after such a life. Their never-dancing "deeds" prove "frail" and far from "bright." "The last wave by" is both the ultimate wave of life's beckoning waters and waving good-by. "Wild men" seem men of action and lovers of living, who, making much of time, find they "grieved it on its way"—as all hedonists, attempting the passing moment, must discover. The grief is more theirs than that of time, the thief. Naturally, they cannot quietly accept the setting of their flying sun.

"Grave men," the most important of all and the climax toward which the poet has been working, must be poets. "Grave," meaning serious, also means concerned with tomb and womb or all life's undertakings (cf. "a grave truth," 112). And the nearness of "death" increases their gravity. But this is a tercet of seeing and light—blinding light. Seeing with "blinding sight" is the artist's vision as gaiety is the quality of the artist and his grave art. Light and blinding as a meteor, art, however long, is short. However blinding the artist's vision for others, his eyes are blind, blinded maybe by too much light. "Blind eyes" and this vision of light ("Bright effluence of bright essence increate") put Milton alongside Yeats, the poet of art's gaiety. If the meteor is from the Ithaca chapter of *Ulysses*, blind Joyce too is of this blinding company.

"Blind eyes" lead Thomas back to his father; for, although no poet, he too was blind in his last years, or so the notes published with "Elegy" (*Encounter*, VI, February 1956) imply: "Although he was too proud to die, he *did* die, blind." As an unbeliever, old Thomas was blind to holy light, but this blindness seems more than metaphorical.

"Elegy," which augments "Do not go gentle," is maybe the last poem Thomas wrote before raging ungently into the dark in St. Vincent's Hospital on Seventh Avenue, as if bounced from a bar on The Bowery.

Watkins, 126. Bill Read, in *Casebook*, 271. Fraser, 26. John Wain, *Preliminary Essays*, 184. Stanford, 116-18. Oliver Evans, in *English Miscellany*, VI (1955). Thomas recorded this poem, Caedmon, 1002.

Deaths and Entrances (1941), *pp. 129-30*

Fear of invasion and incendiary raid, late in 1940, occasioned this poem. The title comes from Donne's last sermon, "Death's Duell," a meditation on womb and tomb that delighted Thomas. "Deliverance *from* that death, the death of the *wombe*," says Donne, "is an *entrance*, a delivery over to *another death*." Delighted too by burning babies and old men, Thomas devoted several poems to the theme, supplied by war, of dying and entering: "A Refusal to Mourn," "Among Those Killed," "Ceremony After a Fire Raid," and "Holy Spring." Recurrent images unite, and differences in value divide, these poems. Womb and tomb may still obsess him here, but these poems, like his funeral services, show progress toward the light. For him, coming up for air raid meant coming up for air—and light. Deaths in London were his entrances.

1: Excessive qualification, uncertain identity, scrambled syntax, quarrels of opposites, and multiple ambiguity establish darkness here. "Almost," "eve," and "near," proving the raid impending, make the poet seem another Stephen Dedalus, who, amid the flux of tide and sand, says: "I am almosting it." Identity, however, is the immediate problem. Who is addressed as "you"—any Londoner? And who is "one," the evident hero? "One" who is a great-least-best-known-unknown friend, about to die with you and certainly "immortal," must be the poet, about to leave the customary "Lions and fires of his flying breath." (Compare the "bonfire [bone-fire] maned like a lion," "In the Direction of the Beginning.") A little displaced, "Of your immortal friends" belongs with "one." The flying poem of the dying poet, assuring resurrection of the body, will "raise the organs of the counted dust." An organ singing praise is what Wallace Stevens called a harmonium; and a shooting organ, creative and destructive, seems phallic. Organ Morgan of *Under Milk Wood* and the burning "organpipes" of "Ceremony After a Fire Raid" confirm the organ's possibilities. Dead and immortal, the deep poet will "hold his peace"—at once silence and what, in a letter to Treece, Thomas called "that momentary peace which is a poem." The "deepest" poem, unable to "sink," must continue to "sing" to London and to the poet's "wound." "Married" and "estranging," disagreeing in the last fine line, make the estranged poet agree with the strangers of London. As common grief brings them together, so the poet's uncommon grief affirms his estrangement. Having become one with the many, "One," including the many, remains one. Whatever his subject, Dylan Thomas remains the subject of his poetry.

2: Having become one with London, this estranged "one" of the "flying breath" becomes one, apparently, with the German flier, a stranger who will drop the bombs. Indeed, the poet seems one with any stranger, down here or up there, yet strange to each. "The murdered strangers" seem Londoners, the poet, his readers, and murdering strangers shot down. As fliers "weave" in their planes, poets weave poems, and Londoners weave tears. The "most unknown . . . polestar neighbor, sun of another street" is certainly the poet; for the polestar is a guide, poles apart from neighbors. In an air raid, above and below and all opposites conveniently unite. The unknown son of another street is also the aviator, guided by the polestar, and the man in the street. When the flier dives to drop his bomb, the poet dives up to his ears in tears, feet first apparently. Aviator and poet "load the throats of shells," both bomb and song. The poet will "wind his globe" or poem out of strangers' weavings and threads of tears. "The male sea" in which he bathes his blood, while winding tears and striding for the dead, seems meant for a creative synthesis of incompatibles; but their confusion is less than mine. "Thunder clapping eyes" of poetic vision, forking godlike lightnings since first light (cf. 128), are thunderclapped by a bomb, directed by the thunderclapping eyes of the airman. Imagery of key and lock, which recurs in "Among Those Killed," unites organs of all kinds with vain shelter from the thunderclapping skies.

3: "Near and strange," in accord with "polestar neighbor," seem important words. London's "waves" may be waves of bombers, floods of blood, sweat, and tears, or air waves of the B. B. C., carrying a poem. The enemy airman—still one with the poet maybe or maybe not—knows that hearts hidden in the dark, locked cave of the shelter are "luminous" (cf. 145), either vital or burning. A thunderclapping eye will direct a thunderbolt to put out your sun (replacing it by another?) and unlock the doors of your shelter by mounting (blowing up, ascending from, establishing?) the keys. This could apply to the poet, but searing "just riders" (of the R. A. F.?) seems a German's job. If, like the poet of "Holy Spring," this poet, winding his globe of tears, is another maker amid destruction, there is hope. But as "the last Samson of your zodiac," his role is as ambiguous as this poem. A hairy strong man, Samson, replacing Atlas, may hold up the thunderclapping skies. (For Samson see 88, 101, 125; for zodiac see 27, 62, 80, 90.) But Samson, a stranger among Philistines, is better known for pulling down than holding up. Is the creative poet as Samson still one with the destructive airman, or is Samson the airman alone? Just what is this Samson doing to the zodiac? An established order of light that rules our fate, the zodiac, whether supported or pulled down, is amazing here. References to sun, polestar, and death from the sky seem inadequate preparation, though chaos may demand some sign of order.

Good, if taken alone, the last line, plainly "worked-upon," seems one of those lines which, Thomas says, approximate true, accidental magic by craft. (See "On Poetry," *Quite Early*.) A poem, he says in "Replies to an Enquiry" (*Quite Early*), should be "a formally watertight compartment of words." But, however reflexive some of the parts, this form is not tight. The uncertain center does not hold or, else, holds amazement alone. Loose windings do not wind a globe, and water threads wind no one through a maze.

Watkins, 101. Geoffrey Grigson, in *Casebook*, 119. Fraser, 25-26. Olson, 97. Treece, 122. John L. Sweeney, Introduction, *Selected Writings*, xix.

A *Winter's Tale* (1945), *pp.* 131-37

"Narrative is essential," said Thomas, speaking of poetry in "Replies to an Enquiry." Though many of his poems are static abstractions of concretions, many show movement in theme from stanza to stanza, and many are dramatic. Few are narratives in the customary sense. There are narrative elements in such poems as "A warring absence," "Once below a time," or even "The Conversation of Prayer." "Poem in October" tells a little story. But the unmistakable narratives are "Ballad of the Long-legged Bait" and "A Winter's Tale."

Narrative in a poem is good, Thomas continues, paraphrasing T. S. Eliot, because, while the mind of the reader is detained by events, "the essence of the poem will do its work on him." The essence of the poem must be the sound of shape and the shape of sound. "A Winter's Tale," a sounding shape, shows a crafty delight in alliteration, rhythm, structure, texture, and concerted vowels. There are many fine-sounding lines: "Torn and alone in a farm house in a fold," or "Though no sound flowed down the hand folded air," or "A she bird dawned, and her breast with snow and scarlet downed." Indeed, this story is more remarkable for craft than for story. Watkins thought it a "masterpiece," but this opinion must express a friend's or a fellow craftsman's approval. Plainly the poem, lacking the magic it attempts, is the deliberate, calculated, and essentially cold product of great skill. An expedition to the heart rests, fully equipped and charts in hand, at the top of the head, where it all but set out from.

Dream fantasy in kind or fairy tale with mythical center, this contrivance is the story of a sorrowing hot-and-cold man, alone by the fire in the cold dark. His prayers for human warmth are answered by a vision of a burning "she bird" in the snow. A dream of quest and capture ends at a dark door, gliding wide. Engulfed by his dark firebird, he dies in two senses, sexually and actually. In this fantasy of love and death, the poet revisits the "asylum" for another look at that "girl mad as birds" (119). The phoenix, Lawrence's bird in pot, has figured in "Unluckily for a death."

Not this strange bird, however, but snow, in contention with fire, is the central image here. Like the snow of Joyce's Phoenix Park in "The Dead" and Mann's snow in *The Magic Mountain*, Thomas' snow holds many things. Frozen water with the possibility of melting, it suggests life, death, and renewal. Like arctic ice, crowded with mastadons, it preserves and yields the past. Seasons and times, seeds and dusts abound, awaiting call, in this white preservative. Through snow's dead white we wade to life and, wading, die. We die to love and love to die and all life long enjoy the fires of ice. The pity that masterful image, variation upon the myth of rebirth, and traditional quest fail to guarantee a masterpiece.

S. F. Johnson, the Shakespeare scholar I consulted, finds no remarkable connection between "A Winter's Tale" and *The Winter's Tale*. Lawrence's "A Winter's Tale" seems equally irrelevant.

The five-line stanza with short first line is that of the ballad, lengthened and given heavier movement by intervention of Hopkins. Five sprung stresses in the long lines give variety while rhyme, both good and approximate, gives the assurance of custom. Internal sounds link the parts. Sometimes end-stopped, the stanzas run freely on sometimes. So moving, stanza is linked to stanza by echo of word and image.

The first two stanzas set the scene by a confusion of snow and water that anticipates melting at the end. The frozen fields float, twilight is a boat, and the vale of the farm a cup. "Snow blind twilight" is better for omission of the hyphen, and so the other unhyphenated adjectives, "Hand folded," for example, which frequently recurrent, suggests white linen or book. "And," which appears four times in the second stanza, introduces the syntax of dream, which, according to Freud, is innocent of logical connectives. This dream poem is a structure of and, and, and. "Flocked with the sheep white smoke" (cf. xvi) sounds like Hopkins himself. Every terminal word of the first stanza contains an a, this rhyme or that, and every terminal word of the second contains an o. As for sense: like Whittier's New Englanders, we are snowbound, and the owl, a-cold for all his feathers, dreams this St. Agnes' Eve.

Stanzas 3, 4, and 5 introduce the protagonist, "a man," evidently a poet since Apocalyptic "scrolls of fire" burn "in his heart and head." Although he is nameless and his story proceeds in third person, first person singular is around, behind the scenes. This man is alone on a "firelit island," surrounded by snow, and, although no man should be an island or on one (cf. 67), there he will sit, insulated, till "cock crow combs" through the white farmyard and the "morning men" (no men for Anthony Powell) go out to dig and the milkmaids go out in clogs to walk "the fallen sky." These lovely oafs at their "white trades" anticipate the boy at his "blue trades" at Fern Hill and the bouncing goosegirls of "The White Giant's Thigh." This bucolic vision, celebrating future dawn, is the happiest of the poem. But back to present night. On such a night Christ, ever in Thomas' service, was born "On a star of faith pure as the drifting bread" of the snowy Eucharist. "Turned old," an ambiguity, may mean grew up, became old, or turned of old. "Food and flames of the snow," going with Eucharistic bread and scrolls of poetry, anticipates the imagery of grain and fire. Notice, in the fourth stanza, the internal chiming of "hills . . . chill till" and "ringed . . . winged."

Stanzas 6 through 10, beginning the action, show its motive. The lonely man, as "forsaken" as Jesus on the cross, weeps. But on no cross, he can kneel and pray for communion. The heaven of his desire, "forever sought," is "the bride bed." As "the believer lost and the hurled outcast of light," he combines, like Stephen Dedalus before him, the conditions of Lucifer and Christ, light and dark. His "cup and cut bread" are the remains of his last supper, and snow, equally Eucharistic, becomes "the bread of water," which birds, "the harvest melting on their tongues," will receive.

The man, beside himself beside homely spit and pot "in the log bright light," is "burning and lost." A "nameless need," plainly romantic, will drive him forth to run "cold as snow" over the glass of the frozen pond, past the icy "statues of the stables and the sky roofed sties," an instructive meeting of above with below. Meanwhile, "on the point of love" (love's cross, its impaling stake, or its almost), he directs his cries to heaven, "the home of prayers." "May his hunger go howling on bare white bones" is the most impressive line of this section. But "the quick of night" is a successful play on the dead of night. Nothing here in image or sound betrays the spurring moment.

The prayer for "bride bed," in the eleventh stanza, is as paradoxical as marriage. Let me be saved by being lost, the man prays with the hero of "Vision and Prayer," and be delivered by being engulfed. His "engulfing bride," certainly carnivorous, seems a flying siren, a Charybdis, or an anemone of the "ramshackling sea" (193). As he like Jesus, so she like the bride of the lamb—a lamb led to slaughter. Syntactical difficulty, intruding for the first time, makes the last two lines obscure. Does "Never to flourish" go with bride or victim? What are we to make of flowering in seed, especially the "white seed" of snow's "bread of water" and the melting "harvest" (stanza 9)? And even if the horseflesh of the last line is allegorical time, what are we to make of a flower at once astride and under it? ("Under," of course, may mean beneath or under the influence of.) "Astride" (cf. "rode," 125, and "riding," 112, 181) is sexual and temporal riding and the riding of dream. Is "flower" a noun connected with "white seed" by "and" or an infinitive parallel to "flourish"? But such problems properly follow engulfing delivery. The word "time," emerging from this puzzle, introduces the recapture of past time in the following stanzas.

Stanzas 12 and 13 concern the past, preserved in the seedy snow and evoked from it. Minstrels sing under Hardy's greenwood tree from now deserted villages, and nightingales, now grains of dust, sing on the winds and "wings of the dead." The voice of snow, "the dust of water" from some vanished "spring" (source and season), magically "spells" and tells this "winter's tale." "Wizened stream," as frozen as the "withered spring" and the "long gone glistening" dews of the past, thaws and rings its bells. The "baying water bounds," and the mouths of the rocks, singing, string along. "Gristed," meaning ground up, recalls the snow as seed, grain, dust, and bread. In short, "Time sings" from the dead and intricate snowflake that preserves it. "Listen," which suitably introduces these two stanzas of past music, ends them suitably and links them by a kind of chiasmus. Stops, falling here and there within the lines, impart an unusual movement to the thirteenth stanza. Alliteration helps the belling, baying, and bounding song along. More than memory, Eucharistic snow is poetry, the music of time.

Time's music of "the long ago land," aided by dissonant "hand or sound" and by elaborate alliteration, glides "the dark door wide." This dark door, that of the past or of death and sex, is connected—who knows how?—with the "burning bride," outside on the "bread" of the snow, toasting it. Stanza 14 heralds this story's heroine, a burning "she bird" like Caitlin (89, 120, 127), a firebird to warm the snowbound hero up. She rises, arrayed in rays of light. Alliteration, ever more intricate, attends this phoenix, in whose light the hero, dazzled by sound, enjoys a vision: "Look."

In Stanzas 15 and 16, "Look," replacing the "Listen" of stanzas 12 and 13, forms a parallel chiasmus. Dead minstrels sing in stanza 12. Here, dead dancers, like those of "East Coker," move on a green now white with snow. Horses, "grave" because dead as centaurs, tread the dead paddocks of dusty birds and "The dead oak walks for love." The centaur, as fabulous and "long ago" as the phoenix, is her fitting companion. Movement in the past has taken the place of past sound, to embody another aspect of the poetic tradition. "Carved limbs in the rock" have replaced its "carved mouths." "Calligraphy" of leaves and "lines of age on the stones" are fossils, as the twenty-fourth stanza proves. (Compare the fossils in "The Long-legged Bait," 173, and "In the Direction of the Beginning.") Emerging from the past with centaur and phoenix, fossils also respond to the harp plucked by "water's dust," the evocative snows of poetry.

That all this is dream or vision seems indicated in stanza 17. "The soft feathered voice" flies through the "house" where the man is still kneeling alone, asleep on his knees or, awake, seeing things. The head of his phoenix is "folded" or enfolded by her wings. "The slow fall" of the slowly falling snow seems pleased by the prayer and vision it inspired. Ands abounding confirm dream, which becomes active in Stanza 18. "Charmed" by the "plumed voice" of this Lawrentian bird, the man runs out like the wind through the windless farm in pursuit of her "kindling flight." He runs, kneeling—or, running within, he kneels without.

A running, ragged "scarecrow of snow" (made of snow or scaring it?), he scares the priestlike blackbirds and runs them ragged.

(For scarecrow as Christ see "scarecrow word," 83, and the "cross-wood," female scarecrow in rags with "fork-tree breast" in "The Orchards." Compare the priestly blackbirds with the "gospel rooks" of "In Country Sleep" and the "reverent rook," xvii.) The "poles of the year," hardly those of summer and winter, must mean the arctic and the antarctic of winter. "The cloth of counties," like the hedges' cloak, is both white snow and the black vestments of priests. A scarecrow's antlers must be his sticks (cf. "combing with antlers," 148). A scarecrow trying to attract a bird is odd, but a phoenix is no crow. "Listen and look" as he chases her through "the goose plucked sea" (cf. 86) of the "slow flakes," through all their "times and lands and tribes," deep frozen and out with the phoenix for cooking.

Stanza 21, beginning with a catalogue, recapitulates. "The fields of seed and time dying flesh astride," for example, repeats elements of the ninth and eleventh stanzas. Heaven, grave, and "burning font," plainly sexual, mark triumph and death: "the door of his death glided wide" (cf. stanza 14). But sexual possession of the bird is in "the far ago land," preserved and revealed by the snow. Retreat to the past is his success—as it was to be that of Dylan Thomas. Indeed, this poem seems an allegory of Thomas' marriage, his recovery of the past, his poetic career, the nature of poetry, and, maybe, his premonitions of death. Poetry, love, and death involve one another.

Descending bird and opening door bring the man to "the last harm / And the home of prayers and fires." Attaining the heavenly womb may mean death in the snow—but no matter. Apparently, he is still safe in the farm as the tale ends in stanza 22. The rest is coda. Stanza 23, reviewing material from stanzas 12 and 15, adds flying fish figure-skating over lakes—a picture by Hieronymus Bosch. The next stanza recalls nightingale, dew, centaur, and fossil. However "shorn" this "rite" of midwinter spring, it continues for two more stanzas, a terminal flourish that adds little to what we know or guess.

We know that the "engulfing bride" is a "whirlpool" (cf. 92). We may guess the heavenly peace in its "wanting" center, where, like Eliot's Chinese jar, a man enjoys movement and stillness, time and eternity at once. Thomas' "paradise" of the multifoliate "bud," we agree, is improved—as a *bidet* would be—by hot and cold running water; and "melting snow," bringing the flow-ers of heavenly spring, is as good a way as any to end a winter's tale.

Watkins, 125-26. Fraser, 31. W. S. Merwin, in *Casebook*, 65-66. Stanford, 99-105. Thomas recorded this poem, Caedmon, 1018.

On a Wedding Anniversary (1941), p. 138

In *New Poems*, "On a Wedding Anniversary" has four stanzas of five lines each. For the present version Thomas omitted one stanza, reduced the others, and made the third stanza the first. Such fussing shows the poem worth it in his opinion. As it stands now, the poem has the virtues of neatness and condensation. We may not be altogether sure what it is about but, surely, a con-centrated enigma with every appearance of clarity is better than a diffuse or muddy enigma, like some. The impression of neatness is owing to simple words and simple quatrains, which, however, are more intricate than they seem. A b b a (of near dissonance and near assonance) becomes a c c a (dissonant and assonant) and b d d b, which combines assonance with conclusive rhyme. Neat, to be sure, but what, we ask, is going on here?

The early version in *New Poems* sheds a little light on the torn and ragged sky, "the crater / Carrying cloud," and the burn-ing doors. An air raid is in progress—as "street of the flares" and "raiding moon," in the early version, suggest. This air raid coin-cides with a third and probably last wedding anniversary. That much is evident, but what precisely happens to these two "in tune" remains uncertain. It is likely, however, that, whether attuned or temporarily discordant, they die in the raid, like some burning baby or old man.

The second stanza strongly supports this probability. Allegori-cally personified, "Death strikes their house" from the sky—from the "true" cloud, carrying rain, and from its more likely opposite, the crater-carrying cloud of a fire raid. Hence "their love lies a loss," and, allegorically personified, Love roars with his chained "patients" or sufferers. That these chained patients are madmen in Dr. Love's asylum (cf. 119) is made clear by "the singing wards of the marriage house" in the earlier version.

With the third stanza we meet Enigma herself, face to face: "They come together whom their love parted." I puzzle over this simple line. Who are "they" and to whom does "their" refer? "They" and "their" may refer to the married pair or their mourning survivors. Or "they" may be the survivors and "their" refer to the pair. How does love part? Have the survivors been divided into two camps, as in Verona, by the love of this couple? Or has the couple been reunited after one of love's warring absences? Does "whom their love parted" mean from whom their love departed? Anyway, it is "too late" and the rain is "wrong." Too late for the pair to do anything about reunion or too late for the others? Rain may be from either a rain cloud or a fire cloud. "Wrong" may mean the wrong sort for this occasion, whatever it is, or wrong in the sense of evil. The colon that promises explanation of togetherness and parting is of little help; for "their" is there again. Either the survivors mourn their loss or the two meet death in their house. Windows and doors, pouring and burning, heart and brain are conjunctions of opposites in accord with the two clouds of water and fire. Since the important and most enigmatic line is new to the present version, the earlier version is no use here.

Like many clear enigmas, this poem affects us. The marriage of neatness with mystery is pleasing. To enjoy a shapely, fine-sounding enigma it is not necessary to solve it; for in the best riddles sense is but an element. Not to know, moreover, is often more pleasing than to know as Sir Thomas Browne affirms: " 'Tis my solitary recreation to pose my apprehension with . . . involved Aenigma's and riddles." He had the Blessed Trinity in mind.

Geoffrey Grigson, in *Casebook*, 120.

There was a saviour (1940), *pp. 139-40*

What Thomas calls "my austere poem in Milton measure" is a metrical parody of Milton's "On the Morning of Christ's Nativity." The indentions are reversed and assonance replaces rhyme, but, on the whole, the stanza remains Milton's. This form is significant. Its adoption helps to prove the "saviour" not some demagogue—a Hitler or Stalin—but Jesus Christ Himself. Here, for those who think Thomas a Christian poet, is the plainest statement of his position: that of an unbelieving ex-believer, with charity for all—except believers. Not only significant in respect of sense, the choice of stanza is ironic and a little wicked.

So is the alliteration of the second and third lines, and so their meaning. "Crueller than truth," the Saviour is this side or the other side of that. "Children kept from the sun" of holy nature by the Son of Sunday school hear the "golden note" of ritual and convention "turn in a groove." (For the image of the phonograph see 39, 42-43.) Children, not only those of Sunday school, are all believers, all "prisoners" of their own prayers. The Saviour's answering smile, whatever our theological studies, is "keyless" or enigmatic.

The "lost wilderness" of the second stanza, resembling the one Christ spent forty days in, is the wasteland where we are. Our unrest at cruelty to man or beast is made calm and inactive by His "safe unrest." "Calm to be done" and "silence to do" are still the safe advice of His "murdering breath" in a world at war—"murdering" because beside the truth. "Lairs and asylums" make our tremendously shouting world bestial and mad.

The "glory" preached in His tearful churches and the sighs of believers as He, apparently responsible, strikes have no relation to stricken reality. "His downy arm" confuses Son with Pigeon or Holy Ghost. Under the protection of this arm, though you cannot cry when men die, you respond easily to "the unearthly flood" of Christ's tears and to a cloud-cuckoo "cloud-formed shell." (Thomas says in a letter that he chose "cloud-formed" in place of "cloud-made" to avoid the too easy flow of "the thin conceited stream.") The pivotal last line of the third stanza (reminiscent of early Auden) begins with "Now," the key word, which will recur twice. "Now in the dark" of the war and of a reality that makes Christ unsafe, "there is only yourself and myself." The coming to light of what Emerson called "self reliance" is the morning of Man's nativity.

"Yourself and myself," the brothers of the fourth stanza, are "blacked" in the black-out, side by side in war's inhospitable first winter. Unable, when sheltering alongside the "sky-blue" wailing wall of Sunday school or of Christian heaven, to sigh over man's "greed," the blacked-out brothers now "break a giant tear," not for Adam's fall but for the "little known fall" of every man, their "near and fire [far] neighbor." Now we are members of each other as the pronouns of all three persons show.

We who under Christian auspices did not cry for the destruction of others' houses and the deaths of others' "only ones," never found in the rubble, "now see" all men in ourselves. Now "our own true strangers' dust," we live in the never-entered houses of strangers. (Thomas says that for earlier "Fly" he substituted "Ride," the very word, "mysteriously militant.") "Exiled in us" means that, relying on ourselves and the brotherhood of mankind, we are exiled from our former Saviour. Our "unclenched, armless," human love—not that of the raised fist—will break "all rocks," presumably Peter's, too. (Cf. "red rock" and "rock arrival," 91.) The movement of this "lyrical poem" is brisk until the straining of the muscular and unmistakably phallic finale.

The hero of "A Winter's Tale" is also "the believer lost and the hurled outcast of light" (133). Yet Jesus remained useful as metaphor for Lucifer.

Watkins, 81-83. Treece, 113. Geoffrey Grigson, in *Casebook*, 121. Thomas recorded this poem, Caedmon, 1018.

On the Marriage of a Virgin (*1941; ms. 1933*), *p. 141*

Inviting comparison with Yeats' sonnet of Leda, this poem, also of fourteen lines, leaves Yeats in possession of the field or bed of divine amours. Yeats' sonnet is great. This poem is clever—witty in the seventeenth-century sense of discovering ingenious analogies or of putting apparent incompatibles together. In this elaborate conceit of conceits, the elements at loving war with one another are the Christian and the pagan, the divine and the human, spirit and flesh, the fabulous and the real, abstraction and individuality, woman alone and woman accompanied, the serious and the frivolous, and more. The air of the seventeenth century, girdling these conceits, is so thick that Sweeney seems justified in detecting the influence of metaphysical Andrew Marvell. Thomas, who read some seventeenth-century poets, certainly found their wit, and what Eliot calls their serious levity, congenial. But, if we demand a source for what seems a habit of Thomas' own mind, Hopkins' "The Blessed Virgin Compared to the Air We Breathe" seems as likely as any.

Not wit alone but clever allusion distinguishes this poem on "a multitude of loves." Iris, Mercury, Aphrodite, the golden shower of Danaë, and Leda's Swan surround the Virgin Mary and the less miraculous married virgin at the end. Less miraculous? All marriage, whether fabulous or real, is miracle, especially the latter. Starting with miraculous sun and dove, we end with miraculous blood. The director-in-chief of this almost-sonnet must be D. H. Lawrence. But jesting Thomas in discordant concord with preaching Lawrence is another conceit.

Not individual woman but "miraculous virginity" is the subject of the first sentence. Virginity, accosted by divine lovers, is "alone," as the married virgin of the last two lines is accompanied by a present husband. (Compare the "virgin married," 102.) "Miraculous virginity," wickedly implying that virginity is a miracle, is but the first of many miracles. Possession of the virgin by divine light is another: "the moment of a miracle is unending lightning"—a paradox of time and eternity. Sun is God the Father here. "His golden yesterday" is the begetting of the Son, "this day's sun," leaping to the sky out of virgin thighs. "Golden" complicates Christian sun by the golden shower of Zeus, god of lightning, as "thighs," an allusion to Yeats' Leda, complicates Mary's Pigeon by the Swan. That this composite virgin is Mary most of all and that the leaping sun is her Son are established by "loaves and fishes" and Galilee.

"Loaves and fishes" stand for multiplication, Jesus, and miracle. Mary's miraculous virginity is no older than her moment of conceiving and multiplying. The "shipyards" of "footprints," a pleasing conceit, construct the boatlike footprints of Jesus walking on Galilee's water. (Compare "ship-work," 105, the building of an ark, xvii, and the "imprints on the water," 27.) These shipyards conceal "a navy of doves." Now naval and plural, the dove is the Pigeon or Holy Ghost, who begot Jesus, and the dove sacred to Aphrodite. As holy bird, this dove includes the Swan. A feathered navy implies "a multitude of loves" and engagements at sea. A flying rather than a sailing thing, however, dove stands for the above, as "blood," the last word of the poem, stands for the below in a transaction between the human and the divine. But as flying the sky descends to become sailing the sea, so blood ascends.

"Iris," not only the center of Mary's light-receiving eye, is the goddess of the rainbow, the virgin mother of Eros, and Mercury's predecessor as messenger of the gods. "Golden" in metaphysical concord with silvery or mercurial Iris anticipates the physical amalgam of mercury and gold in the second stanza. What so clever as this, what so playful, and what so witty? To have looked into some dictionary of classical myth, however, is no sure sign of erudition.

The "vibrations" of the desiring sun and the virgin's "deepsea pillow" combine male fire and female water. Mary is star of the sea. "Married alone," the paradox of "miraculous virginity," reveals the trouble with divine love and adds emphasis to introductory "alone." Her gold-catching eyes are now accompanied by no less receptive ears and lips. According to a legend that Yeats refers to, Mary conceived through her ear. Whatever the catcher of the sky, it catches "the avalanche / Of the golden ghost," a union of Holy Ghost, Zeus as shower of gold, Danaë, and Mary. "Ringed" means married, and a wedding ring is gold. His gold alchemically weds her mercury. But "mercury bone" is complicated. Mercury's crucial bone is a winged heel, like that, no doubt, of Iris, his predecessor. Does wing imply the elevation of mercury to gold by transformation? Since bone is both deathly and phallic, did she put on mortality with his power? Anyway, like a porter, he delivers his "golden luggage" through her eyes, below the "lids of her windows." "Hoisting" places the above below again, for convenience.

Such falling, hoisting, and vibrating will occur no more; for now, instead of abstract and composite virginity, we have to do with an actual, though nameless, woman, a veritable "she," no longer miraculously alone but miraculously with a husband in bed, his arm around her. Man, as good as sun or better, replaces sun. The coursing blood of Lawrence is "unrivalled" by divine light, showering gold, or Pigeon. A product of many comparisons, this blood is incomparable. But possessive and triumphant blood, as Thomas knows, is "jealous" of rivals entering bed (119, 125), of all rivals, human or divine—as jealous as Joseph's were Joseph not a saint.

Some commentators think this poem an epithalamion. Thomas may have written the poem to celebrate the marriage of a friend, as, on another occasion, he wrote to celebrate an anniversary. But without knowledge of the occasion and taking the text alone, we must find this poem a conceit and the serious poet a wit.

Two stanzas of seven oddly-rhymed lines do not make a sonnet. But, as in a Shakespearean sonnet, the two last lines are conclusive. Thomas' sonnets are unorthodox, and who knows if this may not have been meant to join that queer company? Sound showers gold in the woven alliteration of the first line. The terminal words of the first stanza are assonant until "doves" breaks the pattern. The terminal words of the second stanza play on o, a, and a nasal until "blood" breaks the pattern. "Doves" and "blood," united by position and assonance, include the theme.

The 1933 manuscript, now at Buffalo, is nothing like the rewritten text of 1941. Thomas rebuilt the poem from "golden ghost" and a few other hints in the original version. Essentially, the poem is a product of 1941.

Watkins, 105-07. John L. Sweeney, Introduction, *Selected Writings*, xvi-xvii. Treece, 115. Stanford, 120-21. S. F. Johnson, in *Explicator*, X (February 1952). Bernard Knieger, in *Explicator*, XIX (May 1961). David Daiches, *Poems in English*, 745. Thomas recorded this poem, Caedmon, 1043.

In my craft or sullen art (1945), *p.* 142

That Yeats is a director of these proud verses seems established by many echoes. Except for the feminine endings, which assure individual movement, the lines of three stresses are those of "The Fisherman." Thomas has caught something of Yeats' coldly passionate feeling and something of his tone, nobly austere. The pattern of five good rhymes lends an air of finality and assurance. All rhymes are good, even that of "psalms" and "arms," which, jarring the American ear, is sound in Britain.

Going naked, suitable for indignation and advice, has other uses. This bare poem concerns poet, poetry, and audience.

The problems that attend the poet's simplest lines begin at the beginning with "craft or sullen art." Does "or" imply the identity of craft and art or a distinction between them? Certainly a craftsman, Thomas, at his best, was certainly an artist. In "On Poetry" (*Quite Early*) he makes a distinction between the "intricate craft" which may approximate accidental magic and art itself. Preserving a distinction, "or" implies a connection. But what of "sullen"? This fine word, for which Thomas must have preceded us to the dictionary, owes some meanings to its Latin and Middle-English origins and others to gradual accretion. Gloomy, morose, peevish, and ill-humored, the meanings that come readily to mind, are secondary. The primary meaning is lonely, solitary, unsociable, unique. Among the accretions are crabbed, obstinate, and austere. Thomas' "sullen art," crowded with these meanings, is lonely and austere from his point of view, and, since this is a poem of artist and today's audience, unsociable, crabbed and maybe morose in the eyes of that audience.

The craftsman pursues his art under Yeats' raging moon, sign of imagination and inspiration here, while lovers sleep. Lovers, for whom he labors, seem lovers of women and life—common men, the "common wages" of whose hearts are commonly no payment at all. "Their most secret heart" implies depth, unawareness, and, like Yeats' "secret rose," a multitude of remote and unknowable privacies. The "griefs in their arms," not only women, are the troubles of life and thieving time— "the griefs of the ages."

By the "singing light" of the moon that directs the tide, Dylan, the lonely craftsman, labors without hope of fame or money, the common incentives. (In "On Poetry," however, he says that foolish craftsmen alone are indifferent to sales.) He dismisses "strut" or the public pretensions of poets and the "trade of charms" or poetry as business, the exchanging of magic spells for cash. "Ivory stages" (cf. "moonlit stages," 126) seem an odd synthesis of the private and the public, of ivory tower and theater. Not floors of ivory towers, these are stages for showing off on, where privacies of ivory towers become public shows. No doubt the ivory gate of dream in the tower's interior is above such staging. *Under Milk Wood*, however, could be called a trading of charms on ivory stages and so could Thomas' recitations at colleges or at the Y. M. H. A. These, of course, came later than this poem, but in "Twenty-four years" the poet confesses to "sensual strut" as in "Once below a time" he confesses to swanking. However noble and austere his tone, Thomas seems torn between the pleasures of strutting on an ivory stage and of solitude in tower or steeple.

There, strutting alone, he devotes his craft to the "spindrift pages" (cf. "steeple of spindrift," 42) of modest, impermanent art. "The proud man apart / From the raging moon" has a Yeatsian sound. Such proud men, account executives or brokers maybe, are not his audience; for, apart from the moon's pull, they are indifferent to spindrift and singing tide. Just as sensibly, Thomas also excludes the dead—even "the towering dead" of poetry: Milton, translating "psalms" in his "high, lonely tower," and Yeats in his, or towerless Keats among his "nightingales." The trouble with the grieving lovers for whom the poet writes is that, heedless of his craft or art, they do not praise or pay. The payment of "their most secret heart," responding beneath their notice to borrowed copies perhaps, seems inadequate. Hence the art of this poet without audience is "sullen" in every sense and his neat structure more ambiguous than his brave airs make you think.

Stanford, 115-16. W. S. Merwin, in *Casebook*, 67. D. R. Howard, in *Explicator*, XII (February 1954). Patricia Meyer Spacks, in *Explicator*, XVIII (December 1959). Thomas recorded this poem for "Pleasure Dome," Columbia, ML-4259.

Ceremony After a Fire Raid (1944), *pp. 143-46*

"It really is a Ceremony," said Thomas, the ritualistic naturalist. Ceremonious "Death shall have no dominion" and "Refusal to Mourn" prepare for this triumph of ritual. "Vision and Prayer" and "Holy Spring" echo it down Thomas' secular cloisters. A sacrificial babe, touched off, maybe, by Robert Southwell's "Burning Babe," burns on every altar but the first. Only a ritualist would burn a baby or, fascinated by such sacrifice, continue to celebrate it. Ritual, myth's likely origin, is a symbolic form, which, like mathematics or music, is a way of knowing what we cannot know. Thomas' services, conducted with "hwyl" and Roman pomp, are forms for embodying and offering the sense of holiness and glory—not Christian holiness, which lends the form, but a holiness like Wordsworth's "spirit of religious love in which I walked with Nature." Hopkins found nature a sign of the glory of God. Thomas found God a sign of the glory of nature. "Glory glory glory," Thomas exclaims, but "Glory be to God," says Hopkins.

In the essay on Wilfred Owen (*Quite Early*), a Welshman "charred" in the flames of war, Thomas hails an affinity. Owen, he says, is "himself the intoning priest over the ceremony. . . . He is the bell of the church of the broken body." Secular, priestly Owen, Thomas continues, rivals Hopkins, Yeats, and Eliot in influence on later poets. Affected by them all, Thomas welcomed Owen's support for what, with all the inclinations of a priest without creed, bishop, Latin, or congregation, he had enough of in himself.

"Ceremony After a Fire Raid," one of Thomas' great poems and one of the great poems of our time, falls, like most rituals—*Ash Wednesday*, for example—into a dramatic sequence, in this case, of hopeful gloom, gloomy resignation, and ecstasy: a convenient, though uncanonical, concentrate of the Masses for Good Friday, Holy Saturday, and Easter Sunday. *Ulysses*, the ritual of another unbelieving believer, offers the same convenience. The first part of Thomas' ritual is a "chant," a requiem chant of despair, relieved by intimations of immortality. The second part combines collect and sermon. The third part combines gloria, communion, and organ voluntary. In a letter to Watkins, Thomas called this *Missa est* a "voluntary" or "the music at the end" of the service.

Each part differs from the others in shape, movement, and feeling. The first, adapting the stanza of "Now," is suitably dissonant ("grieve . . . grave," "death . . . mouth," "hours . . . fires") in the manner of Owen, whose "dark, grave, assonant rhythms" are Thomas' own. Like Owen's words—as Thomas describes them in that essay—words here are "purged and sinewed" for "wrathful pity and prophetic utterance . . . driving towards the final intensity of language: the words behind words." However dark the words and rhythms of these poems of war, Owen's and Thomas' alike, "everything, as Yeats once said," says Thomas, "happens in a blaze of light."

The second part, though freer in rhythm than the sprung stanzas of the first, moves more slowly through its two parallel, incantatory sections. In the third part, breaking through the vain restraints of ritual repetition, the organist pulls out all the stops.

I

1: Grieving Thomas, made plural by romantic inclusion of all mankind, stands in the rubble of a street that "among" makes all streets burned to "tireless death." "Kneading mouth," "black breast," and "dug" (which, though a verb, implies the noun) prove the child unweaned. "The grave / The mother dug," making womb tomb again, means that "spade-handed" mother buried the child she bore; for birth, we remember, is the beginning of death. "Arms full of fires" on the black edge of a crater (cf. "rim of the grave," 109) combines the despair of literal burning with the hope of eternal life. These destructive fires, like those of the phoenix, are the fires of life. (Compare the "infants of pure fire," 177, and "The majesty and burning of the child's death," 112.) Notice the alliteration in the last two lines.

2: Let this service begin with singing of "Darkness kindled back into beginning." Darkness is death and beginning is genesis; but darkness, as we know from "A Refusal to Mourn," is also our origin. Genesis, as dark as death, is bright as "darkness kindled." The caught, nodding, blind, tongue, a synthesis of burning head, eye, and voice, says and nods yes to death and life. "The star," literally a bomb, is also the star of divine conception and birth, the star of faith and the star of beginning (cf. 27, 131, 141). As the child embraces life's dual fires, so he includes, by heredity, the "centuries" of mankind. So strong our grief, for the moment, that no "miracles" of the creative star can "atone."

3: "Myselves the believers," rising above grief and guilt, pray for forgiveness and renewal. "The great flood," anticipating the waters of Part III, combines water to put fire out, tears of grievers, and Noah's flood, that destroyed the guilty and saved mankind for this. Let the grains of dust become seed and blood spurting through our hearts. (For grains, dust, flame, and blood see 24, 112, 133, 141, 158.) Touched by death, our hearts' blood will save. "Blow" and "grows," united by sound, unite dust and bloody seed.

4: Compare the dying cry of the burning baby of "The Burning Baby": "A flame touched its tongue. Eeeeeh, cried the burning baby, and the illuminated hill replied." Depressed again by immediate grief, we who believe without belief think the child "beyond cockcrow"; yet in fire, we "chant the flying sea" (cf. "flying grail," 44, "flying heartbone," 49, "flying garden," 85), which, along with fire in the child, will put the bad fire out. The consolation of eternal life conquers thought of death at last: "Love is the last light spoken." (Compare "In the Beginning.") Love is the last word, as in the beginning it was the first. The "last light" before darkness becomes the first light after darkness. The word of light and love, for God and poets, ends with Alpha and begins with Omega. Hopkins' "Oh," less magical here than where it came from, heralds "seed of sons"—of suns and lovers in the "black husk."

I I

1: Once plural, first person becomes singular. The singular congregation, becoming priest, rises in the pulpit for a discourse that is meditative, incantatory, sad, and rhythmically free. The child, sacrificed on London's altar, says the preacher, includes all victims on all altars: holy bullocks, lambs, chosen virgins, and Adam and Eve, victims of the serpent and victims by association with the others. (Bride and groom are in chiasmatic relationship with Adam and Eve.) Parents and victims, concentrated in the child, died in the black "cinder" of its skull, which becomes the white "head stone" of buried Eden. That the preacher does not know which of the child's components was first to burn does not matter.

2: Nor does it matter that, commencing the second section, he knows; for to know and not to know in matters like this are the same thing. We too know that the "legend" of Genesis is never silent in Thomas' "service." Eden serves his purposes, particularly those of this ceremony. The child, who includes Adam and Eve, includes Christ, "the one child," whose legend, too, is always of service to Thomas. The serpent who undid our first parents is undone by Christ, "fruit" of their fall, and "sun" or Son. The compendious victim now becomes "priest and servants" at the altar, "Word, singers, and tongue"—or Thomas, ever his subject and object.

Parallel structure and repetition connect the two sections of this soliloquy. "Beginning crumbled back to darkness," a reversal of "Darkness kindled back into beginning" (Part I), resumes the play of Alpha and Omega. As the first section of Part II ends hopefully with "the garden of Eden," so this, darkly, with "the garden of the wilderness," a barren nursery of plant and child. "Wilderness," the Biblical word for wasteland, reminds us of Christ's forty bedeviled days (Matthew 4:1) and of Isaiah 51.30: "he will make her wilderness like Eden, and her desert like the garden of the Lord." Isaiah hopes for green renewal. The gloom of preaching Thomas, less dismal than it seems, is only what, by the laws of drama and music, must precede joy and light. Consider K. 516 and how Mozart there is darkest before the bright gaiety of the final movement. Consider Bloom's K. 11.

I I I

The hallelujah, magnificently rendered on the "organpipes" of "luminous cathedrals," affirms life and joy. Jubilant is the word we seek. Beethoven found words in Schiller.

Ritualistic parallels and incremental repetition, toward the end, lead to climax. Note the pattern of opening words: "Into," which begins three lines, resumes for two more after interruption by triple "Over." After this interweaving comes repetition of definite "The" to establish, maybe, what Wallace Stevens calls "The the."

Burning in the fire raid, the cathedrals are "luminous" and the "weathercocks" (not crosses) on the steeples are "molten." Time and space, represented by clock and weathercock, burn too. (For the twelve winds and directions see 41, 63, 69.) The "urn of the sabbaths" is for the ashes of all those dead Sundays in the chapel. Light of daybreak, increasing the brightness of flaming slum, gilds the molten pavements. Eucharistic "bread" and "wine," or Christ's body, burn with church, slum, time, space, and child. (Compare snow's "bread of water," 133, with this "wheatfield of flames.")

Burning Eucharist cries for holy water. To put the fires of destruction out and make way for the fires of life the creative waters of "the infant-bearing sea" erupt like a volcano. (Compare the waters after the fires of "A Refusal to Mourn.") The "masses" of the holy sea remind us that we are attending a service in a cathedral now "luminous" with altar light. Our Easter candles, both holy and natural, will "erupt" and "fountain" to refill the font. Rhythm, as well as image, proves our resurrection an erection and our Easter a begetting. The organ, like Organ Morgan's, is organic.

This Lawrentian concert of the natural and the divine ends rapturously in "a storm of singing" (153), like that of the Ninth Symphony. "Erupt . . . enter to utter for ever" prepares for the greater symphony of a last line not unlike that which ends "The Wreck of the Deutschland." Thomas' last line, as long and ponderous as creation, owes some of its effect to the short line that prepares the way, and some to conspiracies of sound and sense. "Sundering" is death, and "thunder" follows the short genetic spark (cf. "thunderclap spring," 193, and "the short spark," 80). The "ultimate kingdom" is heaven and earth, end and beginning. But the penultimate line that serves the ultimate kingdom is less preparatory than climactic. Once "Glory cracked like a flea" (105). Now, cracking like thunder, triple "glory" is the poem's triumph and, to shift metaphor, its distillate. To achieve glory by naming it thrice seems the unlikeliest thing in the world. But the recording proves the achievement. To hear Thomas rolling these glories out is to recover "the sense of glory" that Herbert Read thought all but lost. I recovered it one night, sitting next to Thomas as, ascending to "the glory of the brightness," he rolled his triple glory out, in the broadcasting studio of WEVD on West 46th Street.

Watkins, 112-14. Stanford, 98. Thomas recorded this poem, Caedmon, 1002.

Once below a time (1940), *pp. 147-49*

Like the portrait of Shem in *Finnegans Wake*, this autobiography is heavily ironic. In tone it differs from earlier autobiographies

("From love's first fever," "Then was my neophyte," "Altarwise," and "Twenty-four years") and it differs in feeling from boisterous "Lament." As estimate and resolve, "Once below a time" belongs with "Once it was the colour of saying."

The metaphor of the dog brings *Portrait of the Artist as a Young Dog* to mind and that "dog among the fairies," as the metaphor of skins, *Adventures in the Skin Trade.* (In this novel, the hero was to shed seven skins until he stood naked in Paddington. Compare *The Dog Beneath the Skin* by Auden and Isherwood.) The metaphor of tailor and clothing, which Thomas also uses in "When, like a running grave" and "Twenty-four years," recalls Swift, Carlyle, Joyce, and Yeats. The metaphor of nautical adventure (cf. 85, 153, 193) heralds "Ballad of the Long-legged Bait," another autobiography.

In "Once below a time" the intricate image strides on three levels, two metaphorical and one literal. What seems at first reading an account of womb and birth, disguised and presented by metaphors of tailor, clothing, cellar, and dog, becomes on second reading an account of the poet's adolescence and early manhood. Clothing means the adolescent's guises, and birth, his emergence from Cwmdonkin Park into the literary and drinking world of Swansea. This poem is about young Thomas astounding parents and the wits of Swansea with his outrageous manners, his pretensions, and his astonishing poems. The estimate is ironic, but bouncing, sprung lines and extravagant images recapture the gaiety of youth and all its strut and swank. High spirits are rarely higher. Telling how he astounded Swansea, the poet astounds again and pleases. Even the irregular rhymes are funny: the rocking agreement of "spirit . . . bit . . . ashpit," in assonance with "hardship," in rocking dissonance with "shop."

I

1: "Once below a time" (cf. "Fern Hill," 178), a play upon once upon a time, is a good way to begin a story of irresponsibility before "time tracks you down." The embryo, suggested by skin-tailoring shop, grotto, and cellar, is below time, but so is the adolescent, embryo poet. His tailored flesh must be paid for by what some call hire purchase and others, time payments, an installment on the first of each month, each month a "hardship."

His "love torn breeches," a gross pretension, are probably lovelorn at this period, and his jacket seems rescued from the rim of time's "ashpit" (cf. "rim of the grave," 109, "time's jacket," 21). "Bit" and "snapping" prepare the way for a dog beneath the skin. A grotto is an unlikely place for a bird dog to work, and a bird dog (a cocker spaniel perhaps) is pretentious and absurd in a mastiff's spiked and tasselled collar. The cellar where this dog was decorated is the womb with which the embryonic poet is obsessed. But he climbs out of the shop, "decked" (decorated and on deck. Cf. "bitten decks," 78) for a voyage at sea on a cloud-swallowing ship—another "hardship" for a shopworn young man; but the sea is as wet as the cellar.

2: The "bursting sea," a metaphor of birth, means leaving home for the pubs of Swansea and their bottlecorks. (In skin-trading London, Samuel Bennet has a bottle on his finger.) Sailors at the bar are as "out-of-perspective" to a drunken eye (cf. "Old Garbo" in *Portrait of the Artist as a Young Dog*) as to an infant eye. The coming out of the fast young man is "swift"; and Swift in *A Tale of a Tub* uses the metaphor of clothing which figures in this tale of a pub. Allusions to other writers prove the pub-crawler literate. "Kangaroo," as Thomas told Watkins, is an allusion to D. H. Lawrence's poem of *Birds, Beasts and Flowers.* "Trailing" appropriately hints Wordsworth's clouds of glory; and "lubber . . . Wales" seems a not inappropriate allusion to *Moby Dick*, for, in a pub, he was all at sea. (Compare "Jonah's Moby," 82.) "Lubber," which suggests blubber, means clumsy or land-lubberly. "Wales" combines crusty, hard-shelled Wales and a child's wails with whales. "Wales" is a "serious joke," said punning Thomas.

At sea in Swansea, the now public, literary boy, assuming disguises, covers the "common clay clothes" of his everyday flesh in a variety of ways. "Scales," a serpent's dress, make him a young devil. The "he-god's paddling water skirts" make him Zeus, the Swan—of Swansea. Swanking in Russian "bear wig" may imply his political opinions. (Compare swank with "sensual strut," 110, 142.)

These disguises astound Swansea and his parents, the "clock faced tailors" of his "common clay clothes," who, still sitting in their chilly, "snipping shop," are in another time, yet aware of time and trying in vain to tell it as he sets them back. These squatting tailors work for the stitch-dropping firm of "Shabby and Shorten," which made the boy's first suit. The "needle rock," though needle goes with tailoring and "flashing needle" may be the Needles lighthouse, remains unclear to me.

I I

And so does the poet's motive for dividing his poem into stanzas of unequal length—unless this and all the flourishes are meant for Swansea baroque.

Now his "silly suit," not the original suiting of Shabby and Shorten but any of his own creations, is that of a coffin-carrying "birdman" (either an aviator or Count Dracula) or of a "told" (storied) ghost, equally high-spirited and reminiscent of dark mortality. His "owl hood" of precocious, dark wisdom ("owl-light") tops a cloak to hide his Achilles' heel. Such disguises "deceived, I believed" the master tailor who, as director of Shabby and Shorten, ordered nerves for thread. Though plainly a god, this maker is not the God of the chapel; for he is a squatting "idol," like one of the stone gods who "thump the clouds" (52). Seeing through this young "pretender"—this "dandy," decked with sailor suit—god's needling eyes find nothing but "the masked, headless boy" (79) of "Then was my neophyte." As a tailor of skins, this squatting idol could be nature's adorable creative power, the unused power within the young pretender. This god could be and, indeed, must be the craftsman's conscience protesting the dissipation of powers by strutting on ivory stages or trading charms in the pubs (cf. 142).

A craftsman's conscience strips him of skins and masks: those of sea bird, stag (cf. "antlered like a deer," 135), and explorer, whether tropical "Columbus on fire" or "cold Nansen" in his snows. "Navigating head" unites explorer with sharklike torpedo. "Beak" of a sea bird becomes the prow of "a boat full of gongs"; and bells, we recall from other poems, are commonly poems. Here, they are also loud noises in pubs and reminders of closing time. Stripped of nautical pretensions, the young sea dog shrinks to what he is, a nervy "boy of common thread" and a landsman, whose destined bed is earth.

The hero of "The Long-legged Bait" comes soberly back to

land after dizzy voyaging. On land, both that great sailor and this cabin boy miss the old delights of water, where "it was sweet to drown." For the fishing sailor water is amatory adventure. For the less experienced "sea dandy," his "readymade handy water" is that of the womb. Still embryonic in his roaring adolescence, he found the amniotic sea a handy and readymade or suitable subject for his poems, which, having emerged from womb and tomb, he now dismisses with an affectionate wave of the hand. Though his early poems summon "a child's voice from a webfoot stone," he cannot regret them. "Webfoot" recalls Thomas as paddling Zeus, the Swan of the second stanza. "Stone" recalls god as "idol"; for "gods are stone" (52). Pretending to be a god, childish Thomas, the "webfoot stone," was a sinking swan.

But it was "sweet to drown . . . With my cheery capped dangler green as seaweed." This fine and outrageously funny line, concentrating feeling, sense, and tone, is the poem's climax. "Green," which means immature as well as vital, is no color for "a cherry capped dangler," seeking cherries. "Seaweed," both limp and feminine (see 2, 12, 55, 83), is not a dangler's proper condition. Since the dangling "triton" (42) is an embryo, this dangler seems embryonic. But the dangler is also a bugle, worn on a swimming arm and blasting in a wave. Blowing the poetic bugle under water is blowing bubbles. And so is blowing one's own horn.

"Never never oh never," a comic sigh for submarine delights, balances and prepares for "Lie down, lie down," a sigh of acceptance. "Now" on land, seen through, shown up, and stripped of masks and cloaks, he resigns himself to reality—to living and dying "as quiet as a bone." Coming from below a time to time's level, he confronts it, as "clock faced" as his tailors now. But the triumph of reality and sobriety is incomplete. "Mostly bare" is not altogether bare. "Would lie down" is not the same thing as lying down. And "bone," both sepulchral and phallic, proves womb and tomb his preoccupation still. Partly regretful estimate of the past and uncertain resolve do not guarantee present or future.

Having discarded his coat of embroideries, Yeats found "enterprise in walking naked." Thomas' resolve is still greater than his enterprise, but knowing the trouble and finding fun in it mean embroidered coat half off. The hero of *Adventures in the Skin Trade* loses his coat and hat, but the story stops before, having lost his pants, he stands bare in Paddington—except for that bottle on his finger.

Watkins, 78-80. Treece, 112-13. Stanford, 127-28.

When I woke (1939), *pp. 150-51*

Like *Finnegans Wake,* this poem is about sleeping and waking. Joyce's wake celebrates waking from the reality of dream to the reality of dawn. But Thomas' wake, not in a pub, celebrates waking from dream to reality. The poet resolves again to leave the chambers of an ignoble past and go out on the town by daylight. (For similar resolves see "Once below a time" and "Once it was the colour of saying.") The first line could serve as epigraph for *Under Milk Wood.*

Thomas wrote this line when a schoolboy of fifteen or so, and, having found a place for it, rescued it from a notebook. A symphony in o and w, this memorable line called for the interwoven alliteration (b c c b) of the second line and the third (d d c c d). The three freely sprung stresses of the first line decreed the rhythm. An earlier version of the poem in *New Poems* proves tinkering improvement.

1: Literally, the first line means being awakened after a night's sleep by the noises of the town. But for Thomas this night's sleep is the dark poetic past from which, summoned by external reality, he is awaking. His past, represented by snakes, pokers, frogs, and satans, is dream and myth. "Poker" goes with sexual and Satanic "flame," snake, and the "tongue peeled" rod of Aaron (cf. 63), at once a magician's wand, a phallus, and a snake. The "subtle bough," not only this wand and Eden's fatal tree, is Fraser's passport to the lower regions, represented by Eve's wrapped figleaf. Satans, frogs, and wands are the matters of Thomas' occult, early stories of witches' brews and sabbaths, magicians, vampires, and mad doctors with their phials, "The Lemon," for example. In "The Orchards" Marlais plans a "devilish story" on waking from a dream "more terrible than the stories of the reverend madmen in the Black Book of Llareggub." But Marlais dreams again, his dream a myth. Waking today to daylight puts an end to Dylan's dreams, myths, and fictions of darkness. Good-by to Aaron and Eve.

Birds, clocks, and "cross bells" (jangling news of risen Christ from churches) bring Thomas back to outer time, but Christ is myth, and what dispells the figments of darkness is the sound of the "next-door sea" (no longer that of the womb but the actual sea under his window) and a man, significantly "outside," working in the morning with a scythe. It may be that the traditional figure of Time ("from a book") also has a beard and a scythe, but this man is real, Time's "warm-veined double," filled with Lawrentian blood to the neck. The scythe of reality, slashing "the last snake through," gets rid of dream and myth.

2: The first two lines are not unlike lines of A *Child's Garden of Verses* in manner, though not in sense. "I" and "God" are in apposition. Like God or God Himself, Thomas is a maker of good and evil. Like Stephen Dedalus, who thought himself Jesus sometimes and sometimes God, Thomas makes a poem, good or bad, every morning in bed. (Sexual making is also possible.) Like Jesus, he has walked the face of the waters of Genesis. Whether he has also walked "everybody's earth" or made it remains unclear. But, like God, he marks the sparrow's fall and the more spectacular fall of the "death-stagged" mammoth. ("Stagged," suggesting killed by antlers, replaces "staggered" in *New Poems*.) God's earth means death or "scatter-breath." But God the poet is a creative "scatter-breath."

The living earth is full of birds, leaves, boats, and ducks. But since a poet's similes, getting between him and reality, distort it, we cannot be sure whether waking Thomas sees birds and boats or leaves and ducks, whether birds like leaves are a reversal of leaves like birds. But, as the "cross bells" wake him "crossly," he hears a voice not his. More like an oracle's than a prophet's, this voice is ambiguous—as ambiguous as the "cross bells" in the "erected air" of the steeples. Voices of town clock and church bell tell him his "sea town is breaking." This town may be the womb or Swansea, Laugharne, and Llareggub. Its "breaking" may mean destruction or dawning. "No Time," say the clocks, paradoxically. "No God," say the paradoxical church bells. No time left to create? It is later than you think and creative power is gone? Or, clock time gone, there is time for timeless poetry; and, the old God of the cross gone, there is room for "god in bed"?

Responding suitably to this message, god in bed draws "the white sheet over the islands." A white sheet drawn up (see "The Visitor") signifies death, but a white sheet is what a poet writes on with the worm of his finger. "Islands" may signify eye-lands, solipsism, or dream, now dead; but since a "two-backed" island lies on the equator of the Map of Love, islands may signify life and love. Whatever the island, the dead poet has pennies on his eyes. Both sheet and pennies prevent vision. Yet these pennies, proclaiming vision, "sing like shells" (cf. "throats of shells," 129, speaking shells, xv). This may mean that death is the mother of poetry or that the poet awakes from death, his beginning. Triton's wreathed horn is a shell, but a shell is a mollusk's skeleton. These teasing ambiguities, carefully devised, replace the unambiguous and less pleasing final lines of the version in *New Poems*.

Watkins, 41-42. Treece, 124-25. Stanford, 127.

Among Those Killed in the Dawn Raid Was a Man Aged a Hundred (1941), *p.* 152

Another wake and waking, this vision of death by bomb and glorious resurrection has images in common with "Ceremony After a Fire Raid" and "Deaths and Entrances." The lack of a burning baby is supplied by a burning man in his second childhood.

Strange among Thomas' fourteen-line poems, this poem is a sonnet, orthodox in all but the rhyming of the second quatrain of the octave, which, plainly separated from the sestet, precedes it—in the teeth of the inverted sonnets of "Altarwise." The structure is tight and crafty. As the first sentence runs into the second quatrain, linking the quatrains of the octave, so imperative "Tell" in the octave, anticipating imperative "Dig" and "keep" in the sestet, links octave with sestet. Within the sestet a little drama of sentences ascends to a climax. The first sentence occupies a single line, the second, two lines, and the third, three. Meanwhile, a little drama of imagery unfolds. From the admirable nakedness of the second line of the sonnet we proceed to splendors by degrees. Ascending through the more or less familiar images of locks and craters, we come at last to astounding conceits.

Octave: As at the end of "Ceremony," dawn gilds pavements already golden with fire. "Waking over," a condensation, means day breaking over and holding a wake over. The locks and keys (cf. 129) imply shelter and body. "Where he loved," involving lock and key in two senses, the domestic and the sexual, is home. "The funeral grains" (cf. 143), those of man and pavement, are dust and seed. A "street on its back" is a "slaughtered floor." The man's eyes, like the arms of the baby (143), are full of fires. But destructive craters, becoming green fuses, erupt "springshoots" or the fires of vegetable life. Earlier poems have prepared us for all this and for this "sun": "he stopped a sun." His sun is at once a bomb and the rising sun of morning, which, since reality depends upon us, he stopped at the moment of death. The sun's fires, like those of the crater, are destructive and, forcing "springshoots," creative. Today's sun, which stopped for him, stopped him, but the sun goes on shining.

Sestet: "Chains" and "cages," like locks and keys, are the man's body, the ribs that sheltered and caged his heart—"his grey-haired heart." This apparently surrealistic image may come from Hopkins, who, in a letter to Robert Bridges, terribly described his heart as "all shaggy with the whitest hair." "Dig no more" in the rubble for this man's cage and "keep his bones" from the ambulance, a queer vehicle that brings us from the surrealistic to the metaphysical. More formidable than the actual ambulance it parodies, this ambulance, assembling "funeral grains," carries them up to heaven for the glorious resurrection of the body (cf. 158, 160). The horse is even more heavenly than the ambulance he draws; for this horse is a "wound," and the "world's wound" (165) is Jesus. Since the poet, always one with Jesus, is also a wound—a "loud wound" (153) and a "gentleman of wounds" (80)—horse and ambulance could be Thomas and this poem, except for "that common cart." Surely there is nothing common about Thomas' carting or horsing here. "Common" must mean the general resurrection. Keeping these bones from heavenly resurrection, we must reserve them for temporal resurrection, here on earth, where holy nature's green and sunny fuse assures "springshoots." The man's age lends wings to the morning of secular resurrection. From burning age a hundred burning infants shoot, flown by a hundred storks, one for every year of this man's life. These flying midwives of the morning perch "on the sun's right hand." The Son's right hand, at which, according to tradition, the redeemed and resurrected sit, becomes that of the secular sun, agent of life, death, and renewal down here. Stopped for the old man as he stopped it, this sun will shine on the bundles of a hundred storks.

Thomas' playful wit strikes some critics as extravagant, fantastic, and disgustingly out of keeping with the solemn occasion. But his ingenious fooling, like that of Donne, Marvell, Hopkins, and Joyce, is serious, however beyond the capacity of common romantics. In the seventeenth century wit meant discovering concords in the discords of nature. Since the idea of nature held by the metaphysical poets has been replaced by later ideas, both classical and romantic, the serious discoveries of these poets have come to seem outrageous or funny. A liberal romantic, Thomas, who understood the metaphysical conceit as it was, also took it as it seems today. His conceits, both serious and funny, suit his theme and his mood. Death and rebirth are serious matters, but that a German raid accomplished the death of a man about to die has its amusing side. For Thomas, in this poem at least, grotesque invention and extravagant ingenuity, express his feelings exactly. Accepting life's seriocomic mixture, he presents his joyous sorrow in this poem's mixture.

Watkins, 108, 137. Olson, 23, 26. Phyllis Bartlett, in *Explicator*, XII (December 1953), Elmer L. Brooks, in *Explicator*, XII (June 1954).

Lie still, sleep becalmed (1945), *p.* 153

This sonnet, as nearly traditional as its predecessor, "Among Those Killed," is notable for rhythm and sound. The sprung lines are symphonic. Remark the heavy alliteration (e.g. "slow sad sail") and this sequence within the second quatrain of the octave: "sound . . . blood . . . loud wound . . . drowned . . . wind." The terminal words, equally dissonant and as craftily chosen embody the meaning.

After many resolves to leave the original sea and come up for air and light, Thomas is still at sea. It is still "sweet to drown" (148), still sweet to sing with the "voices of all the drowned" among sunken bells, cathedrals, and ships. After many resolves to abandon myth, Thomas is still the "wounded surgeon." Jesus, the "world's wound," has five stigmata. A wound in the singing throat is the poet's stigma.

This dramatic sonnet is a dialogue between the wounded sailor and his auditors. Shut your singing wound, "we" pray, lest we sink with you. Indifferent to his effect on us, he replies: "My voyage . . . to the end of my wound" is just beginning.

Octave: "Becalmed," which introduces the metaphor of voyaging, disagrees with "burning and turning" (cf. "the burn and turn of time," 154). Plainly, the poet is tossing at sea in bed and the "salt sheet" that wraps his wound is a wept-upon bedsheet, a sail for his boat, and a sheet of paper to write a poem on. The sea is silent, but we hear the sound of the "loud wound," a bloody "sea sound" that makes us tremble. Still "tide-tongued," Dylan is far from tongue-tied. ("The salt was singing," 83.) Indeed, the winds of this "storm of singing" break the sheet. As the hurricane breaks the sail, so the poem breaks through paper meant to contain it. Whether "the mile off moon" of imagination, which controls the tongue of the tide, is near or far is a puzzling question. But it is clear that the poet who once abandoned blowing his submarine bugle (149) still has a drowned, though swimming, voice.

Sestet: We hear the sea-sounding reply of the "salt sheet," less a reply, however, than a prayer: "Open a pathway." A pathway to let more wind through an already broken sail or a pathway up to light? "Throw wide to the wind the gates of the wandering boat." The wind is the divine breath of poetry, but what are a boat's gates unless the boat is a ferry? No ferry, this "wandering boat" is suitable for following in the wake of Rimbaud or for fishing with long-legged bait. "Wandering," opposite to "becalmed," implies movement and the repair of torn sails for fresh winds. Wandering means no direction. Yet the navigator has set a course: "to the end of my wound." Ambiguous "end" may mean exploring his wound to the bottom, fulfilling his wound's purpose, or dying— beginning a voyage to an end which is his beginning. (Compare "As I sail out to die," 193.)

Sleeping "becalmed" and silent in bed, we conclude, ending with our beginning, is better than such nautical ends; for so persuasive this singing salt that we must "ride" through the drowned with him unless he hold his peace and his sheet, his wind.

Geoffrey Grigson, in *Casebook*, 119. Treece, 119. Stanford, 126-27.

Vision and Prayer (1945), *pp. 154-65*

Two things detain us first: the shapes of the stanzas and the theme. Taking the second first, we ask if this poem celebrates the poet's religious conversion or if, as earlier poems suggest, religion serves again as metaphor for something else—something secular which, feeling holy, demands holy metaphor: secular enlightenment, the birth of a child, the making of a poem? A child's birth seems the occasion. The making of a poem, parallel to the birth of the child, seems a way to the poet's remaking. Jesus seems the light to which child, poet, and poem ascend. These seemings amount at last, like circumstantial evidence, to all but certainty. Here is another poem about the poet coming—this time by the aid of child and poem—from original darkness to the holy light of nature. All the rest is metaphor.

After "There was a saviour" what forgiveness? Before "Lament" what conversion? These and the other poems, as the prefatory "Note" proclaims, may praise God, who, in many poems, however, cannot be distinguished from the poet as maker or from nature's creative power. Thomas never went back to the chapel. But Jesus, encountered there, remained handy for secular matters of comparable holiness. The chapel, abounding in conversions, made conversion handy for the poet's burning turnings from darkness to the light of art and nature. Nature is holy, and so are child, poem, and poet.

The shapes of the stanzas are significant and ambiguous. A diamond, carrying for Thomas the meaning of Hopkins' "immortal diamond," must stand for light, vision, and eternity. Yet Thomas' diamonds are often black as coal. Even such diamonds, however, hold light, promise vision, image art, and bring things forth. By shape, a diamond represents the womb, which, as we know from other poems, is heavenly. But why diamonds before wings? Why not wings before diamonds? Answers to these questions depend on which of the several meanings of diamond and wing you prefer. If diamonds are black and temporal, wings bring the poet to light and eternity. If diamonds are heavenly, black wings arc the temporal vehicles to diamond light. In the first case, wings are better where they are. In the second, not. In either case, the poet meant them to be where they are; but what he meant and meant us to conclude remain dark.

The wings of the second part owe something to George Herbert's "Easter Wings," which, like the Mouse's Tale in *Alice in Wonderland*, belongs to the tradition of "figured" poems—poems that take their shape from what they are about. Thomas, who had read some of Herbert's poems (see "Welsh Poets," *Quite Early*), must have known "Easter Wings," a poem of two ten-line stanzas in the shape of wings. "Advance the flight in me," Herbert prays, and "imp my wing on thine." Vaughan's "Ascension-Hymn" and "Night" (quoted by Thomas in "Welsh Poets") also concern flight from darkness to glorious light. Vaughan calls for "wings" to bear him to "the world of light" and the "dazling darkness of God." Even dark wings suit a poet's Eastering. But shapes aspiring to eternity can be the hourglasses of time. As ambiguous as diamonds, wings include the opposites of time and eternity, light and dark. Maybe the poet's eternity is temporal, and his road through time "as long as forever is" (110). What shapes more suitable for a double-talking poet than diamonds and wings?

What shapes more suitable for a story of process? A diamond, rising from point to climax, descends to point. A wing, descending from climax to point, ascends to climax. Each part of the poetic process is a miniature of a whole process of one kind or another. The important points of diamond and wing are beginning, middle, and end, the first, ninth, and seventeenth lines of these stanzas. Diamonds ascend and fall. That wings fall and rise seems more triumphant. But sands in Hopkins' hourglass fall and accumulate. Reversing the hourglass leaves time on our hands. But, since preachers used to pray by the hourglass, what shape more suitable for prayer? Who knows what Thomas had in mind as he played with diamonds, wings, and time's glasses? That he liked to play with beginning, middle, and end is plain. "Author's Prologue," which rhymes beginning with end, the penultimate line with the second, and so on, comes to a rhymer's climax in the middle.

The rhymes of Thomas' diamonds, setting the points apart from the rest, emphasize them. In the first diamond, for example, a symphony in m, n, and dark vowels begins with "Who . . . you" and ends with "wild . . . Child." The points, so set off, are more important than the undistinguished middle. In the second wing, a symphony in m and n is interrupted at the middle by "bore . . . For." But this distinction gives the lowest point more emphasis than the climax of beginning or end. With some variation, this system of emphasis and de-emphasis persists throughout the sequence. That the process of sounds is out of accord with the process of sense (or what can be taken for a sense of these shapes) might be expected in a poem so ambiguous as this.

The trouble with a double or triple-talking poem is that, saying too many things at once, it says nothing in particular. From the concerns of this poem—obstetrics, making love, writing a poem, and seeing the light—little emerges but the poet's burning and turning. We hope that, unlike Eliot, Thomas hopes to turn again, burning with a single flame. For the time being there is less illumination than prayer.

I

1: "Who are you?" the question of Alice's Caterpillar, is answered in the second half of the diamond by "wild Child," whose identity is our problem. Plainly the occasion of the poem, this child is being born in the next room—a loud, bloody room as dark as the obstetrical diamond that brings him to light. "Dark" is the important word. The "wren bone" wall is puzzling. Thomas' bones commonly imply sex and death, but the bone of this domestic bird suggests a former or future wing. A wall as thin as a wing transmits sounds; and sounds, like "the heart print of man," are poems. (Compare "handprint," 84, "heart bone," 160, 162, "flying heartbone," 47. A "heart print" must be a footprint of the sacred heart.) Not only the poet's fate, burning and turning in time (cf. "burning and turning," 153, and "My voice burns," 165. For turning see 111, 114-15) also refer to sun and world, unknown to a son still in the dark, below a time. No promising rainbow of seven lights arches ("Bows") and blesses the unbaptised or nameless child (cf. "christens," 165). But that this unchristened "dropped son" is like the Christ Child seems confirmed by the presence of "ghost" and father, who complete a trinity.

Since father is one with son (see "Altarwise," 80) and things above are as things below, this "wild child" suggests the poet or his poem, burning and turning in the throes of origin before heart-printing. Jesus and child are comparable because Jesus saves and the child will save the father by bringing him to the light of reality. So poetry saves the poet. Jesus, here, seems to be what Thomas the father makes, whether son or poem. Before such incarnations, Jesus is the saving principle within the godlike poet and his inner light. The reincarnated wren bone may fly again, guided by light, to light. So the enlightened poet may shape the flashing diamond he is trying to shape. His shaping spirit comes from the diamond womb of the imagination.

2: "I" and "Light," the first and last words of this shape, are not only its points but Thomas' Alpha and Omega. Still in the dark by his grounded wren bone, the poet attends the birth of child, self, and poem, who or which will overthrow the dark. (Compare "head of pain" with the head hurting the hair's foot.) The mother's "casting" could mean shaping, casting out, or forecasting agony for child and poet: the crown of thorns ("thorn" and "torrid crown"). "The midwives of miracle" (cf. "Music of elements, that a miracle makes!" 185) could be Muses, attending the birth of a poem, or angels singing the birth of the Holy Child, as "turbulent" as Yeats' Jesus, heralded by singing Muses in "Two Songs from a Play." The no-longer-nameless burning baby of this obstetrical ceremony is Robert Southwell's Jesus, Thomas' poem, and Thomas himself. The torn "winged wall" of wren bone (cf. the broken sail, 153) bears these fliers to the light, and the dark-dispelling "loin" is equally creative.

3: Affected by that "loin," the wren bone, becoming a phallic snake, "writhes down" to its "kingdom come," the heaven of the womb. The "dazzler of heaven," one with snaking wren bone, is sun and Son or Thomas and son and poem. Each has a "bonfire in his mouth" (cf. 143, 152, 177). The watery, loin-splashed maiden, who bore the burning baby, will rock him, and receive him, is Virgin, Muse, and Nature. But the "shining" of this Great

Mother's three-headed child is terrible to one so long in the familiar safety of "the hooded room"; for rebirth is as frightful to a poet as birth to a child. The birth of a poem is no less frightful. Becoming the hound of heaven (cf. 165) or, better, that of the Baskervilles, the flaming child pursues the poet fleeing the light that saves.

4: The lost poet reaches haven, the sun's high noon, where, not only found, he is dumbfounded (cf. "high noon, the story-killer," "The Orchards"). Plainly, the sun is Son and son, whose "man drenched throne" is at the still center of a cyclone's wing (cf. "cyclone of silence," 183, and the heavenly "whirlpool," 137). Salvation is by adorable light; but light so blinding that it strikes a poet dumb (cf. "dumbstruck tree," 94) seems an impermanent haven for poets. "Black silence" has been replaced by white. Since Jesus and poet enjoy wounds, the blinding "wound" may mean poetic enlightenment beyond words or without words to fit. Permanent for saints, this difficulty is temporary for saintly poets.

The "fury of his stream" (cf. "Furied by his stream," 156), recalling Yeats' fury of human blood and Lawrence's organic sun, brings sun to earth and water to fire. Above and below, Jesus and poet, sun and son are confounded in dumbfounding light. "The dazzler of heaven" (156) has shaped a diamond with too many facets—one of which is sexual; for the dumbfounding haven of the wound may be the poet's wife, open again after obstetrical leave.

5: "There," in the shrine of the blazing baby, the found, dumbfounded poet enjoys heavenly bliss among the saved, who, by general resurrection, have also ascended to the light. "The judge blown bedlam" of the last judgment, announced by Gabriel's horn, combines Bethlehem with madhouse. Divine birth joins love in the poet's asylum (119). To this domestic bedlam the "bidden dust," each grain a flame, has risen from the "exhaling tomb" and from the Apocalyptic sea, which gives up its dead. The diamond is loud with wings. Turning and burning in Yeats' "widening gyre," the wings ascend from "the vultured urn," at once tomb and womb. (Thomas may have read Browne's *Urn Burial*.) This carrion bird, uniting death and sex, vultures the urn of man's "morning" in Eden. From the Alpha of Genesis we have reached the Omega of Apocalypse. First is last, death is life, and bottom is top. Of such is the kingdom of Thomas' heaven.

6: The "born sea" of Genesis praises its sun in songs of origin. "Upright Adam," the unfallen one who finds, seems Jesus and phallus. The salty voice singing of origin and seeking the sun could be that of Thomas' early poetry of womb and tomb. Indeed, the first six lines of the diamond seem a history of his poetic development and the plainest statement of his central theme: his progress from dark, watery womb to the fire and light of noon. His obsession, this theme emerges again to direct "Vision and Prayer."

The flying dust of the previous diamond becomes flying children, as ancient as Eden. (Lines seven to nine, recited with *hwyl*, are magnificent.) Reborn or born, dust and children fly flaming from canyon and urn, along with soldiers and saints, happening upon vision. Their "woundward flight" is toward Christ in heaven or toward the wounded poet, whose materials they become. The world of the poet winds home to his poem, "the shrine of his world's wound" (162).

Poetry as prayer, vision, and pain is but a facet of this diamond. Another is sex. The winding home of the writhing bone is the phallus entering its heaven, which "flows open," splashed with the furious stream. Ecstatic "I Die," uniting tomb and womb, is sexual dying to live and create. As the child saves the poet, bringing him to light, so the making of love and poetry. Holy metaphor suits triple salvation.

Conceits maybe but also significant shapes, these diamonds are what they are about—or so they seem for the time being. The bottom point of the last diamond is "Die" as the top point of the first diamond is "born." The six diamonds compose a great diamond of which the third and fourth constitute the middle. The top points of the third and fourth diamonds and the bottom point of the fifth lack distinction by sound from the nasal continuo.

I I

1: "Not wholly" lost, the poet is not wholly saved. The ascent to light in the ultimate diamonds has left him in a dark relieved somewhat by "joy" in his son's birth. "Birds of burden," the bestial vultures of the fifth diamond, have failed to carry him from the "plains of carrion" in which the wholly lost glory. The "burial song" of these dark birds of resurrection implies birth as well as death; for tomb is womb. Their black plumes, suitable for hearses (cf. the "ambulance," 152), bear "green dust" from the Apocalyptic sea and ghostly pollen from the ground. Their beaks of slime, suitable for carrion, are phallic. The "heart bone," another union of death and life, is the poet's creative instrument, of which his son and this poem are products.

The ascent of vultures requires a stanza in the shape of a wing; and the poet's prayer requires a stanza in the shape of a preacher's hourglass. Whether wing or hourglass or both together, the shape and its effect are dark; but "From," the pivotal word, promises change. That "dust" and "ghost," the words out of key with the terminal nasals, are above the wing's lowest point may be hopeful. That "heart bone" in the wing's climactic lower tip balances and replaces "the lost" in the upper tip may be encouraging—or only inevitable, like Yeats' "widening gyre." Thomas' flying hourglass may owe as much to Yeats as to Herbert.

2: The poet prays for his son, who, unweaned, thinks his mother's milk the sun and moon. May he return to the birth-bloody, wren-boned room, and may the womb "Yawn to his upcoming." What sounds like a prayer for regression must be a prayer for the "upcoming" of sexual fulfillment. Resurrection is erection and return is new adventure. Not only the womb that bore him, this womb is general: that of the son's future wife or mistress and that of the Virgin Mary. Jesus, born by the general womb, is plainly parallel to Thomas' son and as plainly the embodiment of light. But His saving light is a "dazzling prison" that blinds and confines (cf. "Blinds my cry," 157, "the dazzler of heaven," 156, and the "Prisoners . . . locked . . . in the jails . . . of his keyless smiles," 139). Saving light is dangerous.

May Thomas' son return to the womb "Before the lips blaze and bloom." These blazing, blooming lips could be those of the womb, those of the hopeful poet, or those of the son as future poet. But the last of these possibilities is made unlikely by "be dumb."

The poet's prayer for a dumb but potent son ascends from the dark center of the lost, in whose name he prays, and with whom he sits on "the unchristened mountain" (nameless or unbelievers' mountain). This dark mount could be Dante's Purgatorial mount, although it has a name and only the christened sit there.

Prayer for the son becomes, in the last word, prayer to "him"; for this son has become the Son, "the adored Infant light," and the glorious sun of heaven. Thomas' prayer ascends to this adorable composite, which, as we shall see in the next wing, includes the poet.

3: Since "he" who is prayed to occupies "the shrine of his world's wound / And the blood drop's garden," he must be the wounded poet as Christ. The garden of the bleeding heart bone could be Gethsemane, fallen Eden, or Thomas' back yard. The "briared," hoisting hands of Jesus could be the suffering poet's hand. Not only son and sun, Jesus seems the poet's creative power and his light within.

Thomas is reluctant to be saved from the familiar dark by his own light and his son's light. Better to let the dead lie, sleeping "stone blind" in the dark of the tomb. Not the rock of ages, the "Rock" that occupies the lowest point of the wing and is properly out of accord with the prevailing nasals, is bedrock or tombstone. Let the poet's heart bone break, unawaked, on his sunless mountain. Let no vultures carry his "beating dust" up to light. "Beating" implies heart and wing. Let the "bidden dust" rest "unbidden by the sun." Below the Purgatorial peak, the "river rooting plain," that of the Styx maybe, extends like "the swinish plains of carrion" in the first wing. "Rooting" is swinish. "Down," "Under," and "forever falling" are sad, dark words to conclude with. But the three last lines, straight from the heart bone, stand out.

4: The fourth wing is a darker elaboration of the third. "Forever falling night" and "endless fall," horrors for Hopkins, suit these sleepers in the tomb, who, feeling at home in a "known" country, under a known, dark star, are reluctant to awake and arise: "For the country of death is the heart's size." This line, one of the best in the poem, must mean suitable to the heart bone as bone alone. Though "common lazarus," a praying concentrate of all the dead, is happy where he lies, he mourns the "deluging light" of resurrection, dead for him and his fellows. Let the "sea" retain its dead and the "soil" enjoy its victory. The "mazes" of the grave (at the low point of this wing) are familiar and pleasing to sleepers provided with charts and clues. Tolling the tongue of those for whom the bell tolls, Dylan is still the poet of tomb and womb. It was hard to abandon the agreeable, intricate darkness of the early poems for the common day of Llareggub.

Starting with customary nasals, the terminal agreements modulate to liquids and sibilants. The final rhyme, surprising in this poem, may affirm the finality and comfort of the tomb, which still inspires the best lines; for the poet's heart is in the graveyard.

5: As the graveyard fits his bony heart, so the dark star, known to the lost, suits his vision. He prays "in the name of the lost" (160), the unborn and the dead, who reject rebirth. "Midwiving morning" with her instruments (cf. "midwives of miracle," 155) is a pleasing conceit in accord with the more obstetrical diamonds. "No," death's word, and a symphony of dark vowels for hollow men occupy the lowest and most impressive point of this wing. "No one now or no one to be," including the dead and the unborn, could also refer to "fabulous, dear God" (191). Let the crimson sun of morning leave the "grave grey." Let "the colour of clay" hide light's "martyrdom"—that of Son, son, or poet. "The interpreted evening," opposite to midwiving morning, is the dark "known" to a poet of womb and tomb and interpreted in his poetry. "Amen" fittingly concludes this prayer for comfortable darkness. But prayer resumes in the last wing—there, however, a prayer in light for more.

6: "I," the first and central word of this wing, is the important word of the poem and the most compendious approach to its theme. So occupied, the middle of the wing becomes the turning point and the lowest point becomes the highest.

Around the corner of prayer comes sudden and unaccountable salvation by light—what Calvinists of the chapel call salvation by grace. "Turn" and "burn," good words for conversion, suitably recall the first diamond, glittering now in retrospect. Still in love with tomb and womb, the poet would "turn back and run to the hidden land" of the lost. ("Yes, the Hound of Heaven is baying there," said Thomas to Watkins.) The sun, who runs the lost poet down and finds him (cf. "the finding one" of the fourth diamond), is a bright composite. As the "world's wound" he is Jesus and the wounded poet, saving himself. As the "loud sun" he is Thomas' son, crying and christening down, as babies will, on "the unchristened mountain." The ultimate sun, however, is brightest and densest of all: the sun that "roars at the prayer's end." Not only the howling baby, this sun is the poem: "My images roared . . . on heaven's hill" (44). Salvation by light, for which sun and Jesus are proper metaphors, means salvation by poetry, son, and self. In the penultimate line, these saviours become "the blinding One," the central and initial "I."

Paradox suits such holiness. No longer lost in one sense, the poet is lost in another. Scalded, drowned, and burning like a baby, he is lost and found at once. Dumbfounded no more, he has found his voice: "My voice burns in his hand"—the hand of a saviour at once three and one. At once two and one, Lazarus and Jesus ascend from the damp, dark precincts of the tomb to a world of light.

Significant shapes maybe, the diamonds and wings now seem to signify the same thing or much the same; for the second part of this poem, like the second act of *Waiting for Godot*, repeats the first with variation.

Watkins, 114, 122-23. Fraser, 29. Treece, 117-18. John L. Sweeney, Introduction, *Selected Writings*, xxi-xxii. Stanford, 94-96. Robin Mayhead, in *Scrutiny*, XIX (Winter 1952-53). W. S. Merwin, in *Casebook*, 66.

Ballad of the Long-legged Bait (1941), pp. 166-76

One afternoon at Cavanagh's on West 23rd Street, sitting at the bar, Dylan told me what this poem is about. A young man, he said, goes fishing for sexual experience—though this is not quite how he put it; but the fisherman "catches the church and the village green." In other words, Thomas meant this poem to be a narrative of the wantoning that leads to the sobrieties and responsibilities of marriage. A happy boy becomes an adult with mixed feelings. The catcher is caught. For us, this is the story of any man, and for Thomas, another autobiography that takes its place with "Once below a time," "Altarwise," "From love's first fever," "Lament," and all the rest in verse or prose, each a portrait of a young dog—sea dog in this case—and each an adventure in the skin trade. Although, sitting at the bar, he did not say this, his "Ballad" is also a portrait of the artist.

The metaphor of a voyage suits the voyage of life. Thomas had sailed the significant seas in "Altarwise," "A warring absence," and "Lie still"; and he was to sail again in "Poem on His Birthday." "Once below a time," the closest anticipation of the present voyage, tells of a "ridiculous sea dandy" who thinks himself "a Columbus on fire." But he is landed at last, as sober as a bone. Consider, too, the angling and the landing of the marine creature in "How shall my animal."

In "The Mouse and the Woman" Thomas speaks of "a sea of mystery and meaning." Sailing such a sea in this ballad is but one of many images. Land is important, and so are fish, bait, and the long-legged girl. Like most romantic images, these are "many sounding minded" (25) and incompletely assigned. "Polysemous," a good word for the many-minded image, is Dante's word for triple-talking allegory. Carlyle called the unallegorical image a "symbol," a thing that conceals and reveals. Limited by reference, a romantic symbol seems unlimited in the suggestions it carries. Indefinite is the more accurate word.

Take the fish for which the girl is bait. This fish must be experience. But a fisherman caught by his bait is a fish—a poor fish. A fish out of water is a husband. A fish in water could be an embryo. A fish is the traditional sign of Jesus, a fisherman of men; and the fisherman of this ballad, like God, has a rod. Since fish is the Word, it can be the word, as Yeats suggests in "The Fish"; and the fisherman, as he suggests in "The Fisherman," can be the poet. Fish, swimming in the deep, suggest dangerous, agreeable freedom, but, as Lovelace says, "Fishes that tipple in the deep know no such liberty" as he in prison. Which of these implications to accept depends upon the context.

The bait is a long-legged girl at the end of a troll. Does the fisherman use a girl to catch a girl? In one sense he does, but in another, he uses her to catch experience. She uses herself, hook, line, and sinker, to catch him. Bait becomes fisher of fisherman and fisherman, fish. Why long-legged? Long legs are good bait, as men know, and good for running after or away from—as the long-legged heart knows. Useful for the race, such running, as we know from "When, like a running grave," is around a track where time tracks you down. A running sea is a climber: "A climbing sea from Asia had me down" (82). The long-legged girl has sea legs, like those the fisherman thinks he has on "the sea-legged deck."

Amniotic woman, moved by the moon with the tides, is no less formidable than all those "scaled sea-sawers," the "bagpipe-breasted ladies in the deadweed" (83). Literally, the long-legged girl is a girl. Specifically, she is Caitlin Thomas, the "sunday wife" of "Lament" (196). But more than this, she embodies the poet's heart, his flesh, his Muse, and his *Anima*. In a sense, she is himself. Caught by her, he finds himself. Finding himself, he grows up, faces reality, and becomes a poet.

Saving him from the amniotic sea of his adolescence, she lands him. Land is what he sets out to sea from—the land of his parents, waving handkerchiefs. The land that sinks his silly sea, though equally domestic, is adult. The sea is enchanting and the land where he is landed is disenchanting. But coming back from romantic sporting to the home he has left, or something like it, he has gained humanity, understanding, humor, and power—all that a poet needs. What if the land proves as amniotic as the sea? What if his end is his beginning? Here, in an image, is the story of any man and of the making of a poet.

Such voyaging with its enchantment and disenchantment is not without literary precedent. Ulysses left home and, after seafaring among ladies, came home, and so did Mr. Bloom. But Ulysses was a sober man, and, in spite of Gerty MacDowell, unromantic. Rimbaud's romantic adventuring on, over, and under the sea and his return to daily earth are a closer parallel. Reading "The Long-legged Bait" brings "Bateau ivre" to mind. But Thomas, who knew no French, could not have read it—in the original. He must have read it in English, however, for there is a translation of "Bateau ivre" by Norman Cameron in *New Verse* (No. 21, June-July 1936). Thomas read *New Verse*, and Norman Cameron was a friend. It is not for nothing that Thomas, in a letter to Watkins (104), called himself "the Rimbaud of Cwmdonkin Drive."

We know that Thomas read *Moby Dick*. He may have read the story of the caught sailor in *Finnegans Wake*, open on the bar before us that day on West 23rd Street. It is likely that he read Shelley's "Alastor," another dizzy voyage. He read "The Ancient Mariner" and Yeats' poems of fishermen. And, since Thomas knew Donne's poetry pretty well, it is likely that he had read "The Baite":

When thou wilt swimme in that live bath,
Each fish, which every channell hath,
Will amorously to thee swimme,
Gladder to catch thee, then thou him.

For thou thy selfe art thine own bait;
That fish, that is not catch'd thereby,
Alas, is wiser farre then I.

There is a story in *Folklore* (XVI, p. 337, 1905) by Thomas H. Thomas about a Welsh boy in a boat on the Towy, who catches a fish that becomes a girl with his hook through her lips. She marries him, and a catcher is caught—caught again in *Saturday Night and Sunday Morning* (1958) by Alan Sillitoe. After roaring search for experience, his amorous fisherman says:

> Whenever you caught a fish, the fish caught you. . . . Mostly you were like a fish: you swam about with freedom, thinking how good it was . . . and then you were hookedup by the arse with a wife . . . the big hook clapped itself into your mouth and you were caught.

Sillitoe may have read Thomas as Thomas may have read Donne. But reading seems unnecessary for an image so inevitable as this for all the caught.

Two stories, "In the Direction of the Beginning" (1938) and "An Adventure from a Work in Progress" (1939), seem studies for "The Long-legged Bait." In these stories Thomas tried the figures—all but the bait—that were to be transfigured in the poem.

The fifty-four quatrains of the "Ballad" are those of a ballad. Sprung and deliberately roughened, the lines have three, four, or five stresses. The rhymes are various: a b c b, a b c a, a b a c, and even a b a b. Sounds, both terminal and internal, are rich—in the manners of Wales and Hopkins. The tone and feeling range from ignorant joy and extravagance to sober irony; but humor, the gift of light, is triumphant. Brightness, falling from the air, is all.

Quatrains 1-3, p. 166: Chiming vowels and consonants provide what Dame Edith calls texture. As the fisherman weighs anchor, the parental shore looks helplessly but affectionately on, dazzled by his enterprise. Parental "good-bye" becomes a motif. "Thrashing hair and whale-blue eye" make the boy a kind of Ahab, but his whaler's eye is a whale's and its color the sea's. (Compare "he was a shoreman in deep sea, lashed by his hair," "In the Direction of the Beginning.") "Trodden," meaning customary and pedestrian, may also imply the sexual endeavor of a town that bravely rings its "cobbles" like coins or bells. One day this boy, who now rejects the familiar shore, will discover the cobbles and cockles of Llareggub. Even now, the poet, looking back and seeing more than that sailing boy, has affectionate understanding of his uncommonly liberal elders. There are several kinds of "looking" here, several kinds of eyes, and several times, one of them told by the "affectionate sand." "Whale-blue" and "fishermanned" are the happiest inventions. "Fishermanned" was hit upon at once, but "whale-blue," as the worksheets show, came after trial of "pale, blue."

The anchor of the "fishermanned boat" (on the "ramshackling sea," 193) is either free (weighed) and made fast or weighed and fast (quick) as a bird. The "hooking" bird, a flying anchor or hook, is a fisher, unlike the black birds of the coast. Hook, anchor, mast, and bird, according to Freud, who directs much of the imagery, are male images. It matters little whether anchor or hooking bird is "high and dry" at the top of the mast. The adolescent display of untried masculinity must dazzle lookers-on. "Look!" says the daring young man. (Compare "hovering anchor" and "a bird above the anchor" in "In the Direction of the Beginning.") It is pleasing to guess that "high and dry," the name of a gin, introduces the "drinking dark" of the fourth quatrain. Exhibiting his hook to the eyes of the town, the boy tries his sea legs out in a pub; for, half-seas over, he is still on shore. Compare the departing hero of *Adventures in the Skin Trade,* the young man of "Once below a time," and the pub-crawling dog of *Portrait.*

Quatrain 4: Drinking sails take the sea dog into "the drinking dark." (Compare the sails of "Lie still," 153, where the winds are those of poetry or life.) "White as milk" makes the voyager an innocent, as white milk makes "the drinking dark" infantile. The last two lines, a synopsis of the poem, predict the sailor's fate: shipwreck of sun or son on a pearl, at once the last segment of the sun as it sinks below the sea's rim and, by metonymy, the feminine sea that, though thought his oyster, destroys him. (For pearls as "sea-girls" and "seashell flesh" see 87, 193.) The long-legged moon swims out of the sun's wreck or "hulk." That the triumphant moon rises in the West is no dizzier than a drinker's dark. This quatrain owes an obvious debt to "The Ancient Mariner."

Quatrains 5-6, pp. 166-67: The "funnels and masts" are those of "the dwindling ships" of Swansea harbour. "Good-bye," say the ships, joining the parental shore, as, also looking, they ("we") see what the boy is up to on that "sea-legged deck"—a brilliant, surrealistic transfer of epithet. (A deck composed of wriggling sea legs makes things hard for the most sea-legged captain.) Looking again, the ships see the bait stalking out of the fisherman's sack. Not only willing, active, and erect, confusing the members of this company, she does the stalking while her prey thinks he is fishing for her with her. "His hooks through her lips" (anchors and fishhooks) are phallic. As this is his first amatory experience, so it is hers; for, as he trolls, she rays the fishes around her in blood. ("Rayed" can mean arrayed, made radiant, or striped like a bass. Compare "the wrackspiked maiden mouth" and "bridebait," 101.) The first line of the sixth quatrain—with four or five stresses as the reader prefers—is a good example of sprung rhythm. The last line dwindles to three stresses with the "dwindling ships."

Quatrains 7-9, p. 167: Less sea-legged than he thinks, the troller bids "good-bye" to the smoking "chimneys" of the land, the smoking "funnels" of the harbour, and the smoking hearths of cottages where "old wives" ominously spin thread, like fatal sisters, and, he hopes, spin old wives' tales about him. Though clear of the smoke, he is "blind" to what he has left: his parents, looking after him from "eyes of candles" and "windows." "Candles" seem paternal, and "praying windows of waves," recalling Virginia Woolf, are maternal. "Old wives," waving a wet good-bye, become "waves." "The eyes of candles," suggesting the eyes of needles, make father a tailor (cf. 147) as well as a lighthouse in the watery window.

Incapable of seeing, the troller hears his bait bucking in a "shoal" of amorous fish, those whom he shows her off to, himself among them. If, like Mr. Bloom, he invites rivals—and whales mean rivals, Thomas told me—a sea "hilly with whales" should delight a whale-blue eye. But whales may give it the blues. He fears "whalebed and bulldance" in "A warring absence" (87); and "Into her lying down head" is a nightmare of rivals. (For whales see 42, 82, 125, 147.) Since whales are not what he is trolling for, he casts down his rod when they appear. Still at the end of his long line, however, the long-legged bait, far from downcast, ambiguously "longs" among sea horses, angel fish, and "rainbow-fish," arching in response to her joyous bucking. She is less promiscuous than she seems; for these poor fish must be the fisherman himself. At once on deck and in the sea, fisherman and fish, he thoroughly enjoys his "shoals of loves." At the center of his joy, his bait becomes his experience, his flesh, his animal *Anima*, his Muse, and his creation. After creating her as she directs, he can cast his rod down like a pencil. (Compare the created woman of "The Mouse and the Woman" and the towering pencil of "The Orchards.") "Rod" is a loaded word. Piscatorial, phallic, and literary, it is also the magician's creative wand and, according to the Psalm, God's instrument.

But over the ecstatic sea come bells of buoys, as if from a sunken cathedral, warning the heedless sailor of rocks or of "the engulfing bride" (137). "Rocked buoys" become boys wrecked on siren rocks. (Compare "swerved past a . . . buoy with cathedral chimes," "An Adventure from a Work in Progress." "Floated," syntactically puzzling, may be an ellipsis. The tide-tongued swan of Swansea liked sunken cathedrals, sunken bells, and sunken pyramids, e.g. 42, 88, 191.)

Quatrains 10-12, pp. 167-68: The anchor, now a hooking gull, soars miles above a boat that is "moonstruck" in several senses: stricken by the moon that wrecks the sun in the fourth quatrain, that rocks the buoys in the ninth, that makes lunatics of men, and, serving as a sign of the imagination, that inspires poets. The sailor is drunk on moonshine, and his *bateau* is as *ivre* as he and as loony. The "squall of birds," bellowing and falling, is plainly sexual; but the "cloud" blowing "rain from its throat" is difficult. Clouds are feminine (e.g. 89) and throats are poetical. A cloudy poet clearing rain from his throat may be a poet, directed by his Muse, emerging from his amniotic obsessions to the concerns of maturity. Taking the metaphors this way makes the ballad another history of Thomas' poetic development. Taken literally, the metaphors describe a storm at sea, a necessary part of any voyage (cf. the storm in "An Adventure from a Work in Progress," 161-62). Taken another way, the storm could mean lovers quarreling and making love.

Like a warship with smoking funnels, "fuming bows," ram, and guns for raking, the storm of fire and ice is both phallic and deadly. "Jesu's stream" and "the water's face," churned by the screws of this destroyer (cf. 12), are waters for walking on and the waters of Genesis. No sun shines on them (for the sun has been sunk by the moon), but only the oily moon, whose "bubbles" could be early poems. (For the oil of life see 27, 29, 38, 42, 63, 107.) But this moon, now one with the bait, has become the sexual aggressor, plunging, piercing, and luring. Confusion of sexes plagues this voyage. Plainly female, the bait, stalking out of the sack and "plunging and piercing," is plainly male. In a sense, the bait that the boy is fishing with is his own member; but, as they say, we are members of one another.

What more suitable for the confusions of this voyage than syntactical confusion? Whatever the syntax of the twelfth quatrain, the sense is clear. Witnessing with a kiss implies both marriage and, in connection with Jesu, betrayal—betrayal of lured fish, of bait, and of fisherman. That he is Jesus and God with a rod, creating waters, sun, moon, and woman, is what earlier poems have led us to expect; for Thomas the Word was creator and sufferer. There is a lot going on here, as in "Vision and Prayer," but here, somehow, the confusion is not confusing. Things work pretty well together.

Quatrains 13-15, p. 168: Once hilly, now Alpine, humpback whales are back, but, with a slip and a dip and "raining lips," the bait avoids all rivals—with such dizzy weavings that little wonder the "sick sea" is seasick. A teaser, revealing and concealing her great pubic bush, she spins on their spouts "in the nick of love" until all the beasts "blared" horns of "Jericho." (Announcing their own fall? Or has she become a walled town to be blasted down? Or is she conductor of brasses?) Her nipping

and tucking, nicking and timing make the horn of Jericho, like
Gabriel's trumpet, a signal for general resurrection and erection.
Turtles emerge from their shells (cf. "turnturtle dust," 191) and
"every bone in the rushing grave" becomes the cock of the morning to announce the grave's victory and death's sting. Thomas'
graves are always running, rushing, climbing, opening, and, like
escaped cocks, crowing.

Read the thirteenth quatrain aloud. Not Hopkins himself could
put sweeter sounds together:

> Whales in the wake like capes and Alps
> Quaked the sick sea and snouted deep,
> Deep the great bushed bait with raining lips
> Slipped the fins of those humpbacked tons.

This symphony of vowels and consonants proves Thomas a
master. Here is the blast of Jericho's horn and Gabriel's too, orches-
trated with the song of the reel and with all those tootling shells.

Quatrains 16-18, p. 169: Recapitulating the fifth, seventh, and
eighth quatrains, the sixteenth is the calm after the storm of love
and music. The "hand on the rod" with "thunder under its
thumbs" is that of God, the maker. It is hardly singular that
God's thumb is plural. His reel singing off its flames is the poem
inspired by the baited hook; for even tide-tongued poetry is a
"burning and crested act" (xv). The "whirled" boat, as *ivre* as
Rimbaud's, sails Thomas' burning arteries now, and, a poem
too, it cries with all its equipment "from nets to knives."

"Shearwater birds," cousins of the albatross, and "the bulls of
Biscay" (a union of "whalebed" of the bay and Spanish "bulldance," 87) have swallowed the bait at last. "The nick of love"
proves vain and vain the skill of the angler. The "huge weddings"
he has invited confirm his worst nightmare (125). Like Theseus,
he hoists a black sail to "break the black news." Since that black
news was false, there is hope, however, that this is nearer fear
than actuality.

"The green, laid veil," which recurs, is the watermarked surface of the sea or poem, decently hiding what goes on below.
"Laid" also seems his bait's condition. "Good luck," like "Good-
bye," becomes a motif to weave in and out. Holding the story

together, it changes with each appearance. But those huge weddings make the cry for luck seem vain. Love and poetry, like the journey of Bunyan's pilgrim, have their ups and downs.

Quatrains 19-21, pp. 169-70: The mariner, emerging from his gloom, is speaking now in the imperative mood, to the accompaniment of bells and drums. His joy over the bait's violation by the "raping wave" (125) makes him her violator and his own rivals. Splendidly one, he includes bait, fish, fisher, and whales, not to mention the octopus, the polar eagle, and the amorous seal. Walking, treading, and kissing, he has laid "the long, laid minute's bride." Laying is short. Its results are long. Death is the end of love; for womb is tomb.

"The gardens of the floor" anticipate the climbing gardens (cf. 85) that will displace the sea at last. "The mounting dolphin's day" must become falling night; for a dolphin's life is up and down—and burdened, as Yeats knew. Compare the phallic, poetical, aspiring, and unsunken "bell-spire" with that of "The spire cranes." Compare the coldness of the hot "polar eagle" and the "salt-lipped beak" of bird and boat with "cold Nansen's beak" of an earlier voyage (148) and "the beaks at the stern" in "An Adventure from a Work in Progress." The contention of heat with cold brings back to mind the "fuming" destroyer with its "ram of ice." The icy North is part of most symbolic voyages, that of the Ancient Mariner, for instance.

Quatrains 22-25, p. 170: "Drifting death" (that of the embryo) and "the graveyard in the water" (womb) suggest that he has got the girl with child. A composite of "nightingale and hyena," the poet sings, howls, and laughs. The "shell of a girl" includes temporal "sand" and engulfing "anemone," desert and fertile valley; for the womb, like the poet, is all-embracing. Not only the womb, this shell is that of marine Venus (63) and a container of shipwrecking pearls (cf. quatrain 4; "closed pearl" and "shell of virgins," 87; and "seashell flesh," 193). The bait and her crowded shell are the fisherman's "wanting flesh," his "enemy," as time will prove. The union of his flesh with his oyster is old as amniotic water and plain as phallic eel. That the shell, brimming with her flesh and his, is also the poem, a form for all the meanings of life and death, is likely.

The fourth "good-bye" and the fifth are sighs for the vanished delights of fishing, which, approaching land, has become sowing—and, alas, reaping. The "long-legged bread," cast upon the waters (cf. "bridebait of gold bread," 101, and "bread of water," 133) is floating home. Bread, of course, is the body of Jesus and poet. "Tall grains," scattered for the salt-lipped beaks, are sprouting. The old "fires of the face" are becoming the face of genetic waters—puddles, like those of disenchanted Rimbaud, on the shore. Harpies of the shore await the eagle of the sea: "Harpies around me out of her womb" (196).

Bearing death in her shell, the bait is scuttled. The "crab-backed dead," scuttling over her "blind, clawed stare" seem ancestors, the forces of heredity, and crabbed age. (Compare "claw of the crabbed veins," 100, "crabbing sun," 19, "scuttled sea," 105, and "crabs clacked from the shells," "An Adventure from a Work in Progress.") But the crab-backed dead, rising from the sea-bed, are also embryos, containers of the crabbed and crabbing past. *Post coitum*, as the Romans say, *tristitia*.

Quatrains 26-28, p. 171: Even the old erotic dreams, fulfilling Freudian "wishes," are dead. "The tempter" under the sleeping eyelid (cf. 125), who once created visions or eunuch dreams of "mast-high moon-white women naked," has shut up shop. (Compare the white moon-woman of "In the Direction of the Beginning" and Samuel Bennet's dream of women in *Adventures in the Skin Trade*. A mast-high woman fits the mast-high "bell-spire" of the nineteenth quatrain.) Lovely Susanna, bathing no more while crabbed elders peep, is drowned in their beards. Sheba's Solomon has yielded to "the hungry kings of the tides," embryos, babies, and moon-driven time. Delightful Sin herself is fleeing the approach of a "sunday wife" (196). The allegorical figures of Sin and Silence recall "The Ancient Mariner" and, not inappropriately, *Paradise Lost*. What Silence is doing in the domestic scene is beyond me—though blowing clouds away and leaping waters sound hopeful.

Quatrains 29-30, p. 171: Since Lucifer and Venus are the same planet as morning or evening star, their juxtaposition here seems a sign of marriage. Lucifer, the light-bringer, heroic rebel, and spectacular faller, leaves the cold, phallic North of polar eagles and rams of ice to melt "in her vaulted breath." "Vaulted" is a good word for womb, tomb, and church. (Lucifer, as Stephen

Dedalus remarks, is the "romantic youth" of Christ. Thomas' Lucifer, the "incarnate devil" who shares creation with God (46), is as good a fiddler as He.) "Lost" maybe, Lucifer is not "the star of the lost" (164). "That bird's dropping" is pleasingly ambiguous—like the condition of any husband. On the one hand, Lucifer may be a falling bird or angel. On the other, he may be bird turd. "Star-struck" Venus becomes the Virgin Mary, who conceived by a star (cf. "A star was broken / Into the centuries of the child," 143). Her "wound," unlike that of her Child, is vaginal. "The sensual ruins" of creative falling bring three "seasons" or nine months (cf. 81) to "the liquid world" of the womb. "White springs in the dark" allows two readings. If "springs" is taken as a verb, the line means the triumph of light over darkness as in "Vision and Prayer." Lucifer becomes the child of light as well as its creator, the poem as well as the poet. If "springs" is taken as a noun, we have a surrealistic picture of bedsprings.

Quatrains 31-32, p. 172: The sixth "good-bye" and the seventh, uttered by poet, fisherman, and reader, are more and more regretful. The fishing is over, the reel is wound, and "the flesh is cast" in several senses: cast by a fishing rod, shaped, forecast or determined, and cast, like bread, on the waters (cf. 54, 93). "The voices through the shell" are those of the ancestor-crowded embryo and the polysemous poem. The second "good luck" is uttered by the hopeful embryo, who, recapitulating phylogeny, is finned and feathered like bird and fish. For drinking sails, thunder, and lightning see quatrains 4 and 16. "Catch" is the important word. What, after all, is the fisherman's catch: his child, his bait, himself, his poem? Whatever the catch, there is a catch in it as there is a rub in "the rub of love." "Catch" splendidly concentrates the meanings of the fishing.

Quatrains 33-34, p. 172: In connection with "freezes fast," the "six-year weather" suggests arctic stasis (cf. "six-year night," "An Adventure from a Work in Progress") and, maybe, the chilling prospect of rearing a young child (cf. "From blank . . . winter sails the child," 93). What the "gold gut" of the sixteenth quatrain drags from the submarine landscape of the twenty-second quatrain is the catch. "The crest" is light, birth, and "crested song." What clings to the child's emerging "hair and skull" seems the crabbed, ancestral past of the twenty-fifth quatrain, "the centuries of the child" (143). In "the six-year weather," we are surrounded with icicles ("statues of great rain") and snow (cf. the "snowstorm whose flakes fell like hills," "glass hills," and "white rain" of the arctic episodes of "An Adventure from a Work in Progress" and "In the Direction of the Beginning"). Plainly, the fisher, as the thirty-first quatrain proclaims, has "no more desire." He has had it. But the boat's "drinking wings" still promise pubs near home and a little relaxation.

Quatrain 35, p. 172: Poetry breaks through. However "heavy" his "haul" and whatever the catch in his catch, the poet sings it. (Compare "strike and smoothe," quatrain 20. To strike, which has a hundred senses, can mean to cause to sound, to cast in a mold, to form, to light upon, to hook a fish. Both fish and fisherman strike.) "The long dead bite" rivals "catch," the other great concentrate. A cockney pun on bait, "bite" refers to the girl. Biting bait becomes the catch and the catcher—and that is the catch. Bite carries suggestions of Eve's apple and the serpent of Eden. That the bait is dead we know from quatrains 21 and 25. But "bite," as the striking catch, can be the embryo, a floating dead man, and, since the fisherman is caught, the fisherman with dead desire.

"The snow of light" combines the six-year weather with Lucifer, fall and death with birth: "White springs in the dark." The miracles are those of birth, poetry, and Jesus as poet and fisherman of men. The "miracle of fishes" is the miracle of loaves and fishes, appropriate here because a fish has been caught, bread has been cast on water, fishes are words, the fisher is the Word, and this miracle is one of multiplication. (Be fruitfly and multiply, as Thomas Morgan, Organ Morgan, or someone else may have said. Compare the "midwives of miracle," 155, "Music of elements, that a miracle makes," 185.)

Quatrains 36-39, p. 173: "The urn" (cf. "vultured urn," 158) is womb and tomb; and so are the "room" (cf. 154) and the "house" that holds "town" and "continent." "Fossil" is the imprint of the past upon the embryo. (Compare "carved limbs in the rock" and "Calligraphy of the old leaves," 134; "the print on the cliff," "In the Direction of the Beginning.") The "insect-faced" forefathers "in dust and shawl" are like these fossils and the crab-backed dead of the twenty-fifth quatrain (cf. "in crabbed burial shawl, by sorcerer's insect woken," 93). The hand of the past conducts the child, who recapitulating the past, becomes the past—all "the centuries of the child" (143). Birth of a child is the rebirth of old men, led as if children and airy ghosts by the dead hand of heredity to "the blindly tossing tops" of the boat's mast. Though waving in the light and air, the mast of this boat is blind as a bat.

Seed and egg are the beginning of death, the old men sing. (Compare "oaks were felled in the acorn and lizards laid in the shell," "An Adventure from a Work in Progress.") In *New Poems* this discouraging song of childbed lacks italics, added here, perhaps, to indicate a climax. (The manuscript has italics.) The "newborn lips" are those of Thomas—or will be once the bait has landed him.

Quatrains 40-41, pp. 173-74: He who blew fire into the watery womb and "died" there is father and the poet as God, walking the earth of Genesis in the cool of the evening—as "cool as a cucumber" in the worksheets—to admire the work of His rod. "Counting the denials of the grains" may hint the parable of seeds falling on barren ground, the noting of fallen sparrows, or the fact that seeds bring death into the world. Yet the godlike poet, dependent on the "drifting hair" of the dead bait, "climbs" it. Now "the risen sun" of dawn or the risen Son of Easter, he laments the songs he has taught his "liquid choirs." These could be his early poems of the womb or his embryos, who, by heredity, are of the tribe. He weeps the death he has brought upon them.

Quatrains 42-45, p. 174: Home from the sea, the sailor changes his manner of speaking. The "liquid choirs" of womb and sea approach the young and easy chorus of Llareggub and Fern Hill. This change of manner, movement, light, and feeling proves the ballad another history of poetic development. Regressive or irresponsible dream has yielded to responsibilities in the light of common day or harvest moon. The light that never was on sea shines out on land.

Now a "divining" rod (cf. 29), the old fishing rod, once pointing to water—as a divining rod should—now points to land. The plug of the tub pulled up, the sea sinks in a "whirlpool of ships." Sinking like Noah's flood, the sea brings gardens to light—

a countryside of men, women, birds, and animals, all "holding to her hand"; for the girl who has landed the catch is as earthy as the Great Mother, rooted in time and place, in valleys and among insects (cf. the "insect-faced" fathers). As his fathers held her hand in the thirty-seventh quatrain, so the garden now—at once Eden and the cool, dry earth of Wales. "The green, laid veil," once that of the sea, has become that of the land, where the landed fish lies "stunned" (cf. "cast high, stunned on gilled stone," 101). The temporal "sand" of the shore (cf. "the affectionate sand," quatrain 3), "with legends in its virgin laps" and on its lips, becomes the Virgin with Child or the girl with her child and her poet, for whom the sunny sand dunes prophesy more light. Her "breaking with seasons and clouds" can mean breaking off relations with or bursting with. A fresh-water girl, she trails her hand in a brook, like the boy of "A Prospect of the Sea." This brook, though on land, is "a separate river," apparently a current, in "the greater waves" of life's salty sea. In lyric grace the forty-fifth quatrain rivals Auden's "Fish in the unruffled lakes."

Quatrains 46-48, p. 175: "His catch of fields" is not far from the sea that has sunk beneath it; for barley grows in "the surge," cows graze on "the covered foam," and horses of the "arched, green farms" (arched, like Fern Hill, with green and golden trees) are as salty as riding gulls. But thunderbolting colts are also related to Lawrence's St. Mawr and Thomas' stallion, who trots "with a loud mate the haybeds of a mile" (100). The fisherman's "haul of miracles," no longer as "heavy" as it seemed, includes the joyous barnyard. "Strike and sing" is to "Sing and strike" (quatrain 35) as this miraculous, bucolic haul is to that miraculous heavy haul.

The gulled and salty countryside becomes the "country tide" of a "cobbled" sea town, Llareggub itself with all its cockles and mussels. Back in the town that "rang its cobbles for luck" as, deaf to their sound, he sailed out to sea, he sees the place with new eyes, hears it with new ears, and sings it with "newborn lips." As it strikes him for the first time, he strikes up. The "country tide" and its cockled town are holy now. Not so the city; for, as God made the town that the poet will remake, so fallen man made the wicked city. This vision of London as tomorrow's Sodom and Gomorrah or declining and falling Rome is that of "Because the pleasure-bird whistles" and "The Countryman's Return." In "One Warm Saturday" a hellfire preacher thunders against Sodom and Gomorrah in the streets of Swansea. But Thomas' moral indictment, tempered by two puns, yields to the gaiety of the cobbled shore. A pity that this countryman had to die at Seventh Avenue and 13th Street.

Quatrains 49-50, p. 175: The "steeples" hint that the church of a "sunday wife" is part of his catch, steeples over the village green. Her steeple-pierced "cloud" (see quatrain 44 and "A warring absence") promises domestic squalls. "The streets that the fisherman combed" become "the thoroughfares of her hair," up which he has climbed (quatrain 41). These streets, that lead him home, make his voyage seem a metaphor for adventure on shore as "his long-legged flesh" makes his bait seem his member.

The glory of the tide-tongued poet's "country tide" pales in the terror of coming home again. (The chiasmus of "terribly . . . home" and "home . . . terror" intensifies the elements by weaving his fate.) "Home alive" is ultimate terror for this poor fish out of water. Like the prodigal son (cf. 95, 177), he has come home to "the furious ox-killing house of love." These oxen of the prodigal son may be fatted calves or Homeric and Joycean beasts, devoted to the sun and sacrificed to love's hunger. The almost zodiacal "house of love" is fated marriage and the "ramshackling" womb. Hence the sighs of "the old ram rod, dying of women" (193, 194). Repeated "And" marks the syntax of dream—bad dream.

Quatrains 51-54, p. 176: "Down, down, down," like falling Alice, goes the romantic sea, leaving nothing but "Land, land, land." This desperate echo is comic. Everything here is a little mixed. The lamented "metropolis" or mother city of fishes has gone under the ground on which agreeable villages float. However lamented, the sea joins Sodom and other rejected cities now. Yet still "loud" from underground, the sea continues to direct "speech" with its "sound": for the manners of womb and tomb, even in a sunny village, are hard to discard. Anyway, the boat is dead, and the "bait" (plainly the poet here) is drowned like a fish among hayricks.

The "seven tombs" are the seven seas; for tomb is womb and womb is sea, which, like woman, is "talkative." The anchor that used to soar like a hooking bird now "dives through the floor of a church"—through the girl (a composite now of church and village green) to the sea below.

The great words of the penultimate quatrain are "the pacing, famous sea." As the worksheets prove, Thomas arrived at "pacing" after trying "stalking," "loud," and "long." Pacing is the right word, one agrees, without knowing why. Pacing can mean deliberately walking, measuring, or setting the speed of a runner; but the magic of the word exceeds these meanings. No less magical, "famous," a word from Yeats' grandest vocabulary, was hit upon at once, as the worksheets prove. Sudden strike and careful angling land equal miracles. We can only admire the miracle of words together; for their sense, their placing, their effect on one another, their rhythm and sound, and all their ghostly attendants work, like that pacing, famous sea, below the threshold.

At the door of his home, hearing the speech of the pacing sea, the fisherman stands alone. "Alone," "door," and "home" are important words. At home with his wife, he is alone. A door is for going into, out of, or standing in. He is "lost on land," but, as we know from "Vision and Prayer," to be lost may be to be found.

The sun, once sunk by the moon, has come up again to shine with the moon on the land. These co-operating shiners may be father and mother, husband and wife, or day and night. "Struck" (cf. "moonstruck," quatrain 10), which puts an end to all the striking and singing, can mean a hundred things; but the effect is final. "Good-bye, good luck," the common strike of sun and moon, brings motifs together in a great farewell to the stricken striker. These unions, like that of thesis and antithesis, have a synthetic air.

But the great, last line, which weds the final to the unfinal, is the fitting conclusion to a story of bait and catch. The "long-legged bait" and the "long-legged flesh" have become the "long-legged heart," which, by the aid of these predecessors, is all-inclusive. Both his wife and himself and parts of each, this heart may be caught, or ready to run away, or caught and ready to run with. Tennyson's Ulysses vies with Homer's and his Penelope with Helen. A heart in hand may be clutched, offered, displayed, contemplated, or about to be thrown away; and since a hand is what a poet writes with, "hand" is the last word, fittingly. A poet's heart is in his hand. A heart with long legs in a hand in a door may mean coming, going or staying. Long legs can mean past or future running. The comic, the tragic, the ironic, the humorous, and the pathetic pace the scene. But from these mixtures of conditions, possibilities, feelings, and tones something like the "yes" of Mr. and Mrs. Bloom emerges—as it emerges from "Lament." Stuck with life, we accept it. Our feelings about it are mixed, but we rage against the dark. Long-legged time has tracked us down, and legs are for arthritis in the long run.

The hundred-and-fifty worksheets (now at The University of Buffalo) that Thomas devoted to this poem show craft and the process of creation. "Dylan & Caitlin," in the center of the thirty-second sheet, shows the meaning of the fishing.

Donald A. Stauffer and W. H. Auden, in *Poets at Work* (1948), 53-54, 164, 178-79. Watkins, 103-04. Olson, 24-25, 44, 50-52. Fraser, 31. Treece, 114. Tindall, *The Literary Symbol* (1955), 155-56. Glauco Cambon, in *English Miscellany*, VII (1956). Richard A. Condon, in *Explicator*, XVI (1958). Stanford, 118-19.

Holy Spring (1945), *p.* 177

Thomas wrote two great poems about the war. Neither of these, "Holy Spring" rivals "Dawn Raid" in fanciful ingenuity. Two seventeenth-century conceits seem the poet's excuse and, maybe, his occasion. The ostensible occasion is waking up and getting out of bed at dawn in spring after a night of fire raids. The sun of morning becomes an image of light, life, sex, and poetry, all of which, like spring itself, renew the dark world of death. Becoming the son of morning, the poet defies death in two long and intricate sentences that crowd two intricate stanzas, introduced by "O" and "No."

"O no" is a likely but premature response. Female "O" (cf. "virgin o," 21) recalls the "O" that begins the eighth chapter of *Finnegans Wake*, Anna Livia's great song of renewal and the most familiar part of the *Wake*. The allusion to Joyce, whether intended or not, is significant; for this poem is another of Thomas' wakes. "No," which serves as the lowest point of "Vision and Prayer" (165), is the word of death in "Now." As there "nay" becomes no to death, so here. The "No" of "Holy Spring" becomes yes to life.

1: The "bed of love" that Thomas gets out of becomes a "hospital"—not unlike that which Eliot took from Sir Thomas Browne for *Four Quartets*. Bed is a hospital for the "cureless" body of "counted" dust. The night's wounding terror came "over the barbed and shooting sea" of the Manche as a trench. "Assumed" ("assured" in an early version) means take up, gather, take the shape of. "I climb" ("out of a bed") is the main clause. "That one dark I owe my light," an elliptical construction, may mean that I owe my light to that one dark night or that, one in the dark, I owe my light to that dark. The dark war, as the end makes almost plain, helps him to emerge into the light of "Vision and Prayer," where he had other assistants. The "mirror," which serves as "confessor" to any narcissist, may be the war, the light, or his enlightened self, probably the last. (Stephen Dedalus was always looking into mirrors for a vision of himself.) It would be fine, the poet modestly says, to have a "wiser mirror" to "glow" with light after this dark night, but there is none around. "God stoning" may be the air raid as an act of God (cf. "gods are stone," 52) or the destruction of God by war.

The last line of the first stanza owes its uncertainty to "struck," a favorite word of "The Long-legged Bait." Does this line mean that, struck by the sun's light or by god-stones, the lonely poet becomes a "holy maker"? Or does the cause of sunstrokes strike him "lonely"? Any poet in our society is lonely without the sun's assistance, especially a holy or druidical bard. Though a "holy maker" must be full of the sun's light, sunstroke should send him back to his hospital. Whatever the meaning of the line, it has a grand sound, the better, maybe, for a little mystery.

2: The second sentence is addressed to the sun. Not spring or dawn is cause for praise, Thomas tells him, but poetry alone and the fact that a lonely maker can stand up and sing after such a bad night. Of spring, dawn, sex, and poetry, the signs and causes of renewal, poetry is the greatest, for it includes the rest; and the mirror-gazing poet is greater than his poem or his tool.

The vision of spring may owe something to Hopkins' juicy, joyous sonnet of spring. "All Gabriel" means spring as annunciation of divine birth and the rebirth of fallen man. "The woebegone pyre," literally burning London, is also the renewing pyre of the phoenix. Compare "the weeping wall" with the "sackcloth" of "A Refusal to Mourn."

The second conceit, that of the sun, is no less traditional than the conceit of the hospital, though more complex. As literal sun, prodigal of rays, he brings light, dawn, and spring to a dark world. As prodigal son (cf. 95, 175), he comes home again after wasting his substance elsewhere. As "Sun the father," he is an image of God, the creator, and Jesus, the recreator at Easter. As son the father, he is the "arising" penis. As creator of light, he is the poet and his poem. The "quiver full of the infants of pure fire" establishes these identities. This pure fire, not that of the fire raid, is what a burning baby's arms are full of (143), the fires of life and love and song. Any father in his hospital bed has a quiver of arrows, but the brightest of all are in the quiver of a fathering poet, the concentrate of the sun in all his capacities.

No praise to the spring, the sunny poet tells himself, but "blessed be" the "hail and upheaval" of the bombed night; for there in the dark is the occasion for the poet's glowing emergence. War has enabled him to "stand and sing alone" in the ruins, to sing the light—"if only for a last time"; for tomorrow he may die. "That uncalm still it is sure alone" may mean, after unscrambling, that although things are still uncalm, the one sure good is to stand alone and sing. Repeated "alone," which echoes "lonely," seems the important word (cf. 176). The "toppling house of holy spring," literally the husk of London, may refer to the zodiac, toppled with things below, amid which the lonely, singing ram stands untoppled and erect, the holy image of recreative light, ejaculating love. By "holy" Thomas means what Lawrence meant.

A good poem by Thomas is a dense and radiant arrangement, a harmony of complications. This poem of the hospital bed of love seems another syndrome.

Watkins, 123. John L. Sweeney, Introduction, *Selected Writings*, xx-xxi. John Wain, *Preliminary Essays*, 183. Stanford, 126.

Fern Hill (1945), *pp.* 178-80

Fern Hill is the farm of Ann Jones, the aunt who is celebrated in "After the Funeral." This farm, the place of holidays from Swansea, glows in memory with even brighter "shoots of everlastingness" than Cwmdonkin Park. In "The Peaches," a recapture of the past in prose, Annie Jones presides over "Gorsehill," which, although it affords a "dingle," is dilapidated and muddy. Yet "there was nowhere like that farm-yard in all the slap dash county." Transfigured by the eyes of youth, "ramshackle outhouses" yield glory. Something of this glory is recaptured in "A Prospect of the Sea" and in the merry barnyards of "A Winter's Tale" and "The Long-legged Bait." Though not devoted to the farm, "Poem in October" and "The hunchback in the park" are comparable visions. Childhood and the cobbles and cockles of Llareggub were the great inventions of ripest Thomas.

"Fern Hill" brings poems by other poets to mind: Vaughan's "Retreate," Marvell's "Garden," and Hopkins' sonnet of "Mayday in girl and boy." "What," asks Hopkins, "is all this juice and all this joy?" But "Fern Hill," needing no more than hints from these or from Wordsworth's poems, is Thomas' own.

Not how it feels to be young, the theme of "Fern Hill" is how it feels to have been young. Time, which has an art to throw dust on all things, broods over the poem. Time is our enemy, yet, as Eliot says, it is only in time and through it that we escape from it. Youth is an ignorant escape that time allows, and wiser memory another. But art, at once in time and out of it, is time's great evader and destroyer. "Fern Hill" is Thomas' victory over what he laments. The green and golden joy of childhood and the shadowy sorrow of maturity become the joy of art. An elder's opinion of another's youth forbids such happiness and art.

The stanza of "Fern Hill" seems a variant upon that of "Poem in October." The young and easy rhythm, below a timing or above it, conspires with alliteration and assonance to shape a symphony in green and gold major. As the poem transcends time and timing, so the craft rebukes analysis. Metronome and caliper find better employment elsewhere. Yet pointing out some parts of glory does not necessarily impair it.

1: "Now" is a storyteller's opening word and a reminder of time, intensified by "was." "As I was young and easy" may be a remote, but not inappropriate, echo of Housman, also echoed in the "many-coloured county" of "A Prospect of the Sea." Although the holidaying boy thinks himself "lordly" (he is also a "prince" in "The Peaches"), it is time that allows this illusion of easy sovereignty. The "heydays" of time's eyes are really the time-permitted heydays of the boy's eyes, which transform temporal reality by projection. His lilting vision makes the ugly house "lilting." "Once below a time," another storyteller's opening and the beginning of a children's tale, suitably modified, means out of time to all appearances (as in "Once below a time"); but "below" also means in time, subject of and to a time and future subject of another. Time, and not the young prince of a fairy story, is the prince of this apple-boughed town.

To heydayed eyes all is "green" and "golden," like the leaves of May in sunshine, seen when skating down the street at the age of six at six o'clock in the morning. Golden brings ripe fruit to mind and Shakespeare's golden lads and girls. Green, not only the color of nature's fuse and the "thought in a green shade" of Marvell's natural Eden, can also mean innocent or immature—as unripe as windfalls. "Windfall light" is that of green apples, which, falling before their time, intimate general fall—like all the apples of this apple-crowded Eden. Marvell's trickier apples are "melons," but Thomas was innocent of Greek. Reading the poems of D. H. Lawrence in July, 1945, Thomas discovered and, in a letter to Oscar Williams, praised this line: "O the green glimmer of apples in the orchard . . . stackyard." Lawrence's apples seem simpler than those of Marvell or Thomas, though just as green.

2: "Green and carefree," echoing "young and easy," anticipates "heedless" and "nothing I cared" in the fifth stanza. Separate "green" and "golden," the thesis and antithesis of this holiday, become "green and golden" in happy synthesis. That the opening words of lines 2, 4, 5, and 6 repeat those of the first stanza lends assurance of permanence, with only the slightest variation, to one who will be "famous among the barns" forever and "honoured among wagons." "As [as if?] the farm was home" also makes holiday forever; but "the sun that is young once only," whatever the harmony of vowels, qualifies the feeling of permanence by maturity's awareness. Thomas in time is hovering above a Thomas once below it. "The mercy of his means," another mature reflection, means the most merciful of the means by which time rules us. "Time let," repeated from the first stanza, rebukes the absolute young prince with the idea of limited monarchy.

"Huntsman and herdsman," in chiasmatic relation to their horns and foxes, are another of childhood's interweavings. Compare the ringing pebbles of the brook with the ringing cobbles of the town (166). Streams are "holy" because "the country is holy" (182), youth trails clouds of glory, and every day of the holiday is sabbatical around here now, far from Sunday school, in the young but aging sun. Thomas is none of those children "kept from the sun" in "There was a saviour."

3: The third stanza shares the delights of day with those of night, which has intruded fleetingly in the first stanza. All the day long underlies and unites "all the sun long" and "all the moon long." Fluid syntax suits holiday ecstasy, for which "lovely" is a word chosen in despair of words; yet "lovely," like "nice" in "A Prospect of the Sea," proves the very word for childish joy: "He could think of no words to say how wonderful the summer was. . . . There were no words for the sky and the sun and the summer country: the birds were nice, and the corn was nice."

"Running," the word for the rhythm of ecstasy, belongs, as well, to the "holy streams." Compare the child's haydayed vision of "hay / Fields high as the house" with "the house high hay" of the fifth stanza. Wind in the chimneys and "fire green as grass" hold but two of the four elements that sing this watery, earthy joy.

The stars of night are as "simple" as their observer from a house as "lilting" as he. Like the girl of "In Country Sleep," the boy rides to sleep—astride no nightmare. He dreams of the farm that owls seem, but fail, to carry away—of birds flying with the ricks and flashing horses. "Blessed among stables" applies to dreamer and nightjar alike. Night is a dream of day, and day itself, golden with the light of holiday, returns as fresh as a daisy and green as the "windfall light."

4: The boy awakes to a dewy, cock-heralded day, as fresh as the first day in Eden. The sky has "gathered" the first "simple light" of Genesis to spin the sun into a ball. But yesterday was the first day of Genesis too, and so tomorrow will be and every day forever. "Warm" in the new sun now, the horses were "spell-bound" by dream in the dark—spellbound too by the magic of youth as they walk (flashing is for the night) from "the whinny-ing green stable." Double transfer of epithet, transforming the stable, reports youth's magic. "The fields of praise" are the meadows of Fern Hill and the Elysian Fields. In "A Prospect of the Sea" the farm is no less paradisal.

5: "And," the opening word, also opens the second and fourth stanzas and the nocturnal half of the third. Freud's dream-connec-tive suits spellbinding youth by night or day. "Honoured" brings the first stanza back, and "foxes" the second, to enrich a day without predecessor by its predecessor. The "lilting house" be-comes as "gay" as its visitor. The clouds of his Eden are "new made" every day, like bread from Annie's oven, and, every day the first, his sun is "born over and over." "Happy as the heart was long," another transformation of the ordinary, recalls "All the sun long"; but heart as day brings time to mind and the short-ness of life.

According to John Malcolm Brinnin, who visited the farm, Thomas winced at "heedless," for which he could find no better word. But the stale and flat may serve as necessary relief. "Heed-less," moreover, is the reflection of the tired commentator on the "sky blue trades" (cf. "the woken farm at its white trades," 132) of innocence. Even the sunflower is weary of time at times. "Time allows," recalling "Time let" in the first and second stanzas, in-troduces Paradise lost. "Green and golden" lads and girls, falling into knowledge, must follow time as he leads them "out of grace." The gates of Paradise bang shut. The eaten apple, if green, will bring discomfort, and, if golden, discord.

But time is not altogether bad. His "tuneful turning" allows "such morning songs" as the child's song of praise and this poem, however "few" such songs. The sun which measures time is all the light we have and the conductor of time's music.

6: Elements from the previous stanzas acquire pathos and new meaning from new context. The "lamb white," careless days of innocence are over. Led by "the shadow" or the dark ghost of his childish hand to the moony loft where he once slept, Thomas, revisiting the farm, finds glory gone. He wakes again—this time to a "farm forever fled from the childless land," which glows in memory alone.

Led by time and at his mercy, even when "young and easy," the poet knows now that time has always "held" him. Once green, he was "dying" like all green things—like the ignorant, green sea itself. As the sea sings in the chains of moon and sun (cf. "moon-chained" sea, 176), so the chained boy sang then. But tuneful time allows "morning songs." Waking to death, the poet still sings green and golden songs: the coins on his eyelids sing "like shells" (151) of the tide-tongued sea.

Sister M. Laurentia, C. S. J., in *Explicator*, XIV (1955). John Malcolm Brinnin, *Dylan Thomas in America*, 125-27, 236. Tindall, *The Literary Symbol*, 261. C. B. Cox, in *Critical Quarterly*, I (1959). Thomas recorded this poem, Caedmon, 1002.

In Country
Sleep, 1952

😾

"Do Not Go Gentle," originally in this volume, is now with the poems of *Deaths and Entrances* in *The Collected Poems*. "In Country Sleep," the last poem of *In Country Sleep*, is the first of the present arrangement. These poems, written between 1947 and 1951, are Thomas at his mellowest. "Elegy," later than the poems of *In Country Sleep*, was published posthumously. "Author's Prologue" belongs with these ultimate poems.

In Country Sleep (1947), *pp. 181-86*

When I told Thomas that I thought this poem to be about how it feels to be a father, he cried, but whether from vexation, beer, or sentimental agreement I could not tell—nor can I now, though I still think this poem to be about how it feels to be a father. Yeats wrote "A Prayer for My Daughter." "In Country Sleep" is Thomas' prayer for his. Fathers worry about daughters.

There are wolves around, except on special days: Fathers' Day at the seminary or at Smith College itself.

Thomas had a "grand and simple" plan for a long poem to be called "In Country Heaven." Of this, "In Country Sleep," "Over Sir John's hill," and "In the White Giant's Thigh" were to be parts, but where they were to go in the structure, he tells us in "Three Poems" (*Quite Early One Morning*), he did not know. This great poem was to concern man and God, "the milky-way farmer . . . the beginning Word, the anthropomorphic bowler-out and blackballer, the stuff of all men." The world He created has killed itself. Memories of the joys, fears, ecstasies, and mysteries of the world, "all *we* know and do not know," were to fill this "affirmation of the beautiful and terrible worth of the Earth." It is a pity that Thomas had no time to complete his "lofty, pretentious, down-to-earth-and-into-the-secrets, optimistic, ludicrous, knock-me-down moony scheme"; for the three parts we have are among his happiest poems.

"In Country Sleep" is divided into two parts, the first of which has nine stanzas of seven lines, one a short one. The second part has eight stanzas of six lines, one a short one. Rhyme, good on the whole, is complicated by assonance. Rhythm, abounding in anapaests, is sprung: five or six stresses—and sometimes more—in the long lines, two in the short. ("Out of a *lair* in the *flocked leaves* in the *dew* dipped *year*." Even if Thomas measured his lines by syllables rather than stresses, syllables in English are stressed or unstressed.) In and out of this flexible pattern, grammatical units weave. The placing of pauses and the short lines affect the movement—and so does the concert of alliteration and internal assonance. These sequences in the third stanza, for example: "rooting . . . wooed . . . plumes . . . broomed . . . spume," "shielded . . . sleep . . . greenwood keep." Agreements and freedoms contending with structural asymmetry, troubled rhythm, and discord present a father's peace and anxiety.

Abundant echoes of Hopkins in rhythm, sound and image seem meant to be recognized. Such echoes, in accord with parodies of ritual, improve the holiness of nature—in Wordsworth's pantheistic sense or Lawrence's, not that of Hopkins, for whom nature was emblem. In Thomas' natural chapel the ministers are rooks. As Hopkins admired Milton for his technical dexterity and detested him as a heretic, so Thomas admired Hopkins for his technical dexterity and detested him as a Papist. The candles and censers of Rome, however, retained their power. Enlarging the chapel, they made it the size of Thomas' back yard.

I

The argument is simple: In the house at Laugharne, Thomas has read his daughter to sleep with folk and fairy tales. However terrible these tales, he says, fear no more. Have no bad dreams of wolves, pigs, ganders, or witches; for these are natural or fictive. Fictions are harmless, boys are boys, nature is holy, and the house secure. But it is wise to fear the Thief, who, left ominously undefined, will find a way into the house, inevitably.

1-3: "Riding," as the spellbound boy of "Fern Hill" once rode, the girl has been "spelled asleep" by "hearthstone" and "hobnail tales" of Little Red Riding Hood and Robin Hood in his "greenwood." But grandma no more, the wolf in the "sheepwhite hood" has become the proverbial wolf in sheep's clothing. Neither wolf should hold terror for a dreaming girl. No danger from the gooseherd and swincherd who, in fairy tales, turn to princes. (There is pretty play with "homestall . . . hamlet," "king . . . prince," "fire . . . ice." But, although a prince, Hamlet seems a little out of keeping with the other personae.) Boys are boys even if swineherd turns to "rooting" pig and gooseherd to plumed gander. ("Ringed" suggests the nose of the piggywig of "The Owl and the Pussycat.") Never need the "rider" fear she will be "wooed / And slaved and riven," burnt and spiked in "dingle" or "spinney" by such innocents. Never need she fear the "spume" or scum of a witch's cauldron—even that of the "broomed" witch of Hansel and Gretel; for, though "ranging the night in the rose and shire" of dream and tale, "country sleep" holds the rider safe in "the greenwood keep," nature's stronghold. Sense is a lesser magic here than glancing hints, reflexive arrangement, rhythm, and sound.

4-6: No danger from "rustic shade or spell" until death tolls her to final sleep. Nothing haunts the eaves or dells but "moonshine," synesthetically echoing. No danger; for "The country is holy." From this statement and a father's prayer the religious imagery proceeds. Angels, saints, grace, cells, nunneries, domes.

beads, chants, lauds, kneeling, knelling, bowing, and the lord's table are metaphors for nature, the *"Sanctum sanctorum"* and the "green good." The "robin breasted tree" with "three Marys in the rays" seems the cross, but the third Mary is a problem, unless quite contrary or followed by a lamb. Not that of the Lamb, the blood before which beasts and woods kneel must be green. The "tales" and "fables," converted by holiness, seem Biblical now. "The prayer wheeling moon" (cf. 92), though as holy as the other machinery, is a Buddhist intrusion.

But into this holy, natural, fabulous peace comes a greater intruder, the Thief, "meek as the dew." Not the "baaing" wolf, the "tusked prince" in love's sty, or the owl but the Thief is "the gravest ghost." Fear him.

7-9: The seventh and eighth stanzas repeat elements met before: grove, thatch, and linen of the bed, all defenses against the "roarer at the latch" and the "dousing" (putting out, striking, drenching) ghost; the "stern bell" of death; and the "hearthstone tales," which, like poems, cast spells. Saying little—almost nothing new—over and over has the incantatory effect of ritual and prayer. The pattern of sounds and movements becomes more portentous than its familiar matter.

"The beaked, web dark and the pouncing boughs" of wood and gander recall the "beak-leaved boughs dragonish" of Hopkins' Sibyl and her "vast night"—as "haygold stalls" and "windmilled dust," in the ninth stanza, have all the air of a happier Hopkins.

The sly Thief will surely fall upon the girl in two senses: pouncing from the dark and falling like snow, hail, rain, dew, dust, and leaves. Falling, the principal motion, is the new and important element. Falling like natural things makes the Thief natural and inevitable. But falling rises to include the fall of man, the fall of stars, and the world's end. The girl's origin was "the falling star" of her begetting (cf. 143), but stars must fall to death. "Morning leaves" and "apple tree" are those of "Fern Hill" and Eden. Gliding and falling, the "Apple seed . . . flowers" in "the yawning wound" of Jesus. (Adam also had a wound—over a rib; the poet, as we know, is wounded; the girl's heart, courted from her side in stanza 2, must leave a wound, and her side is wounded in stanza 15.) Wounded Adam, poet, and girl amount to Christ, man's great composite. But Easter flowering from Christ's wound only precedes the world's fall and "the cyclone of silence," the paradoxical end of everything. (Compare God's "whirlwind silence," 189, the "cyclone" and "black silence," 157.) The "stern bell" has announced ultimate, whirling silence.

"The wind-milled dust" and the "pounded . . . leaves" come from nature's mill, turning before that cyclone. "Haygold," returning to childhood's spells, suggests Goldilocks, as "Sleep spelled," the Sleeping Beauty.

Of the Thief, all we know so far is that, falling like everything in nature, he is silent and sure as death. Maybe he is death's agent or death himself. Maybe he is time or grief, its thief. But since the Thief is in close proximity to Jesus here, and since "the day of the Lord so cometh as a thief in the night" (1 Thessalonians, 5:2), the "meek" Thief may be Jesus or religion—deadening formal religion as against natural holiness and its metaphors. The Thief is easier done than said. An unassigned symbol, he suggests many things—all beyond proof, whatever the assurance of our guesses.

I I

10-13: There is more news of the Thief in the ambiguous statement (stanza 12) that ends a series of thirteen ambiguous exclamations. "Night," which introduces the first and fifth of this series, grows darker over a more menacing countryside. As obscurity deepens in nature, making all uncertain, so obscurity deepens in the poem; and with dense night, poetic density. Exclamations may be enthusiastic. Not so these thirteen, which come to seem shouting in the unlucky dark. The holy book of nature opens to a text upon which dark birds and black boughs preach sermons. These sinister ministers prophesy the Thief, whose coming, however, may not be so dark as it seems.

The first exclamation (stanza 10) serves as transition from children's tales to nature's tale and sermon. "Reindeer" above "haycocks" have abandoned the night before Christmas; and the ribbons of Sinbad's "roc" do little to make it harmless. Flying reindeer and roc introduce rooks, "soaring" as high as "The leaping saga of prayer!" "Saga" unites children's story with the darker story of nature, and "prayer" unites a father's prayer with that of

the black rooks. That "The leaping saga of prayer" is also a definition of poetry seems established by "The saga from mermen /
To seraphim / Leaping!" in the twelfth stanza and the "Illumination of music" in the thirteenth. Uniting merman and angel,
above and below, sea and air, poetry rises in the dark. Internal
rhyme ("prayer . . . there . . . hare," "cocks . . . fox") brings
a craftsman's gaiety to relieve the tenth stanza.

"High, there, on the hare- / Heeled winds" is an obvious
echo of Hopkins' "Windhover," as "sloe," in stanza 11, recalls
"The Wreck of the Deutschland," where it serves as an image of
the Eucharist. (Compare the echoes of "The Windhover" in
"Author's Prologue," xvii.) Hopkins' Christian and priestly falcon,
multiplying and changing feathers, has become Thomas' rooks,
soaring from "black bethels." Bethel (literally house of God and
geographically where Jacob based his ladder) has come to mean
a Protestant chapel. "Gospel rooks" should be at home there, but
not in priestly black (cf. "black birds . . . like priests," 135,
"reverent rook," xvii). The confusion of Protestant with Catholic
seems confirmed by the burning cocks and fox of D. H. Lawrence.
Presiding side by side over the black bethels, Protestant Lawrence
and Catholic Hopkins do a useful job in these three stanzas. To
put it into the language of critics: the allusions to Hopkins and
Lawrence are functional.

That the ministrations of these holy men are not altogether
benign seems implied by their apostolic beasts, the rook and the
fox. A fox is sly and thieving, and a rook is deceitful, cheating,
and thieving (cf. "rooking," 13). Though acquiring clerical and
literary associations, the Thief has not abandoned nature altogether; for bird and fox are natural, and "the holy books of
birds" seem books in the running rooks, which, after all, are as
"hare-heeled" as their winds.

"Priest black" trees, "laced" and "surpliced," combine with
birds to sing and preach. Both priest and nature are "Pastoral."
The precious blood in the sleeved, bird-winged wrists of the
boughs and in the veins of the leaves is green. But black sleeves,
laced with frost that denies the sap, are funereal. So is the "tale"
of Keats' nightingale, and so "the surpliced / Hill of cypresses," a
probable echo of Lawrence's "Giorno dei Morti." The "dingle,"
giving up its ghost, preaches a sermon of death, yet a Lawrentian

"sermon of blood," still leaping—and falling, as in "the skimmed / Yard of the butter milk rain on the pail!" Even the happy barnyard, confused by transferred epithets, sings a song as dubious as the nightingale's "din and tale."

Sermon and hymn of bird and tree, of Lawrence and Hopkins, "all tell" of a Thief as red and foxy as Lawrence's fox and as sly, black, and rooking as Hopkins' wind-heeled rook. But the statement that condenses and concludes thirteen exclamations is not so dark and anti-clerical as we may think; for Lawrence's burning fox gives light and Hopkins' rook soars high there in the wind. Hopkins may have been a black priest and Lawrence may have been an unordained preacher, but both were poets. The "saga of prayer" leaps from their black Christian bethel to air and light. However clerical, nature is still holy; but poetry, holier still, saves us from the natural dark and the dark of church and chapel.

13: Exclamations, no longer ambiguous, revive in light and air. Poetry, the product of musician, magus, and seer, is the "Illumination of music," the "Music of elements, that a miracle makes"—made by a miracle and miracle-making. By the magic of poetry the four elements of nature, becoming one, sing into the "white act" of light. So, too, the elements or parts of a poem. In this light the black gull, gulled, rooked, and blinded by "sand in its eyes," awakes from sleep and time. A foal from the stables of Fern Hill prances, like Pegasus, in moon, water, and wind. The music of poetry is illustrated by "lulled black-backed / Gull," an interweaving of sounds in the Welsh manner of Hopkins. The miracle of poetry, that of all creation, becomes the miracle of a daughter.

14-17: The intruder who threatens her centers father's anxiety and directs his prayer through the loosening, repetitive remainder of the poem. In the fourteenth and fifteenth stanzas, the haygold-haired, high-riding sleeper, with eyes as blue as a "rift" in the clouds, unites the above with the below, sky with earth, like a poem. ("Tide raking" in the sixteenth stanza unites sea and sky.) "Cross its planets," evidently astrological opposition, brings "star-crossed" to mind. One with the earth, like Mrs. Bloom, the girl receives the snow and wave of the Thief. "The wound in her side" (cf. stanzas 2 and 9) makes her one with mankind. "Only," in the fifteenth stanza, means But; and the disagreeable rhymes ("holy. . . truly he . . . ruly sea . . . Oh he") seem to fit a father's agitation. So, too, the hissing of the last line of the fifteenth stanza and the troubled, halting movement of the last two stanzas.

"Willy nilly" and "designed," the Thief inevitably "comes . . . comes . . . comes . . . comes" to destroy her "faith," but in what is not altogether clear. The Thief is "unsacred" though as natural as holy, dark nature. Her faith seems to be that the unholy one will "leave her in the lawless sun awaking" and that he will come; for she grieves, "forsaken," if he does not. Now the Thief seems to represent growing up. You must "believe" in the Thief's coming, says father, and "fear" it. He prays that her awaking from country sleep will not impair a faith "as deathless as the outcry of the ruled sun." "The ruled sun" (cf. "ruly sea") could be poetry, imagination, and the beliefs of childhood—in short, "the saga of prayer." "The lawless sun" could be the world of fact and nature's apparent disorder. Is father praying that, growing up and gaining knowledge of fact, the girl may keep her faith in the realities of imagination and in what Yeats called "the ceremony of innocence"? The Thief could represent the knowledge that destroys innocence and glory. When Thomas waked the second time in Fern Hill, it was to glory gone. Some thief had stolen the farm away.

"Shall wake" seems an appropriate echo of Hopkins' "Margaret." "Ever and ever," going back to the beginning, echoes "Never and never." "Vast night" and "last night," echoing with the rest, leave us lost among echoes, hints, and dark anxieties.

Better not try to pin that Thief down. Enough that, associated with many things, he seems to include whatever menaces all of us, sleeping or waking. Our certainty is that things around here are uncertain, though sure someday, as Joyce said, to be "dead certain." Like Joyce in *Finnegans Wake*, Thomas, in his degree and kind, found a form for how we feel and are and for how a father feels.

Stanford, 132-35. Tindall, in *American Scholar*, XVII (Autumn 1948). Thomas recorded this poem, Caedmon, 1043.

Over Sir John's hill (1949), *pp. 187-89*

Thomas was always writing elegies. This one is for the birds. Like God, Thomas marks the sparrow's fall and, like Hopkins, the buckling falcon. Sir John's hill and the river Towy, at Laugharne, are parts of a landscape whose inscape is life and death. Of these, the secretaries are Thomas and a companionable heron.

Their elegiac celebration falls into five stanzas, as irregular in appearance as regular in pattern—a pattern woven of alliteration, internal assonance, and stresses more flexibly sprung than those of Hopkins. Whereas he worked out his rhythms by rule, Thomas probably felt his out. The result of each method is richly symphonic. Thomas' "shapes of sound" are "ruly" in shape and, while not unruly, liberal in movement and sound.

"The hawk on fire hangs." From these words two systems of metaphor exfoliate. "On fire," or bright in the sun as dusk falls below, becomes the flashing, flaming, and exploding of a firebird. Remember "the fire that breaks" from Hopkins' buckled windhover. "Hangs," literally hovering in the wind, leads to an elaborate metaphor of hanging: "hoisted . . . drop . . . gallows . . . tyburn . . . noosed." In subsequent stanzas the hawk becomes hanging judge and hangman. These exfoliations are good examples of method. Starting with a word, Thomas let it suggest another word and another until a thing of words came miraculously from the word.

Under their hangman, the sparrows, blithe as Shelley's skylarks, "swansing," about to die—like the birds of Swansea, it may be, and its swan. Meanwhile the "holy heron" fishes the Towy, bowing his "headstone" for those about to be hanged. His "headstone" is his head, their memorial, and this poem; for a heron is first cousin to the secretary bird. A fisher like Thomas in "The Long-legged Bait," the heron is no less "holy" than the stranded poet he accompanies. (Compare "druid herons," 192, "heron priested shore," 113, "steeple stemmed" herons, 190.) Thomas, the druid, made his headstone for Ann Jones a "monumental argument of the hewn voice." The tombstone of sparrows tells where they fell, as an earlier tombstone "told when she died."

"Stalking" like a long-legged bait, the heron stalks fish and walks like a heron. The "noosed hawk," dangling a noose for birds, is noosed himself and condemned to death. A concert in o suitably darkens the quiet last line. But penultimate "flash . . . Crashes," the lightning swoop of the fire hawk, has prepared us for the crashing that whacks the second stanza open:

> Flash, and the plumes crack,
> And a black cap of jack-
> Daws Sir John's just hill dons,
>
> . . . .
> In a whack of wind.

These sounds are not unlike those of Joyce's comment on Jack (*Ulysses*, 388): "A black crack of noise in the street here, alack, bawled, back." The metaphor of hanging, revived by "black cap," continues through "just" and "halter." The "gulled birds," haring, are one with Thomas' other gulled birds and his "hare-heeled" rooks (185, 192).

As the "elegiac fisherbird" stabs the "dab-filled shallow" (dabs are peck marks), the fisherman lost on land, opens "the leaves of water" to read death's duel, his own funeral sermon; for " 'dilly dilly,' " the call of the hawk, not only a duck call, as Webster affirms, could imply Dylan, Dylan, " 'Come and be killed.' " One with sitting ducks and falling sparrows, Thomas is their secretary. His sepulchral delight prances like an articulate, articulated crab from the interwoven alliteration (ps-s-p-s-p) of the final line.

The sense of the third stanza runs as fluidly on from the second as the waters in which Thomas reads his "shell." Not only a wreathed horn for poets, a shell is a marine skeleton. For another "buoy's bell" see "The Long-legged Bait." While Thomas and the heron "praise" the fiery hawk with his snaky, hanging "fuse," they "grieve" over the "green" chicks who innocently echo the hawk's "dilly dilly." Both "green" and "fuse" belong to life. Both call for praise and grief. As "young Aesop fabling," Thomas draws morals from creatures. But the "saint" (*sanctus* or holy) heron hymns in "the shell-hung" harbor as a poet should. "Dingle" and "cobbles," favorite words of dying Thomas, carry us under

Milk Wood to Llareggub. At Laugharne the "sea cobbles sail"
through Hopkins' "cobbled foam-fleece."

Syntactical pauses smoothly evade ends of stanzas and lines as,
in stanza four, the poet and his long-legged *Doppelgänger* mark
the sparrows' fall. Both these "tell-tale" knellers keep their distance—artistic distance, the one grieving on the "verge," the
other looking through metaphorical windows, not at the falling
birds but at the heron's "tilting" headstone. The heron's eye is
on the object, but the poet's on the poem.

Proceeding through a courtroom, the metaphor of hanging
yields "judging," "guilt," and "Have mercy on." "Have," "save,"
and "hail" are optatives; but "the sparrows hail," condensing
noun and verb, implies the sparrows' icy fall. Compare God's
"whirlwind silence" with "the cyclone of silence" (183).

Notice the assonance of "grieves . . . weeded" in the eleventh
line of the fourth stanza and the interwoven alliteration of the
third line: "And wharves of water. . . ." The third and fourth
lines of the last stanza ("Only a hoot owl / Hollows . . . looted
elms") rival Tennyson at his most mellifluous. Alliteration slows
the ponderous movement of the final line.

No "green" birds have survived the windhover. As their "snapt
feathers snow" the Towy, the fishing heron "Makes all the music."
The poet, hearing this tune and that of the "Wear-willow" or
mourning river, sets the notes down on the heron's "time-shaken"
headstone. "I . . . grave" means gravely engrave with mallet and
chisel; but "grave," a forked word, also serves as adjective and
noun. Plainly, the elegist is masonic secretary to his secretary bird.
The tombstone he chisels is "time-shaken" in two senses: moved
by the death of birds and subject to the paradox of art, which,
though timeless, is of time and in it. Records of time hewn on
stone are no solider than sparrows. "He who marks the sparrow's
fall," says ApLlewelyn in "The Horse's Ha," "has no time for my
birds," from which death pulls "a last fart."

We may speculate about the choice of heron as alter ego and
co-operator. It is true that herons, stalking under the windows at
Laugharne, were handy; and it may be, as Robert Graves assures us in *The White Goddess*, that the ancient Celts found
mana in crane and heron. But Thomas was not an ancient Celt

He had looked into a book or two on ancient Egypt, however, and he was on more or less familiar terms with Joyce's *Portrait of the Artist* and *Ulysses*, where "hawklike" Stephen Dedalus proclaims devotion to Egyptian Thoth or Hermes Trismegistus, god of writers and secretary to the gods. Hermes wrote on a tablet of stone. His companion was the ibis, and this bird is first cousin to the heron. If the heron of Laugharne is the Hermetic ibis, Thomas must be Hermes and his stone the Emerald Tablet, on which Hermes wrote, "As above, so below." While the transaction between Thomas' hawk above and sparrows below is not Hermetic, there is Hermetic correspondence between this transaction and man's fate.

Stanford, 135-36. Ralph Maud, in *Explorations*, No. 6 (1956). Thomas recorded this poem, Caedmon, 1043.

Poem on His Birthday (1951), pp. 190-93

Here is the fourth and last of the birthday poems. Birth and autumn again put Thomas in mind of death and "fabulous, dear God." From under Sir John's hill the heron comes to speed a more desperate voyage than those of "Once below a time," "Lie still," and "The Long-legged Bait." Now, crossing the bar that detained him, Thomas puts out to sea in Lawrence's ship of death. The twelve stanzas, crowning years of experiment in assonance, alliteration, and rhythm, are dense and clear. Syntax weaves freely in and out of prosodic pattern.

The scene is Laugharne with its "full tilt," swiftly running river and its "switchback sea," where tides and waves go up and down like a roller coaster. The poet's ramshackle, seaside house is high "on stilts" among "steeple stemmed" herons. These holy birds, who assisted at an earlier birthday (113), bring each of the first three stanzas to a close. Companionable images of the poet, the herons pursue life's activities: aspiring, killing, and walking in shrouds. As the poet "celebrates and spurns" his birthday, herons, parodying him, "spire and spear." The time is October, whose sun is as small, yellow, and hot as a "mustardseed." Inconsiderable as a "sandgrain" and yellow as the sun, the day is "mined with a motion," like sand in Hopkins' hourglass. "Thistledown fall" is seedy October and the thistle's downfall. "Driftwood," turned by sea and wind, prepares us for the voyage in a "drowned ship." Remark the assonance and woven alliteration of "sandgrain day in the bent bay's grave."

In the sepulchral second stanza, flounders, gulls, curlews, and eels of "the congered waves"—all those dying animals, "doing what they are told" to do by life, "Work at their ways to death." So too, in his "long tongued room," the wounded poet, toiling and tolling, works his way toward death's "ambush." The bell of poetry, celebrating and lamenting birth and death, rings from the herons' steeple. Dying herons and tolling poet "bless" life.

As he "sings towards anguish" in the third stanza, the hawks of the "seizing sky" kill finches, as in Sir John's precincts, and otters kill fish. Shells in the "wynds" (winding streets) of sunken towns bring thoughts of shipwreck and death to the craftsman at "the hewn coils of his trade" (cf. xvii). "Hewn" implies headstone cutting (cf. 189), and "coils" are art's intricacies and all its troubles. One with dying animals, the poet sees "herons walk in their shroud," as John Donne once walked in his to preach "Death's Duell." (Compare "Sewing a shroud for a journey," 110.) More than their flesh, the herons' shroud is the water in which they wade and fish; for their trade and way will be the death of them as the poet's way and trade of him.

"The livelong river's robe" of the fourth stanza is the short-lived heron's shroud. Praying for life and prey to herons, minnows prepare wreaths for their funerals. As the water of herons is their shroud, so the water of dolphins is their "turnturtle dust," or water turned on its back to die. What we live in is our tomb; and our work our death. Seals, at their trade of fishing, will be food for sleeker and larger mouths than theirs. "Far at sea" with minnow, dolphin, and seal, the poet works like his marine parallels to a common end. But, more than death, his "eternal end" is poetry. "Crouched" is the posture of poets, tailors of shrouds, and dying embryos. "Under a serpent cloud" could be the place of fallen man and his climate. Adam, who brought death into the world, must sweat to die.

In Thomas' early poems there is a multitude of images in violent disagreement. Here so far, a multitude of images has been in general agreement—an agreement that, like blood, "Slides good in the sleek mouth." Yet relics of old disagreements survive, along with old paradox and ambiguity. Context makes the "cavernous" wave of stanza five the tomb. The "angelus" is Gabriel's announcement of the womb. But the momentary disagreement of tomb and womb, of "silence" and bell, of white tears and black, is quickly settled by "angelus knells," a synthesis of birth and death that agrees with everything said so far.

In the "drowned ship" (see stanza three), the voyager hears his age struck by a sunken ship's bell. Little wonder; for a navigator who fixes his position by "falling stars" must expect to founder. Better navigators use sextants at noon. Just as well to be sunk, however; for the morrow holds terror—of atomic war, maybe. The imagery of cage, chain, and bolt has served Thomas' earlier vision of war (e.g. 107, 129, 152). Like unbolting "love," the "hammer" (cf. 8, 22) seems both creative and destructive. Having forged burning Tygers, it knocks them to bits.

Emerging in stanza six from his dark immersion, the poet of "Vision and Prayer" is lost in light again. "Dark is a way" to the light of God and heaven. As in the earlier poems, both God and heaven remain uncertain. A "fabulous" god, both wonderful and mythical, sits in a heaven "that never was / Nor will be ever." Yet God and heaven are "always true"; for myth is truer than fact. Although a "void," heaven is, paradoxically, a crowded blackberry patch, where the dead "grow" for God's joy. "Grow" means thrive and heap up. Once again Thomas' long struggle through the dark towards the light seems over; but as he comes to light, what comes to light is light's ambiguity. In the "unknown, famous light" he is lost indeed. "Famous," "great," and "fabulous" are words from Yeats, not T. S. Eliot.

Since "air shaped" or imagined heaven (cf. "air-drawn . . . fibs of vision," 48) is a blackberry patch, "There," which commences the seventh stanza, includes heaven and earth or the place of the dead. Thomas felt at home in graveyards. Laugharne's shore, no less sepulchral than the blackberry patch, is littered with dead horseshoe crabs and starfish. ("Horseshoe bay" is also the "bent bay" of stanza one.) "Roots of whales / And wishbones of wild geese" also litter this littoral graveyard, which, since whale suggests Melville and wild goose Joyce, could be the graveyard of letters too. Except in the most literal sense, the "marrow of eagles" escapes me; for the eagle is associated with numberless men, Dante, for example, and that aged eagle of Russell Square. Devoted to marrow bones, Yeats once saw a singing bone upon the shore, and cruel death brought three things back. As for "Le Cimetière marin," Thomas told me that he ranked Valéry with Yeats and Joyce.

In Laugharne's heap of marrow bones, the poet, wandering with the spirits of the dead, is not, but might be, at peace with "blessed, unborn God and His Ghost." "His Ghost," even if the Holy Ghost, means that God is as dead as the horseshoe crab whose ghost haunts the shore; but dead God is "unborn." Referring maybe to Jesus before the Nativity, "unborn" also means non-existent. The souls of the dead are fit priests for such a god; for every soul is "gulled and chanter." "Gulled" means winged, eaten with the other garbage, and fooled. "Chanter" may mean a celebrant at the altar or, as Webster tells us, a deceitful horse-dealer, who gulls the gullible. "And chanter" implies enchanter; and in this context a magician is another deceiver. "Young Heaven's fold" may mean Eden, the manger, or an enclosure for leading foolish sheep into. The "cloud quaking peace" of heaven is no less dubious. A quaker is not at peace; clouds could make heaven quake; heavenly peace could make the serpent cloud of stanza four quake; and "cloud quaking peace" could be cold war.

"But dark is a long way," which the poet is still pursuing. Being lost in such light as he knows, he is lost in the dark, "on the earth of the night, alone / With all the living"—like the rest of us. He is aware of the general resurrection that will bring all the dead to light; for he has read the Apocalypse. But waters giving up their dead and "rocketing winds" blowing bones out of the grave seem more natural than supernatural, more suggestive of future wars than of any but "cloud quaking peace." Whatever the agency of resurrection, it will bring the dead "Faithlessly unto Him." Thomas' dark way seems a faithless, hopeful approach to a light that never was nor will be. But Dante's stars are still "quick"; and on the dark way up, hope has charity by the hand. Continually praying, Thomas "prays" again. A colon in the ninth stanza, introducing his prayer, marks a necessary but surprising shift from third person to first. Stephen Dedalus commends a poet who, in the course of a poem, shifts from lyrical first person to dramatic third. But what more fitting for a lyric poet than to be lyrical?

"Midlife" (thirty-five years) in stanza nine recalls Dante's journey from dark to light, as "voyage to ruin" recalls the "voyage towards oblivion" of Lawrence's "ship of death," which, breached in autumn by "wounds," is unsteered in the dark towards problematical light and peace. (Compare "my voyage . . . to the end of my wound," 153. Baudelaire had undertaken a more expansive voyage in the same direction.) Though already wrecked, the poet's "tumbledown," long tongue continues, like those of his "druid herons," to bless and count blessings.

Those counted in the tenth stanza are mostly temporal: the four elements, the five senses, and love of the "spun slime" that Joyce calls "whorled without aimed." "Tangling" through the slime of man and nature, the poet proceeds with little faith but great fortitude toward the Cloud-Cuckoo-Land of "kingdom come." Its "lost, moonshine domes" are from dreams of Coleridge and Yeats. Such domes are moonshine, but the Freudian sea is a real blessing; for it hides man's "secret selves." Though the sea's "black, base bones" seem another graveyard—for old ram rods this time—there are "spheres" (pearls or microcosmic spheres) in the flesh of skeletal "seashells." Pearls and moonlit domes offer hope for those sunk by Prospero's tempest or tangled in slime.

The last and greatest blessing (stanza eleven) seems delight in nature. "Hulks" (cf. 166) may be "sundered" and the poet may be "one man" alone with all the living, but sun, sea, and world are joyous. The "louder" the synesthetic sun "blooms," the more it brings Lawrence and Joyce to mind. The "ramshackling," long-legged sea may menace tumbledown old ram rods, but, nautical to the last, they "tackle" the gale. As the sea exults and the world, revealing faith in itself, gives praise, the exultant poet echoes the praise. "With more triumphant faith," the flattest line of the poem, can apply to world or poet; but, whichever our application, such faith is a secular, not a theological, virtue. The "triumphant faith" of things going "Faithlessly unto Him" is paradoxical enough to demand paradoxical flatness for climax. Faithful in its fashion, the world of "spun slime" spins words of praise; for "the world was said" by the Word of Genesis. World, Word, and poet are romantically one.

The "bouncing hills" of Laugharne triumphantly become "heaven's hill" (44) where images roar. Autumn, as in "Poem in October," is transformed into "thunderclap spring." "Mansouled" islands, the voyager's landfalls, become angelic, "shining men." (Compare Phineas Fletcher's "Purple Island," Bunyan's "Mansoul," and Jarvis Island in "The Map of Love.") No longer alone, the charitable captain, almost like Noah of "Author's Prologue," welcomes all men aboard as passengers or crew for a voyage to death in a sunken, drunken ship. God grant them sextant, compass, and waterproof chronometer until eight bells.

Bill Read, in *Casebook,* 269-70. Stanford, 136-38. Thomas recorded this poem, Caedmon, 1018.

Lament (1951), *pp.* 194-96

Black humor is the saving light of "Lament"—humor, irony, gusto, and bouncing rhythm. Humor had lightened earlier autobiographies: "Once below a time," "The Long-legged Bait," *Portrait of the Artist as a Young Dog,* and *Adventures in the Skin Trade.* Humor's triumph in "Lament" clears "spun slime" from the poet's brightening way. The outrageous, the ribald, and the grotesque, changed utterly, put brighter faces on. Maybe humor is all the light that Thomas found and all he needed.

Here the amatory adventures of "The Long-legged Bait" proceed on shore in acres of imagery which, though dry, mean the same thing as before. The fisherman with rod and black ship has become the old ram rod lamenting black sheep. As the fisherman is caught, so a lamb is staked out for harpies. Both end up in front of a church on the village green and both more or less accept what they lament. Thomas was obsessed, like any man, with freedom and marriage.

Of the three conflicts that make the ram rod's story dramatic, the first is between present and past; the second between chapel and black sheep; the third between black mask and white self. Some of these contenders must be protagonists and some antagonists, but it is hard to say which is which. Contending with black, white seems to win the day. But black remains dominant, and the ram rod is too old to be white sheep. The thesis of white and the antithesis of black, or vice versa, produce synthetic grey —light grey with a little pink in it.

1: Plainly potent, the old ram rod is dying of what he has tried his potency out on. Remember "The black ram . . . Alone alive among his mutton fold" (81); and remember Joyce. When I called attention (in 1952) to "Ramrod the meaty hunter," Thomas, surprised by Joyce, called *Finnegans Wake* the best of books and the only one worth reading; but we are apt to leave our favorites unopened. A rod, creative tool of God and man, may be fishing pole or gun, Freudian equivalents; and ram, a thing for knocking down or up, is the sign of spring. (Compare "ram rose," 74; and "rod," 167, 169.) But rams are shackled by the "ramshackling sea" (193) of woman and time. Hence these sighs for a past that is lamentable two ways.

The "windy boy" whom the ram laments is loud, full of hot air, poetic, and a "boy and a bit" in his own eyes. The "chapel fold" is for white sheep. But Thomas was always egregious. As the chapel's "black spit," the boy and a bit is at once black sheep, something spat out by a chapel among coal mines, and the spitting image of what has spat him out. Black without, he is chapel white within. A "shy" innocent, he blushes under his coal black mask of outrageous wickedness. Recall "the lamb on knocking knees" (81), the "sunday faced" (21) boy whom the chapel prefers. Thomas commonly wore a mask, white or black, like the rest of us.

When I first met him at a party, he looked like, and acted the part of, an amorous Volkswagen, driven by Harpo Marx. Chasing the girls round the room, he blew down their dickies. Everyone, wives and husbands alike, took this in good part, except John Malcolm Brinnin, who sat frowning in a corner. Thomas was a poet, after all, and we were academic bourgeoisie, except John Malcolm Brinnin. It was plain, moreover, that the harmless poet, doing his best, was doing what he thought expected of him or else was hiding shyness under what he thought its opposite. (This party at the house of Marshall W. Stearns, 32 West 10th Street, February 22, 1950, was Dylan's first in America. Mr. Brinnin's report leaves the place, the poet's deportment, and the company out, save for two nameless "Joyce experts," of whom I may be one or the other —or both.)

The shy, blushing boy of the first stanza is content to observe bucolic amours. In Milk Wood or near the White Giant, we too shall observe his big girls of "gooseberry wood" and "donkey's common," whose "little weddings" in the black bushes have other grooms than he, their lover and leaver in fancy alone. "Seesaw sunday nights," long after morning chapel, are for tipsy peeping at ups and downs. His eyes are "wicked," but his pants are but-toned "with a virgin o" (21). Here is all the blackness of white-ness.

Sprung rhythm suitably changes pace in the penultimate line. Internal rhyme ("bit . . . spit," "wooed . . . would") and heavy alliteration relieve pathos by gaiety. "Poetry is sound," said Thomas, pausing for ambiguous breath at that party.

2: As the "windy boy and a bit" grows to be a "gusty man and a half" in his own estimation, the "chapel fold" for white sheep turns into black "beetles' pews." It is hard to say whether his ex-ploits in the "twisted flues" and on "clover quilts" are real or imaginary. "Quivering prints" may indicate passion or terror; but the progressing rake is certainly "drunk as a new dropped calf." With this calf the zoo shows signs of overcrowding; for, besides calf, ram, and sheep, it holds owl, tit, donkey, beetle, bitch, a shoal of fish, and an unidentified black beast. It is about to open the gate to cat, mouse, bull, cow, dove, and harpy. "How shall my animal?" asks Thomas. How indeed, and which? It is certain, however, that no poet since Lawrence has loved beasts more or watched more birds. I once saw Thomas kick a cat and, on a happier occasion, fondle an aluminum fish.

3: A man at last, "the black cross of the holy house" (chapel) is hot as a tomcat in spring or a ballocky bull in the summer. The "welcome" the old ram rod is dying of, by women when he was in heat, is now by strangers and women in the cold. "Brandy and ripe in my bright, bass prime," a line notable for assonance and interwoven alliteration, and, indeed, all the other lines of this stanza and this poem were shaped to come out "brandy and ripe" when Thomas read them aloud in his deep "bass prime."

4: The "preachers" of the chapel have warned of the "downfall" that makes him half the man of his red hot days. "Crumpled horn" (of little Boy Blue's cow?) and "limp time" show this downfall's nature. The "foul mousehole" is an image of horror in "The Mouse and the Woman." Clearly it is time for marriage—a marriage of souls as black as freedom; but shoving the soul's "gristle and rind" up into the black sky is more or less than metaphysical. Marriage is a sublimation which "slashed eye" (cf. 42, 43) proves blind. "Slung," a misprint in the American edition, should be Slunk, and "roarers'" should be roarer's.

5: There he lies in the cold bed he once put off the thought of, a man no more, still less a beast; yet roaring lamb is one at last with old ram. "Death," the final word, has lost at last its sexual implication. The "strangers" he is dying of may be wife and children, the Americans who, in 1950, welcomed him almost to death, or his readers (cf. xv). "A sunday wife" means the chapel's victory and good-by to "seesaw sunday nights." The juxtaposition of "angels! / Harpies" is shattering and just; for both have wings, both descend from a "coal black sky," and both are connected with harps. Surrounded by children, his angelic harpies of the shore, and by the seven deadly virtues of the chapel, the sacrificial, harping ram draws a "last black breath," to be exhaled in this black, hilarious poem. Breath, long-legged heart, and hand, more or less at home where they are in "dove cooed" peace, make poems despite the waving of Modesty's wings and those of harpy and dove. Life's mixture accounts for mixture here, as in the final stanza of "The Long-legged Bait." Rhythm, responding to admixture, presents it by regularity and violation. The agitated fifth and twelfth lines are masterly intruders.

Oliver Evans, in *English Miscellany*, VII (1956). Stanford, 138. Thomas recorded this poem, Caedmon, 1018.

In the White Giant's Thigh (1950), *pp. 197-99*

This elegy is for barren women, whose tombstones, on which even "the names . . . are rained away," tell where they died and suggest how they lived, doing their best. A primitive design on the side of a hill, cut through turf to the chalk beneath, like the famous White Horse of England, the White Giant is supposed to confer fertility. Thomas told me that he had never seen the White Giant and had no idea of its location, if any. (Guidebooks to England and Wales—those, at least, that I consulted—do not mention it.) But an immemorial, fertility-promoting icon, whether real or imaginary, offered another occasion for the thoughts of life and death that obsessed him. When the barren girls came hopefully to the Giant, Thomas told me, they expected boys to jump from the bushes, where they had lain in wait, to serve the Giant's promise. Boys and girls did what they could to foster life, but their efforts, however lively and diverting, were fruitless. These lusty efforts, amid the scenery of Fern Hill, Milk Wood, and Llareggub, are the joy of this poem, which praises life in death's despite. Humor, humanity, and charity—good ingredients for literature—help assure the success of this elegy.

In a letter to Oscar Williams, Thomas dismisses the poem as "conventionally romantic," and in his preface to "In Country Heaven" (*Quite Early One Morning*), he deplores some of the poem's "more obviously overlush, arch and exuberant, mauve gauche moments." But the theme and life itself demand what he apologizes for. Something less abundant would impair the glory. A romantic poet should be romantic.

This joyous lament consists of fifteen quatrains, regularly rhymed a b a b, but oddly spaced to conceal their shape and to vary their movement by the pauses that spacing, in spite of syntax, demands. Regularity and its violation seem the principles again. Concerts of alliteration and internal assonance enrich the texture of the freely springing, sprung lines. Consider the second quatrain. From the concerted vowels and consonants of the first line and from "meet" and "pray" in the second, this quatrain proceeds through two systems of assonance: "meet . . . pleading . . . seed . . . weed"; "pray . . . waded bay . . . names . . . rained away"—with "grown stones" for good measure.

1: Long after the death of these longing women, their elegist walks on "the high chalk hill" in the Giant's inviting crotch. "Barren as boulders" then, the women, still longing for love and labour, lie under barren tombstones now. "The conceiving moon," propitious for those women once, helps poetic conception now. The river-throated curlews, one with the women once, are one with the tide-tongued poet now. Rivers, whether Nile or Towy, bring fertility; and throats are for conceiving, crying, and the sounds of poetry. Conceiving, as Wallace Stevens said, is the great word of poetry and life.

2-3: "The waded bay" at the mouth of the Towy, for curlews and herons to wade in, is also woman for wading boys, "the unconceived / And immemorial sons" of the hill. "Immemorial" means ancient, dateless, beyond memory. Hardly unimagined here, "unconceived" must mean never begotten, conceived, and born. These are never-never boys, conceived by the poet and the women. The "curving act" seems that of world, moon, and love. A cudgel is love's tool as a hacker is the sculptor's for White Horses and White Giants.

4-7: The conceiving, curlew-tongued poet, doing his best, imagines these long-dead boys and girls doing theirs. In "East Coker" Eliot sees "dung and death" in the "country mirth" that inspires the human and happy lines of Thomas' elegy. Whether in "gooseskin winter . . . all ice leaved" with frost or in "ox roasting" summer, Thomas' sportive rustics pursue life and joy. In the high-tonned hay under "pitching clouds" or "in the after milking moonlight," they "lay . . . gay" and young. Their "lighted shapes of faith" must be sun and moon. As the "moonshade / Petticoats" of the girls rise up, the boys ride down. "Rough riding boys," recalling San Juan Hill, must be "Teddy boys." Friends in London used to call the poet "Teddy boy" Thomas. Teddy meant discreditably Edwardian there and then, but Roosevelt's word was "bully."

In "the gigantic glade" of the White Giant, the women clasp him to their "grains": seed and dust (cf. 112, 133, 143, 170). Once this "dust was flesh," rooted by the sly swineherd (cf. 181, 184) under the "dunghill sky" of the "wiving sty"—dung and death, to be sure, but of another kind. (Like "pitching clouds" and Eliot's privileged moments, "dunghill sky" suitably unites above and below.) The swineherd's thigh and the orchard man's "core" are torches. Here, under the greenwood tree, are "hedgerow" joys lustier than Hardy knew "green countries since" or many summers ago. Many winters, too; for the "ducked and draked" lake lies white beneath the hail, and the boys of summer are now on ice. Interwoven alliteration distinguishes the seventh quatrain. "Spinny" rivals "cobble" and "dingle" among the favorite words of Llareggub's poet.

8-10: "Hawed" implies hipped and rosy. A sequence of religious images, like those of "In Country Sleep," proves the country holy again: "friars . . . aisles . . . crossed their breast . . . vaulting . . . chime . . . pilgrimage of domes." The "friars"— any small beasts—can hardly be chipmunks (monks) as an ingenious commentator guessed; for chipmunks, alien to Milk Wood, are North American. Literally, the "domes" are molehills. "Dowse" means end or close. The "torch of foxes," burning in the forest of the night, anticipates "Fawkes fires" (quatrain 15). Compare "like fire the red fox" (184), "fox light" (xvii), and the "rush / Light" of the swineherd's thighs (quatrain 6). "Linked" links torch (link) with loving congress.

Thomas told Oscar Williams that "gambo bed" means "farm-cart." But Thomas, according to old habit, was translating his metaphor. Since "gambo" is a kind of goose, and since the context ("goose-girls . . . gander king . . . hissing shippen") fixes the meaning, the literal farm cart is a metaphorical feather bed for pastoral use. Compare "barley dark" with "buttermilk manes" and the other unions of displacements that thicken a juicy, joyous confusion where "butter fat goosegirls bounced in a gambo bed." The poem's concentrate, this symphonic, great line is one of many shapes of sound. This for example: "And heard the lewd, wooed field flow to the coming frost."

11: But all these joys are dead and gone, and all these exercises vain; for the girls "nothing bore." Their cupboards remained as bare as Old Mother Hubbard's (cf. 65); and Jack and Jill tumbled down the White Giant's hill with an empty bucket clattering after. "Mother Goose," recalling the "gambo bed," makes this reading certain. (In 1930 Thomas devoted a free-verse poem, still in manuscript, to themes from Mother Goose.) The "boulder of wives," recalling the tombstone, is bare and sterile. "Veined hives" are the wombs of girls with "breasts full of honey" (quatrain 10; cf. "hives," 1). Putting the main sense paradoxically into a parenthesis is not without precedent: Virginia Woolf's Mrs. Ramsay dies in a parenthesis. Death and sterility become parentheses in the triumph of life and fertility. Virginia Woolf may not have meant this by her parenthesis; but Thomas probably meant something of the sort by his.

12-15: The curlew, serving as invoked Muse, introduces the conclusion. Hortatory "cry me down" seems paralled to "hold me hard" and "Teach me the love," although the latter two may also serve as indicatives. "To these," in the final quatrain, may follow "hold me hard" or go with "do . . . Love" and "flame." Though syntactical uncertainty disagrees with the hope that love is "evergreen," this is a working disagreement, carefully designed.

The barren girls lived so long ago that their kitchens, too, are dust, and hay grows where their houses stood. Time's "billhooks" (cf. 150) have cut the loving hedgerows down. The "faded yard," farmyard once, is graveyard now, where inscriptions on the tombstones ("Beloved . . . Daughters") have been scrubbed away by sun and rain. Yet the daughters' "long desirers" in the foxy streets of the now "crumbled wood" live on; for they are "immemorial," and "evergreen" love is "for ever meridian." Dead maybe, the girls still flame through darkness like "Fawkes fires." The fires of Guy Fawkes burn in "fall leaved" November, death's season; yet fires, whether of burning babies or foxes, are as vital as spring. On the other hand, please to remember that foxy Guy Fawkes, Eliot's hollow man, is a stuffed effigy now, like the fox in Ann Jones' parlor; and even when he was man alive, his fuse, insufficiently green, failed to touch the powder off. Past and present, hope and fear, life and death, certainty and uncertainty fittingly unite and contend in the final image.

The dying poet is still around to sing life in death and death in life. "Hold me hard" (cf. 58), he states or prays—who knows which? He has heard "the tall bell sail down the Sundays of the dead" and the tolling rain "wring out its tongues." He knows for whom these bells toll. "Teach me," he states or prays, that love and life are eternal, and the "Hale dead . . . deathless." Let death have no dominion and grave no victory. What better than syntactical uncertainty, ambiguity of image, and violated quatrains for thoughts so double as these?

Oscar Williams, in *New World Writing*, No. 7 (1955). William T. Moynihan, in *Explicator*, XVII (1959). Marlene Chambers, in *Explicator*, XIX (1960) and *Explicator*, XIX (1961). Ralph N. Maud, in *English Studies*,

XLI (February 1960). John Davenport, in *Twentieth Century*, CLIII (February 1953). Edith Sitwell, in *Casebook*, 126. Olson, 46. Stanford, 140-42. Thomas recorded this poem, Caedmon, 1002.

Elegy (1956), *pp. 200-01*

A grief ago, Thomas addressed "Do Not Go Gentle" to his dying father. "Elegy," the old man's elegy, is simple and moving even as it stands, unfinished. A more or less completed fragment of seventeen lines precedes what Vernon Watkins put together from lines and words in the worksheets. This excellent but hypothetical construction is distinguished from Thomas' own by parentheses. What we have of the poem suggests what it might have been had Thomas had world enough and time. But what we have is very good.

The notes by Vernon Watkins make further comment all but unnecessary. Enough, maybe, to direct attention to some shapes, sounds, and matters: to the modified terza rima that Thomas elected and to the elaborate pattern of alliteration and internal echo that proves craft equal to grief. The first four triplets, for example, are remarkable for internal balancing of sounds ("die . . . died"; "way . . . away"; "day . . . may"; "last . . . crossed"; "young among . . . long . . . longed"; "rest . . . dust"; "kind ground") and an intricate pattern of alliteration in d, b, l, g, and f. As for composition: a few elements (pride, cry, eyes, wound, grass, water, darkness and light, maternal grave and God the father) are arranged as a classical composer arranges the themes of a symphony.

The rejection of maternal womb-tomb for salvation by fatherly light recalls "Vision and Prayer" and "I fellowed sleep." Thomas prays again: let fabulous, dear God raise unbelievers from their darkness to His light. Love of two contending fathers, "He and he," one of light and one in darkness, leaves Thomas where he always found himself, betwixt and between.

Bibliography

Works by Thomas Now in Print:

Collected Poems, London, J. M. Dent, 1952; New York, New Directions, 1953.
Adventures in the Skin Trade and Other Stories, New York, New Directions, 1955; paperback: New York, New American Library, a Signet Book, 1961. (This volume contains *Adventures in the Skin Trade,* London, Putnam, 1955, and *A Prospect of the Sea and Other Stories,* London, Dent, 1955.)
Portrait of the Artist as a Young Dog, London, Dent, 1940; New York, New Directions, 1940. (Also in paperback.)
Quite Early One Morning, London, Dent, 1954; New York, New Directions, 1954. (The English and American editions differ considerably in contents.)
Under Milk Wood, London, Dent, 1954; New York, New Directions, 1954. (Also in paperback.)

Letters:

Watkins, Vernon, editor, *Dylan Thomas: Letters to Vernon Watkins,* London, Dent and Faber and Faber, 1957.
"Seven Letters to Oscar Williams (1945-1953)," *New World Writing,* No. 7, New York, New American Library, 1955.

Bibliographies:

Rolph, J. Alexander, *Dylan Thomas, a Bibliography,* London, Dent; New York, New Directions, 1956.

Huff, William H., "Works About Thomas," in Elder Olson, *The Poetry of Dylan Thomas*, Chicago, University of Chicago Press, 1954.

PMLA (Publications of the Modern Language Association). The Annual Bibliography lists most of the essays on Thomas.

Chronology:

Maud, Ralph N., "Dylan Thomas' Collected Poems: Chronology of Composition," *PMLA*, LXXVI (June, 1961).

Critical and Biographical Studies:

Adam, No. 238 (1953), Dylan Thomas Memorial Number.

Brinnin, John Malcolm, *Dylan Thomas in America*, Boston, Little Brown, 1955.

Brinnin, John Malcolm, editor, *A Casebook on Dylan Thomas*, New York, Crowell, 1960.

Dock Leaves, V (Spring, 1954), Dylan Thomas Number.

Fraser, G. S., *Dylan Thomas*, London, The British Council, 1957.

Olson, Elder, *The Poetry of Dylan Thomas*, Chicago, University of Chicago Press, 1954.

Stanford, Derek, *Dylan Thomas*, London, Neville Spearman, 1954.

Tedlock, E. W., editor, *Dylan Thomas: The Legend and the Poet*, London, Heinemann, 1960.

Thomas, Caitlin, *Leftover Life to Kill*, London, Putnam, 1957.

Treece, Henry, *Dylan Thomas: "Dog Among the Fairies,"* London, Lindsay Drummond, 1949.

Index of Poems

Index of Names